"This remarkable and unique collection to people wherever they are on their journey to becoming psychoanalysts. The diverse experiences, challenges and struggles of a diverse group of accomplished analysts, narrated with remarkable candor, will promote reflection in candidates, colleagues and patients as they navigate their own paths."

     – **Robert Prince**, Adjunct Clinical Associate Professor, NYU Postdoctoral Program in Psychotherapy and Psychoanalysis

"What does it take to become a psychoanalyst or psychotherapist? This collection of personal narratives by individuals steeped in different theoretical traditions reveals no singular developmental explanation. Some become therapists after experiencing youthful trauma. Others took on an instinctive role of caretaker in early life. Still others came to their vocation with a predisposition for the arts – music, literature, theatre, or photography – and even the priesthood. What all had in common was curiosity about and empathy for the human condition. Further, they all manage to engage the reader with their life stories, so generously shared in this volume."

     – **Jack Drescher**, MD, Clinical Professor of Psychiatry, Columbia University

"Arnold Rachman and Harold Kooden masterfully pulled together a collection of twelve chapters, compellingly written by distinguished psychoanalysts and psychotherapists, from a wide range of cultural backgrounds and various disciplines. In this unique and comprehensive book, each contributor offers autobiographical details of early and painful subjective life experiences, illuminating their resilience and post-traumatic growth. The crucial impact of the analytic interaction and influence of mentors, teachers and theorists are emphasized, as well as their creative and innovative ability to integrate their personal history with translated knowledge from their professional discipline to enrich, deepen and expand their use of self in a two-person therapeutic experience. This is an important book for clinicians of all levels of experience, inspiring for those contemplating entering this field and reassuring for anyone embarking upon psychotherapeutic treatment."

     – **Susan A. Klett**, PhD, PsyD, LCSW-R, Training and Supervising Analyst at the Institute of Contemporary Psychoanalysis LA, Faculty at the Institute of the Postgraduate Psychoanalytic Society, former President of Postgraduate Psychoanalytic Society

Different Paths Towards Becoming a Psychoanalyst and Psychotherapist

This book describes the personal journey of a collection of contributors, detailing their pathways to becoming psychoanalysts and psychotherapists, with insights from many of the most interesting analysts in the field.

The history of psychoanalysis and psychotherapy indicates that the pioneers were individuals who came from different pathways, such as medicine, law, education, and art. The integration of men and women with different educational and career backgrounds enhance the intellectual and clinical evolution of the field. Here, Arnold Rachman and Harold Kooden have invited a diverse group of practicing clinicians to demonstrate that psychoanalysis and psychotherapy continues to welcome and integrate individuals with a wide variety of intellectual interests and atypical career pathways.

In showing how varied and personalized the route into analysis can be, this book will be of great interest to clinicians of all levels and experience, and will offer inspiration to those just entering the profession.

Arnold Wm. Rachman, PhD, FAGPA, Training and Supervising Analyst, Postgraduate Psychoanalytic Institute, New York City; Clinical Professor of Psychology, Gordon Derner Institute, Adelphi University Postdoctoral Program in Psychoanalysis and Psychotherapy; Associate Professor of Psychiatry, New York University Medical Center; Board of Directors, Sándor Ferenczi Study Center, New School University, New York City; Donor of the Elizabeth Severn Papers to The Library of Congress, Washington, DC; Honorary Member, The Sándor Ferenczi Society, Budapest.

Harold Kooden, PhD, is a Clinical Psychologist in private practice and a Fellow of the American Psychological Association. He was a founder and board member of the National Gay and Lesbian Education Foundation, board member of the New York State Martin Luther King, Jr. Institute for Nonviolence, and founding member and community activist of Services and Advocacy for GLBT Elders (SAGE). Besides having authored many articles on gay psychology, in 2000 he published *Golden Men: The Power of Gay Midlife.*

Psychoanalytic Inquiry Book Series
Joseph D. Lichtenberg
Series Editor

Like its counterpart, *Psychoanalytic Inquiry: A Topical Journal for Mental Health Professionals*, the Psychoanalytic Inquiry Book Series presents a diversity of subjects within a diversity of approaches to those subjects. Under the editorship of Joseph Lichtenberg, in collaboration with Melvin Bornstein and the editorial board of *Psychoanalytic Inquiry*, the volumes in this series strike a balance between research, theory, and clinical application. We are honored to have published the works of various innovators in psychoanalysis, including Frank Lachmann, James Fosshage, Robert Stolorow, Donna Orange, Louis Sander, Léon Wurmser, James Grotstein, Joseph Jones, Doris Brothers, Fredric Busch, and Joseph Lichtenberg, among others.

The series includes books and monographs on mainline psychoanalytic topics, such as sexuality, narcissism, trauma, homosexuality, jealousy, envy, and varied aspects of analytic process and technique. In our efforts to broaden the field of analytic interest, the series has incorporated and embraced innovative discoveries in infant research, self psychology, intersubjectivity, motivational systems, affects as process, responses to cancer, borderline states, contextualism, postmodernism, attachment research and theory, medication, and mentalization. As further investigations in psychoanalysis come to fruition, we seek to present them in readable, easily comprehensible writing.

After more than 25 years, the core vision of this series remains the investigation, analysis and discussion of developments on the cutting edge of the psychoanalytic field, inspired by a boundless spirit of inquiry. A full list of all the titles available in the *Psychoanalytic Inquiry* Book Series is available at www.routledge.com/Psychoanalytic-Inquiry-Book-Series/book-series/LEAPIBS.

Different Paths Towards Becoming a Psychoanalyst and Psychotherapist

Personal Passions, Subjective Experiences and Unusual Journeys

Edited by Arnold Wm. Rachman and Harold Kooden

Routledge
Taylor & Francis Group

LONDON AND NEW YORK

First published 2021
by Routledge
2 Park Square, Milton Park, Abingdon, Oxon OX14 4RN

and by Routledge
52 Vanderbilt Avenue, New York, NY 10017

Routledge is an imprint of the Taylor & Francis Group, an informa business

© 2021 selection and editorial matter, Arnold Wm. Rachman and Harold Kooden; individual chapters, the contributors

British Library Cataloguing-in-Publication Data
A catalogue record for this book is available from the British Library

Library of Congress Cataloging-in-Publication Data
Names: Rachman, Arnold W., editor. | Kooden, Harold, editor.
Title: Different paths towards becoming a psychoanalyst and psychotherapist: personal passions, subjective experiences and unusual journeys /
edited by Arnold Wm. Rachman and Harold Kooden.
Description: MIlton Park, Abingdon, Oxon ; New York, NY : Routledge, 2021. |
Series: Psychoanalytic inquiry book series |
Includes bibliographical references and index.
Identifiers: LCCN 2020022929 (print) | LCCN 2020022930 (ebook) |
ISBN 9780367523053 (hardback) | ISBN 9780367523046 (paperback) |
ISBN 9781003057383 (ebook)
Subjects: LCSH: Psychotherapy–Vocational guidance. |
Psychoanalysis–Vocational guidance.
Classification: LCC RC440.8 .D34 2021 (print) |
LCC RC440.8 (ebook) | DDC 616.89/14023–dc23
LC record available at https://lccn.loc.gov/2020022929
LC ebook record available at https://lccn.loc.gov/2020022930

ISBN: 978-0-367-52305-3 (hbk)
ISBN: 978-0-367-52304-6 (pbk)
ISBN: 978-1-003-05738-3 (ebk)

Typeset in Times New Roman
by Newgen Publishing UK

Cover image by Arnold Wm. Rachman

Contents

List of contributors   xi

Prologue: different paths towards becoming a
psychoanalyst and psychotherapist: personal passions,
subjective experiences and unusual journeys   1
ARNOLD WM. RACHMAN AND HAROLD KOODEN

1 My traumatic journey towards becoming a
   psychoanalyst: from phenomenology and person-centered
   psychotherapy to Sándor Ferenczi and the Budapest
   school to relational psychoanalysis   5
   ARNOLD WM. RACHMAN

2 Comprehending: harnessing oblique defiance in the
   formation of an analyst   30
   FERGAL BRADY

3 Family gifts and the artful practitioner: a journey of
   personal, professional and artistic growth   56
   ALAN D. ENTIN

4 Imagining the impossible: creativity in psychoanalytic
   practice   81
   DAN GILHOOLEY

5 My dual journey: an autobiographical account   102
   HENRY KELLERMAN

 6 Improvisational play for a psychoanalyst-musician   115
    ROBERT J. MARSHALL

 7 A Parisienne's passage through an American
    psychoanalytic world   131
    ROBERT J. MARSHALL FOR SIMONE V. MARSHALL

 8 How I became a psychoanalyst: from Shakespeare to
    psychoanalysis, from Freud and Lacan to Ferenczi and
    beyond   150
    CLARA MUCCI

 9 Journey to peace and love: from priest to psychoanalyst   178
    BENITO PERRI

10 Wilderness and psychoanalysis: a journey of aesthetics,
    desire, and ethics   187
    JOSEPH SCALIA III

11 My path to and within psychoanalysis   199
    FRANK YEOMANS

12 The scarecrow's search for a brain: a gay man's odyssey
    for validation as a psychotherapist   212
    HAROLD KOODEN

    Conclusion   261
    MELVIN BORNSTEIN

    Index   271

Contributors

Melvin Bornstein, MD, Training and Supervising Analyst, Michigan Psychoanalytic Institute.

Fergal Brady, MA, President of the Irish Psycho-Analytical Association. He is a psychoanalytic psychotherapist working in private practice in Dundalk and Dublin, Ireland. He has presented at the International Sandor Ferenczi Conference and organized the 2019 Conference "The Budapest School of Psychoanalysis: Ferenczi the Balints and Beyond" in Dublin. His paper "An extract of the analysis of the Monkey Puzzle Boy" is published in the *International Forum of Psychoanalysis*, Volume 28, 2019, Issue 4.

Alan D. Entin, PhD, ABPP, a graduate of the University of Chicago, is a licensed clinical psychologist in independent practice specializing in marriage, family and relationships in Richmond, VA, and Fellow of the American Psychological Association. A leader in local, state and national psychological associations, Dr. Entin served as President of the Virginia Psychological Association, and President of the APA Divisions of Psychologists in Independent Practice, Family Psychology and Media Psychology. His awards include: Distinguished Psychologist of the Year by Psychologists in Independent Practice; Distinguished Contributions to Media Psychology by the Division of Media Psychology; the 2008 Rosalee Weiss Award by the American Psychological Foundation for his leadership and contributions to psychology and the arts; and the Virginia Academy of Clinical Psychology Award for Extraordinary Contributions to Practice in Clinical Psychology. His photographs have been shown in national and international exhibits. He is a pioneer in the field of phototherapy, the use of photographs and albums in psychotherapy to understand family relationships, and his work has been featured extensively in the popular media.

Dan Gilhooley is an artist, psychoanalyst and teacher. He graduated with an AB and MA in Studio Art from Hunter College, earned an MA and doctoral degree in psychoanalysis from the Boston Graduate School of Psychoanalysis, and a certificate in psychoanalysis from the Center for Modern Psychoanalytic Studies in New York. Since 2000 Gilhooley has practiced as a NYS licensed psychoanalyst and since 2006 has taught at CMPS and the New York Graduate School of Psychoanalysis. Gilhooley has published 10 papers focusing on clinical process and has spoken at a dozen national conferences on topics such as telepathy, dreaming and creativity, and intersubjectivity. In 2019, in collaboration with his patient Frank Toich, he authored *Psychoanalysis, Intersubjective Writing, and a Post-Materialist Model of Mind: I Woke Up Dead*, published by Routledge.

Henry Kellerman, PhD, Private Practice; Postgraduate Center for Mental Health; Advisory Board, American Mental Health Foundation.

Robert J. Marshall, PhD, ABPP, in private practice since 1959; certificate in Psychoanalysis from the Postgraduate Center for Mental Health; faculty and training psychoanalyst at Center for Modern Psychoanalytic Health; cofounder of Northern Westchester Center for Psychotherapy; Chair of APA Div. 39 Publications Committee.

Simone V. Marshall, PhD, from Teachers College, Columbia University; Fulbright Scholar in Clinical psychology; Certificate in Psychoanalysis, William A. White Institute; Founder of Croton-Cortlandt Women's Center. Deceased August, 1996.

Clara Mucci, PhD, is Professor of Clinical Psychology at the University of Chieti, Italy, where she served as Professor of English Literature. She is also a psychoanalyst in private practice in Pescara and Milan, Italy, a member of the Italian Society for Psychoanalytic Psychotherapy and a supervisor and training analyst for the Italian Society of Psychoanalysis and Psychotherapy – Sándor Ferenczi.

The author of several books on Shakespeare, Psychoanalysis and Literary theory, her fields of expertise in Psychoanalysis are trauma of human agency, personality disorders, affective neuroscience and attachment.

Benito Perri, STB Theology Catholic University, MSW Hunter College, PhD in Psychoanalysis from Union Institute and University; practicing psychoanalysis since 1969; certificates in Psychoanalysis, NPAP and CMPS; certified Focusing Trainer and certified Teacher of Mindfulness Meditation; founder Touro College School of Social Work.

Joseph Scalia III, PsyaD, is a psychoanalyst in private practice, treating children and adults. Originally having studied Modern Psychoanalysis, and later, with Christopher Bollas, object relations theory and practice, in the last 12 years Scalia has studied with the Freudian School of Quebec and now the Lacan School of Psychoanalysis in San Francisco. The author of books and articles within psychoanalysis, Dr. Scalia's writings these days have been in environmental criticism and activism, appearing in *Mountain Journal*, and on Wilderness Podcast and Rendering Unconscious. A former president and current critic of Montana Wilderness Association, Scalia is now President of the Gallatin Yellowstone Wilderness Alliance. He lives and works in Livingston, Montana, The Greater Yellowstone Ecosystem, in the shadow of the Absaroka-Beartooth Wilderness.

Frank Yeomans, MD, PhD, Clinical Associate Professor of Psychiatry, Weill Cornell Medical College; Adjunct Associate Clinical Professor of Psychiatry; Department of Psychiatry, Columbia University Vagelos College of Physicians & Surgeons; President, International Society for TFP.

Prologue

Different paths towards becoming a psychoanalyst and psychotherapist: personal passions, subjective experiences and unusual journeys

Arnold Wm. Rachman and Harold Kooden

Psychoanalysis and psychotherapy became cordial to including individuals of varying backgrounds and education when Sigmund Freud published his ground-breaking essay, "The Question of Lay Analysis" (Freud, 1926), advocating the right of non-doctors or "lay people" to be psychoanalysts. It was written in response to Theodore Reik's being prosecuted for being a non-medical or lay analyst in Austria. Although Freud and many of his early followers were psychiatrists and neurologists, there were a group of pioneers, such as Otto Rank, Anna Freud, Melanie Klein and Erik H. Erikson, who were not medically trained but took different paths towards becoming a psychoanalyst.

Otto Rank was part of Freud's inner circle, the Society of Rings, which was formed to defend the psychoanalytic mainstream as disputes with Adler and Jung developed. Freud viewed Rank as brilliant and creative, encouraging him to pursue graduate education. Rank received his PhD in Philosophy from the University of Vienna. At the age of 21, Rank asked Freud to read a manuscript he had written on the artist. Freud was so impressed he invited Rank to become secretary of the Vienna Psychoanalytic Society (Lieberman and Kramer, 2012). Rank went on to contribute to an important re-evaluation of psychoanalysis towards integrating the emotional and subjective dimension. He also went on to develop his own theory of the birth trauma.

Freud's youngest child, Anna Freud's journey towards psychoanalysis began with her becoming a teacher of children. She first passed the test to work as a teaching apprentice at her old school, The Cottage Lyceum. She rose to head teacher in three years (Young-Bruehl, 2008). She developed an interest in her father's work and writings and was in analysis with him from 1918 to 1921 and from 1924 to 1929 (Roudenesco, 2016; Young-Bruehl, 2008). In 1922, she presented her paper, "Beating Fantasies and Daydreams" to the Vienna Psychoanalytic Society, then becoming a member. In 1923, she began her own psychoanalytic practice with children. By 1925, she was teaching at the Vienna Psychoanalytic Training Institute on child analysis. Subsequently, Anna Freud became one of the founders of child psychoanalysis.

Melanie Klein did not have a bachelor's degree. She sought psychoanalysis for herself from Sándor Ferenczi while she was living in Budapest during World War I. There she became a psychoanalyst and began analyzing children in 1919. In 1921, she moved to Berlin, where she studied with and was analyzed by Karl Abraham to become a psychoanalyst. Ernest Jones invited her to come to London in 1926, where she worked until her death in 1960 (Grosskurth, 1986). Klein, therefore, had exceptional intellectual talent which she combined with her analysis with Ferenczi and Abraham. As in Anna Freud's case, Klein's personal analysis became a training analysis. Along with Anna Freud, she became one of the founders of child psychoanalysis and object relations theory.

Elizabeth Severn, Sándor Ferenczi's controversial analysand, had a unique journey towards becoming a psychoanalyst. When Severn entered into her analysis with Ferenczi in 1925, she was a pioneering psychotherapist. From 1908 until 1920, she became a self-taught therapist, using the intellectual frameworks of Mary Baker Eddy's Christian Science and the French psychologist, Emile Coué, who introduced a method of self-improvement. Combining her natural interpersonal skill, capacity for empathy and creative use of medical and psychological methods, she developed an active therapeutic methodology which made her a successful clinician.

Her analysis with Ferenczi became an historic three-prong experience: she had a successful personal analysis; she co-created with Ferenczi a methodology, Trauma Analysis, and a new theory, The Confusion of Tongues (Rachman, 2018).

Erik H. Erikson, who lacked a bachelor's degree, served as a professor at such prominent academic institutions as Harvard University, University of California at Berkeley and Yale. As a youth, he lacked a general interest in school and graduated without distinction. He attended art school and dropped out (Stevens, 2008). He became one of the "Wandervogel" (Roaming Artists) in Germany and Italy until his friend, Peter Bloss, invited him to Vienna to tutor art at a school whose parents were in analysis with Anna Freud. Anna Freud observed his sensitivity to children and encouraged him to study psychoanalysis at the Vienna Psychoanalytic Institute. He was analyzed by Anna Freud and supervised by a host of outstanding early analysts, such as Hartman, Aichorn, Federn, and Deutsch. He also studied the Montessori Method. In 1933, he received his diploma from the Vienna Psychoanalytic Institute. This and the Montessori diploma were his only earned academic credentials.

Erikson's development of his theory of human development and his other contributions ranked him as the twelfth most cited psychologist of the twentieth century (Hoare, 2002).

Our issue will present a contemporary group of psychoanalysts and psychotherapists who view the therapeutic experience as a human enterprise. They reveal the personal struggles which they needed to traverse to become therapists. Psychoanalysis had in the beginning, as it should sustain today, a psychosocial space for a human experience between analyst and analysand. To believe in empathy and a necessary positive emotional connection as the vehicle for therapy, our contributors were able to go beyond what they were originally taught. Coming from different intellectual perspectives, our contributors had to cross-fertilize their ideas with material from a wide variety of disciplines: biology, the humanities, literature, philosophy, psychology and sociology. They demonstrate their capacity to integrate their own personal journey into a therapeutic encounter which emphasizes a two-person experience. Both members of the therapeutic dyad contribute to the understanding and change experience in a creative mutuality. These essays reflect the intellectual breadth of psychoanalysis and psychotherapy as well as its emotional heart.

References

Freud, S. (1926). The question of lay analysis. *Standard Edition*, XX (1925–26): 179–263.

Grosskurth, P. (1986). *Melanie Klein. Her world and her work*. New York: Alfred A. Knopf.

Hoare, C.H. (2002). *Erikson on development in adulthood, new insights from the unpublished papers*. New York: Oxford University Press.

Lieberman, E.J. and Kramer, R. (Eds.). (2012). *The letters of Sigmund Freud and Otto Rank: Inside psychoanalysis*. Baltimore: John Hopkins University.

Rachman, A.W. (2018). *Elizabeth Severn, the "evil" genius of psychoanalysis*. London: Routledge.

Roudenesco, E. (2016). *Freud: In his time and ours*. Cambridge, MA: Harvard University Press.

Stevens, R. (2008). *Erik H. Erikson: Explorer of identity and the life cycle*. Basingstoke, England: Palgrave MacMillan.

Young-Bruehl, E. (2008). *Anna Freud: A biography*. New Haven: Yale University Press.

Chapter 1

My traumatic journey towards becoming a psychoanalyst

From phenomenology and person-centered psychotherapy to Sándor Ferenczi and the Budapest school to relational psychoanalysis

Arnold Wm. Rachman

My grandmother as a therapeutic role model

In the days of my grammar and high school years, I remember being most interested in two areas of study, history and archeology, which seems, in retrospect, academic areas well suited to the eventual study of psychoanalysis. In addition, to my intellectual interest, I believe my emotional/interpersonal experience with my maternal grandmother, Bertha Metsch-Beispiel, whom I called "Granny," was significantly connected to my becoming a helpful professional.

When I was 8–9 years old, the closest adult males in my family, my maternal grandfather and father, died. Consequently, my mother became intensely depressed. She also had the task of becoming the family provider. My grandmother then became the central figure in our household for my sister and me. We generally had contact with my mother on the weekends. During the week, she held down two jobs: one in the daytime and one at night. On the weekends she seemed depressed, distant and detached. She rarely planned any activities with her children. I grew up feeling she was not interested in me.

My relationship with Granny was emotionally nurturing. When I began to discuss my relations with my grandmother in my personal analysis, I began to think of it as a "Life-Saving Force," an idea I developed during my first year of analytic training (Rachman, 1969). My grandmother, in all the reflections I have done on my own and other peoples' lives, was not only a necessary and sufficient condition for emotional growth, but became a therapeutic role model in becoming

a psychoanalyst. I believe all helping professionals have had a therapeutic role mode in their lives that helped them define their attitude,
beliefs, and feelings toward being a person who devotes their life helping others. Granny helped forge a "curative image" for me as an internal emotional/intellectual map of what it takes to help someone who
is in emotional difficulty.

My first experience of a therapeutic contact between two individuals
came when I was a teenager and witnessed my grandmother's loving
and therapeutic contact with a male cousin. He emotionally unrave-
led when he was contacted by his draft board to report for the armed
services. First, he became intensely anxious and then very angry with
his mother (my grandmother's sister). He began to carry a knife and
openly threatened to use his knife to kill his mother. No one could
calm him down. He barricaded himself in his room. The extended
family that tried to help him was in chaos. Then, one day, my cousin
asked to speak to his aunt, my grandmother. At this time, I witnessed
the "therapeutic presence" of a healing person (Rachman, 2017). The
family could overhear the conversation between my grandmother
and my cousin held in his room. Gradually, the door to his room was
opened and we saw that Granny held his hand, as she talked to him
in a gentle empathic, loving way. He calmed down. My grandmother
was not critical or afraid of him. This 5′2″ demure person was able to
quiet the demons of the 18-year-old, near-psychotic person who bran-
dished a knife. My cousin's murderous rage was boiling over after he
realized that he could not emotionally face a separation from his damaging mother, who had dominated, controlled and infantilized him all
his life. His father was also dominated and controlled by his mother.
My cousin felt so emotionally crippled that he could not tolerate the
idea of having to leave his mother, who he needed for his existence.
Then, when he was faced with separation from his mother, he realized
she had robbed him of the capacity to be an independent person. My
grandmother was the antidote to his mother.

I witnessed in that turbulent time in my adolescent years the "therapeutic presence" of my grandmother with another person. She was
able to help my cousin, when he had turned away from everyone else in
the family. One of the most salient things I had always said to myself
about my grandmother has been, "I love being in the same room with
her, I felt her love, warmth and kindness." I completely understood that

my distraught family member would find a haven in my grandmother's presence. When I told my analyst, Betty Feldman, MA, about my grandmother and her therapeutic presence in my life and my cousin's, she agreed. She provided me with the necessary tenderness, warmth, affirmation, praising and responsiveness that were not provided by my mother (Rachman, 1997, 2003; Rogers, 1959).

Finding psychology as an academic major in college

As I journeyed through my college, graduate school education and analytic training, it is clear to me now, that I was attached to teachers, courses and academic majors that provided for my need for responsiveness, warmth, and affirmation. The dawn of my intellectual consciousness occurred at the University of Buffalo (UB) in the 1950s. The University was a liberal academic institution, at a time when the United States was going through a conservative political period with "McCarthyism" predominating. UB was known at that time as "the Berkeley of the East." The psychology department was headed by Olive Lester, PhD (1903–1996), a kind and interpersonally responsive person. Lester was a friendly, warm presence who parlayed her assertiveness, emotional courage, and intellectual interest into championing social issues. She made it clear that she liked me and added a note on a paper I submitted to her, for which she gave me an A, with the following statement: "Arnold, this is a very fine paper. You have the talent to be a psychologist." There is no question this unsolicited compliment was a gift to me that I have always cherished. I tucked it away in my heart and mind as a motivator towards a career in clinical psychology.

Olive Lester came from a distinguished American WASP family who helped organized Lancaster Presbyterian Church in Lancaster, New York. She graduated from the University of Buffalo in 1924, as the first person to earn a bachelor's degree in psychology at the school. She was the first woman to serve at the College of Arts and Sciences at the University of Buffalo and one of the first women in the country to lead a psychology department. As a social psychologist she was an outspoken advocate for women (Meachem, 2006). As the chairman of the Psychology Department at the University of Buffalo, one of the special contributions that Olive Lester made to the training of psychologists was to teach the introduction to psychology course. This pioneered providing the most experienced and gifted psychologist to teach the introduction to freshmen rather than a graduate student. She brought enthusiasm, experience and a kind and gentle manner to her teaching, which helped me to develop an interest in psychology. When she wrote on my final exam paper I should consider thinking about psychology as a major, I felt very lucky to have her as a teacher in my freshman year because she took the time to set me on the path towards a career in psychology. Buffalo also provided me with the opportunity to have Marvin Farber, PhD, Professor of Philosophy, and a student of Edmund Husserl, the founder of phenomenology, as a teacher (Farber, 2006). Farber taught "Logic and the Scientific Method," and introduced me to phenomenology (the study of immediate experience), empathy, and intersubjectivity. He helped open up a world of intellectual inquiry by his elegant enthusiastic presentations where one's emotional and intellectual life could be integrated. I am also grateful to Walter Gruen, PhD and Aron Herskovitz, PhD for their guidance and support when I was a young psychology student.

The University of Chicago: Committee on Human Development, Person-Centered Psychotherapy, and democratic and liberal philosophy

My education for a doctorate at the University of Chicago enhanced the democratic and liberal ideas and experiences which began at the University of Buffalo. There were three levels of education that occurred at Chicago, interaction with scholars and clinical experiences at Chicago while I pursued a double major in clinical psychology and human development in the Committee on Human Development. The first level of education emerged from the Committee on Human Development, where I received a broad intellectual training in the social sciences where psychology, cultural anthropology, sociology, biology, and any area of study that made a meaningful contribution to the scientific study of human behavior. We had the privilege to be taught by scholars in a wide range of science: the late Robert Havinghurst, PhD, a pioneer in the study of child development; the late Samuel Beck, PhD, one of the world's experts on the Rorschach Test; William Henry, PhD, world expert on the TAT test; and Erika Fromm, PhD, an academic psychoanalyst who was an expert in clinical hypnosis. Secondly, at Chicago, we were taught the American philosophical tradition of Pragmatism, which anchored the study of human behavior in the ideas of William James (McDermott, 1977), John Dewey (McDermott, 1981) and Herbert Mead (1934). These philosophical attitudes provided a democratic, liberal, phenomenological and person-centered attitude toward human relationships.

The third level of training at the University of Chicago was the introduction to the theory and clinical experience of Client-Centered Psychotherapy, now termed Person-Centered Psychotherapy, developed by Carl Rogers (1959) and extended by students such as Eugene Gendlin (1962). The Counseling and Psychotherapy Research Center was the facility established to teach, train and research the Person-Centered Perspective.

My introduction to the Person-Centered perspective occurred during my clinical internship requirement to receive my doctorate in clinical psychology approved by both the American Psychological Association. This 12-month internship occurred at The Counseling and Psychotherapy Research Center at the University of Chicago. At the Counseling Center, I naturally immersed myself in the intellectual interpersonal, and compatible emotional climate of Client-Centered Psychotherapy. A fellow doctorate candidate decided he was going to medical school after finishing his doctorate because he felt he was treated like a second-class citizen as a psychologist. I felt completely different from him, as I was being treated like a young psychologist who has the intellect, temperament and emotional/interpersonal capacity to be a Client-Centered Psychotherapist. This initial acceptance, affirmation and empathic response to me by Rosalind Cartwright, PhD and Fred Zimring, PhD allowed me to enter analytic training with a therapeutic attitude of respect for the subjective experience of the individual, the importance of empathic understanding and the importance of a democratic attitude in relationships.

My first contact with a psychoanalyst which was very positive involved Erika Fromm, PhD, who was an associate faculty member of the Counseling Center, although she was not a client-centered psychotherapist. The University of Chicago was known for developing courses and departments that cut across different disciplines. Fromm offered courses in psychodynamics and hypnosis, provided supervision and was available for dissertation committees. She was also a faculty member in the clinical psychology department. I studied psychodynamics and hypnosis with Erika and she supervised my clinical practicum paper which was experimental design using the Thematic Apperception Test. We enjoyed a very proactive and friendly relationship. I encouraged my former wife to consult with Erika to use self-hypnosis to prepare for the birth of our first child. As a result, the birth process was very enjoyable and our son was born under ideal physical and emotional circumstances, for which I have always been enormously grateful to Erika.

Finding Ferenczi

During my analytic training and for about 10 years afterwards, I was searching for a way to integrate my Phenomenological and Person-Centered Perspective with what I felt was meaningful in my study of psychoanalysis. I had become interested in the encounter and marathon movement of the 1960s and 1970s because it integrated experiential and active measures with a psychodynamic framework (Bach, 1966; Mintz, 1971; Stoller, 1967). During this period, I was in this new kind of group therapy experience with Elizabeth Mintz, PhD, which integrated an analytic approach into her Marathon Group Therapy (Mintz, 1971). During the 1970s, using Mintz as a role model, I began to experiment with the Intensive Group Experience (Rachman, 1970). In my desire to write an article about my experience, I ran across a paper on Active Psychotherapy, which listed a reference to someone called Ferenczi. In the autumn of 1976, in the Institute's library, I discovered who Sándor Ferenczi was. None of my colleagues or former teachers or supervisors ever referred to him or used his ideas or contributions in their work (Rachman, 1997b). So, one morning, I found myself pouring over Ferenczi's Collected Papers (Ferenczi, 1950, 1952, 1955). Before I began reading this material, I was curious about who else at the Institute had read it. When I looked at the library card, which noted the name and date of the book borrowers, to my amazement, I was only the second person to have checked out the Ferenczi volume in about ten years. I did not know, at that moment, if my search would lead to anything fruitful.

I sat down with Volume II, which contained the paper on Ferenczi's "active therapy" (Ferenczi, 1920). Everything that Ferenczi had written in this article was compatible with my developing active analytical perspective and my previous Person-Centered Approach, which I developed at the University of Chicago. I sat in the library reading room all morning soaking up the Ferenczi material. I was convinced at that time that Ferenczi was a clinical genius, a significant figure of psychoanalysis, and a forgotten pioneer who deserved the attention of contemporary psychoanalysis (Rachman, 2016). When I would mention my research on Ferenczi, many felt I was on a wild goose chase. They felt I was wasting my time and energy on an insignificant figure of psychoanalysis. One such scholar was a researcher on the history of Freud's life, Peter Swales. He told me a story of his efforts that, for a time, gave me hope I would be able to find some meaningful material about Ferenczi. He said he wrote a letter to the Secretary of the Library of Congress and simply asked for all the boxes which contain the Freud materials in which he was interested. This direct correspondence produced a surprising result. One day he received all the materials he requested, Xeroxed. We decided I should do the same and request all the Ferenczi materials.

I became ecstatic, just thinking about the possibility I would have the same luck. If I got the same package of Ferenczi materials, I could enlist Paul Mattick, an esteemed German-speaking colleague scholar and friend, to help me translate it. (Paul did not know at the time, I was planning his future.) My enthusiasm waned because I never received a response from the Library of Congress. These were the days when the Library of Congress was unresponsive, which changed dramatically when Harold Blum because the Director of the Freud Archives.

Why was Ferenczi's work unknown to generations of psychoanalysts and psychotherapists? And if he was known to others, such as Heinz Kohut, why didn't Kohut mention Ferenczi when he discussed the issue of empathy (Rachman, 1989)? When I uncovered the answers to these questions I was, frankly, appalled. Ferenczi's suppression was due to the politics of psychoanalysis. The suppression had nothing to do with the merit of Ferenczi's ideas or his clinical abilities and research. The more I discovered, the greater became my admiration for Ferenczi's creative and innovative ideas and for the emotional courage he showed in standing up for his dissident beliefs (Rachman, 1999). Each time I unearthed new data about Ferenczi, I became more committed to my mission and my admiration for Ferenczi as a person and a visionary.

Ferenczi began his analytical career on Sunday, February 2, 1908, when he was introduced to Freud by a Hungarian colleague (Rachman, 1997b). Ernest Jones described the first meeting between Freud and Ferenczi as "electric" (Jones, 1955, p. 34). Freud called Ferenczi "my dear son" (Jones, 1955, p. 89), wishing him to marry his eldest daughter, Mathilde. Freud invited him on his family's vacations. They would become best friends, teacher and student, analyst and analysand (Roazen, 1975). Ferenczi was described by many as the warmest and most likeable of the early analytic pioneers (Grosskurth, 1988). Even Ernest Jones, who later became Ferenczi's foremost citric, said that when Ferenczi entered a room, he would kiss all the analysts gathered. Although it is hard to imagine kissing Jones, Ferenczi was a prototypical romantic, expressive, warm and friendly Hungarian. Interestingly, one of the innovations that Ferenczi pioneered was the integration of his warmth, tenderness, and expressive and outgoing personality into his clinical behavior as an analyst. He was the "analyst of tenderness and passion" (Rachman, 1997b). He was very different, perhaps, the only analyst of his generation to relate as a human being to his analysands. Remember, Freud was the prototype for the demeanor and behavior of an analyst in those pioneering times. Without stereotyping him, Freud by all accounts was a reserved intellectual, and a distant figure (Roazen, 1975).

Ferenczi became the first analyst to experiment with the analytic method. On Freud's suggestion, Ferenczi introduced "activity" into psychoanalysis. Freud had noted that by 1918, interpretation had its limitation in the analysis of compulsions and phobias (Freud, 1919 [1918]). In a series of innovative measures, Ferenczi began his successful work with "difficult cases" by introducing active verbal and physical measures into psychoanalysis (Rachman, 1997b). He was the first analyst to use heightened emotional interaction, intense emotional expression, confrontation between analyst and analysand and the active engagement of the analyst in the analytic process. Non-interpretative measures, as Ferenczi developed them, changed the structure and process of analytic sessions. Freud was so enthusiastic with these developments that at the 1918 International Psychoanalytic Conference in Budapest he announced to the analytic community that "Developments in our therapy ... will no doubt proceed along other lines: first and foremost along the lines which Ferenczi ... has lately termed 'activity' on the part of the analyst" (Freud, 1919 [1918], pp. 161–162). With this address to the analytic world, he passed the mantle of analytic technique to Ferenczi.

Ferenczi's Confusion of Tongues paradigm

One of the greatest contributions Sándor Ferenczi has made to psychoanalysis and human understanding has been his idea of the importance of actual trauma as a central psychodynamic in human relationships (Ferenczi, 1933). He was not emotionally involved in the clinical interactions with his analysands because he was acting out his unfulfilled need to find nurturance in his analysands, as Freud had accused him. Rather, he combined his natural love of personal interaction, his robust Hungarian personality, his astute clinical observations and his identity as a "healer" to become a clinician working in the here-and-now of an analytic encounter (Rachman, 1994). These qualities allowed Ferenczi to become successful with patients who were victims of childhood trauma. He became "the analyst of difficult cases," the analyst among Freud's original circle who was able to treat non-Oedipal cases. These turned out to be what we now call severely neurotic, narcissistic borderline and psychotic-like disorders (Ferenczi, 1988; Rachman, 1997a).

After working with these difficult patients for years, this work reached a crescendo in the analysis with a unique analysand, Elizabeth Severn, who was a survivor of severe childhood traumas. She was herself a pioneering therapist who became a collaborator of Ferenczi. Together they retrieved and analyzed her severe childhood traumas. Out of their analysis came The Confusion of Tongues Theory and Trauma Analysis Methodology (Rachman, 2018).

My Confusion of Tongues trauma

The Confusion of Tongues paradigm is a meaningful way to understand the trauma I struggled with and overcame during my analytic training. From the first day of my training at the Institute, I was haunted by a series of traumatic interactions with the Dean until my last days. There were a series of traumatizing encounters, the first of which occurred on the first day of training. Our first contact began when the Dean assaulted me with a series of verbal attacks, when he falsely accused

me of coming to the Institute not having fulfilled the necessary doctoral requirements. His rage toward me started when I volunteered
that I came to the Institute without completing my doctoral oral
examination. My doctoral committee was not available before I left the
University of Chicago. In actuality, I had contacted the Head of the
Psychology Department of the Institute and was given the permission
to come to the Institute, because I had made arrangements with her to
take my doctoral oral examination in the fall of the year.

Before I could explain the approved plan to the Dean to complete
the doctoral exams, he became enraged with me. He yelled at me,
"Young man, you are a psychopath. I am not going to let you ruin
my postdoctoral program." I could sense that I was dissociating as his
tirade began; I felt his loud voice being lowered, feeling I was being
lifted into a distant place; the words being spoken did not make sense.
When I returned from the dissociated experience, the Dean was still
shouting at me and I felt emotionally wounded. I was hurt, dejected;
beaten up by a mean bully, when as a first-year candidate, completely
new to psychoanalysis, I desperately needed a helping hand with my
oral exam issue. My need for empathic understanding was met with
abuse. Rather than affirmation, I was assaulted.

This first traumatic experience with the Dean is exactly what Ferenczi
described as the Confusion of Tongues experience. I was looking for
empathy and affirmation from an authority figure, the Dean, especially
at a time of emotional need. Instead of understanding my need for
empathy, his narcissistic need for self-aggrandizement became paramount. The Dean was emotionally blind to my need, fulfilling his own.
In a therapeutic encounter, the authority figure, the analyst, attunes to
the need of the analysand. He/she remains attuned to the need of the
analysand, so they can prevent their needs from predominating. The
theory of the Confusion of Tongues is that the analyst guards against
retraumatizing the analysand. The Dean did not understand what
Ferenczi discovered, that a therapeutic interaction demands a two-
person psychology. Both members of a therapeutic dyad contribute to
change. There were more traumatic encounters to come, but as I was
embraced by my personal analyst, as well as psychoanalyst/members
of the Institute and my fellow analytic candidates, I began to have the
necessary curative experiences to work on and through my Confusion
of Tongues trauma.

My personal analysis with Betty Feldman, MA

The Dean to whom I have referred as the traumatizing agent in the development of my Confusion of Tongues experience made another disturbing contribution when I had to choose a personal analyst. He had vetoed three choices I had contacted as a potential personal analyst. The fourth choice, which was going to my last, was Betty Feldman, MA, Head of the Social Work Department at the Institute, who was one of my first-year teachers in the analytic curriculum. I decided to have a consultation session with her because of the positive feelings I developed for her as a teacher. I explained the disturbed interaction I was having with the Dean and the fact he vetoed my three other choices for a personal analysis. These were analysts, as best I could tell, who showed some signs of empathy, compassion and responsiveness. In addition, he had sent me to two other analysts whom I intensely felt were cold, distant and detached. I refused to see them for an analysis. I am sure he had developed an idea that I was a difficult, rebellious candidate who needed to be contained. Finally, I told Betty, I believed the Dean would not let me see her, if I chose her. After carefully listening to me, she said the following in an empathic and assertive voice.

> I used to be good friend with the Dean. He is someone who needs power and control over people. He has been combative with me. Your situation with the doctoral exam made him feel threatened that you were spoiling his program. You didn't do anything to put the program in jeopardy.

What Betty then said endeared her to me forever:

> Arnold, if I want to see you for analysis, I will see you. The Dean cannot veto it, I can assure you of that. And – after the consultation session, we just had, I would like to begin your analysis.

Today, 54 years, later, Betty Feldman's empathy, compassion, self-disclosure and affirmation at a crucial moment in my journey helped me turn a corner toward becoming a psychoanalyst. The course of my analysis with Betty, which included four individual sessions plus one group session each week over a four-year period, helped me

understand, accept and develop an analytic perspective. Most importantly, my analysis was a living therapeutic experience with an open,
caring, accepting human being who believed I was an intelligent, creative and emotionally well-functioning individual. My grandmother
helped me become a "a mensch," a good human being; someone who
believed in helping people. Betty Feldman helped me become "a psychoanalyst who could be a mensch." My experience at the Counseling
Center at the University of Chicago helped me integrate being a
mensch as a psychologist and clinician. When I was first puzzled at
what I should say to a client when I began a clinical session, I would
say to myself: "What would Granny say or do to help this person?"
I always followed Granny's words that emerged in my head. The final
formation of becoming "a mensch who happens to be a psychoanalyst" was aided by my discovering Sándor Ferenczi.

Curative relationship at the Institute, teachers, supervisors, peers

My Confusion of Tongues trauma developed, I believe, because the
Dean instituted a vigorously non-empathic series of interventions with
me, which was a shock to my intellectual/emotional system. I entered
my analytic training believing in the empathic and the person-centered
approach, which led me to believe the Dean was concerned with the
welfare of his analytic candidates more than himself. My developing
anxiety, confusion, anger and depressive feelings in the early stages of
my training did not happen because I was not an intellectually limited
analytic candidate. I was a graduate of one of the most important and
innovative programs in the United States. What is more, I was awarded
a National Institute of Mental Health Postdoctoral Fellowship in
Psychoanalysis and Psychotherapy to study at the Institute, which was
considered an academic honor. Neither was I considered an emotionally unfit candidate, as I was admitted to the program based upon the
results of the required projective testing and personal interviews I had
taken. In fact, during the first of several planned interviews, Ted Reiss,
PhD, Head of the Psychology Department, spontaneously offered to
me the following assessment:

> Arnold, you do not need to see anyone else. You're fine. I will rec-
> ommend the Institute should take you without reservation.

I did not need to have any other interviews. As a result of these positive experiences, I was under the impression I was entering the Institute under favorable circumstances. Just imagine the emotional shock I experienced when my first actual contact with the Institute was the Dean assaulting me with his criticisms of me and labeling me as a "psychopath." The Confusion of Tongues trauma emerged from this kind of abusive behavior form the Dean. He developed a narcissistic, paranoid preoccupation with me because he falsely believed his post-doctoral training program was in jeopardy because I left the University of Chicago without finishing my doctoral oral examinations. His narcissism took precedent over the reality that I had sought and received approval to attend the Institute without the exam. What is more, I had made realistic plans to the finish the exam while attending the Institute.

Although the Confusion of Tongues Trauma I have described was the most difficult part of my journey, it is important to note that there were positive experiences and relationships during my analytic institute training that served as a positive alternative to the traumatic interaction with the Dean. Alice Hampshire, MD, was my assigned comprehensive analytic supervisor for the first two years of my training. Our first meeting started out to be what seemed to be, at first, a repeat of the trauma with the Dean. At our first session, Alice began our supervision session with a series of confrontational statements towards me. As I spoke, she said, "Strike One!" As I continued, she then said, "Strike Two!" Before she could continue, I said to her: "Before I get strike three from you and strike out, I would like to know what game we are playing." Alice then took a step back in her interaction with me and explained what she was doing. She said her experiences with psychologists indicated they were, "all head and no emotions." She thought she was going to have that kind of interaction with me. When I told her I was trained at the University of Chicago's Counseling and Psychotherapy Research Center to be empathic, responsive and compassionate in my clinical relationships, and that I would strive to do so in my experiences at the Institute, she became more relaxed with me, as I chronicled in an article I later wrote about this experience (Rachman, 1969).

After this problematic start, we developed a positive and loving relationship. Alice took me under her wing, and became very interested in me as a person as well as my training and career as a psychoanalyst. When my daughter, Rina Beth, was born during my training years, she bought her a beautiful blue and red velvet baby blanket with the logo of a princess, which became part our family's treasured possessions. Midway through my first year of supervision, Alice told me something that was extraordinarily positive, but contributed to another traumatic moment with the Dean. She began a supervisory session by saying:

> Arnold, I do not think you belong at the Institute. I know you are having difficulty with the Dean and I can see from your clinical work you have a more humanistic orientation than this Institute. My husband went to the William Alanson White Institute. I think you would be more comfortable theoretically and clinically studying there. I think you should leave here and go to White.

I felt at this moment that God had sent me an angel. I was so warmed and affirmed by Alice's evaluation of my functioning that it provided an "emphatic shield" to the Dean's abusive behavior towards me. Alice, as a supervisor, had given me what Betty Feldman, my analyst, had provided: the affirmation necessary to believe I had the emotional and intellectual capacities to be a psychoanalyst.

What happened next was to become another difficult part of my journey. I couldn't wait to tell my analyst what Alice had proposed about my transferring to the White Institute. Betty listened to the transfer proposal to White and then, without a moment of hesitation, told me the following:

> Arnold, if you propose a transfer to White, the Dean will stop you. Then he will have your blacklisted from any other analytic training institute in the country. He would not tolerate having his reputation stained by a candidate leaving his program. I cannot say, you should not do this, but, you should very carefully think about it. I do not want something bad to happen to you.

At first, Betty's response enraged me. I thought to myself:

> What kind of fucking prison am I in? I can't leave the Institute because that asshole Dean would feel insulted.

When I settled down, I realized that Betty's cautionary statement had the ring of truth. I realized that if I transferred to White, the Dean would go after me and that the emotional chaos that would ensue would probably cause me to leave the field of psychoanalysis. I decided to stick it out at the Institute, continuing to integrate the curative experiences with Betty Feldman, Alice Hampshire, and the others who helped affirm me and provided a personal and professional opportunity to become a psychoanalyst.

My initial trust in my analyst, Betty Feldman, and the affirmation by Alice Hampshire was matched in the later part of my training program by the very special experience I was able to have with Alexander Wolf, MD, the founder of Psychoanalysis in Groups (Wolf and Schwartz, 1960b). He was a revered figure at the Institute. Everyone respected him because of his accomplishments as a pioneering figure in psychoanalysis, and his personal warmth, emphatic clinical presence and his inviting teaching method. Our relationship was highlighted by a dramatic event that occurred during my third year of training. He had decided on the advice of the Dean to conduct a group experience interaction by remaining silent. The group experience was a required sequence, to give candidates an experience of analytic group therapy as well as an opportunity to have a therapeutic opportunity for candidates to express and explore their difficulties with each other, teachers, supervisors, and the program. It will come as no surprise that the Dean had used the group experience to experiment with the candidate. In one of these experiments, the Dean as the group experience leader offered only Oedipal interpretations to any statements made by the analytic candidates in group interaction. The candidates were a captive audience to the Dean's desire to experiment. Apparently, Al was tired of offering the standard group experience and consulted with the Dean. They decided to experiment with my third-year class. In the first two sessions of the group experience, Al interacted with us in his usual style, which everyone enjoyed. Then in the third session, he suddenly stopped talking. He remained silent for the rest of the 12 sessions of the group experience which ended the first semester. After various group members attempted to get Al to talk to no avail, the group splintered into three segments: some members gave up and remained silent; some began to interact with each other, as if Al was not in the room; and a third group, of which I was a member, became openly angry. Then we plotted to retaliate against Al by locking him out of the group session towards the end of the semester. This had never been done, before or after, in the Institute's history. Al was shocked and hurt by our retaliation as we found out the next semester when we analyzed what had happened.

I cite the example in our training to illustrate how I was recovering from my Confusion of Tongues trauma with the help of my peers. I was able by my third year to respond to the Dean's negative influence by assertive behavior rather than being a victim. What is more, Al Wolf and I had a series of interactions in the second semester and beyond that helped me develop my relationship perspective. In the interaction during the second semester, when we analyzed the silent group experience, I confronted Al with the idea that during the silent group experience he suffered from a countertransference reaction, which he did not recognize, and consequently did not analyze. I told him I believed this was operative because he was not moved to speak, even though he saw the emotional damage he had created by his continued silence as group members started to cry, became angry, were distraught, or remained silent. Furthermore, I said, maintaining the experiment became more important than responding with empathy to the group's need for a therapeutic response. Al was very receptive to my interpretation of his functioning which I so admired that we began meeting regularly to continue our discussion.

For several years, we met on a bi-weekly basis where Al was completely open and accepting of my idea of what he needed to analyze his countertransference to the group experience. We discussed these issues over lunch, with the two of us taking turns paying. Al created a peer-to-peer relationship with me, leaving our formal teacher/student experience behind. He told me I could call him Sacha, his nickname. Our meetings became a mixture of intellectual and analytic exploration and the development of a warm, humorous, friendship relationship between a senior distinguished psychoanalyst with a worldwide reputation and a young man, just graduating from analytic training, 40 years her junior. This relationship was curative for the Confusion of Tongues trauma. Alexander Wolf was warm, emphatic accepting, loving and an affirming father figure. Al became the growth-enhancing figure in contrast to the Dean who was the traumatogenic agent. My relationship with Al lasted for years after my graduation from the Institute, highlighted by Al and I giving a presentation and publishing a paper about the silent group experience, the group's reaction to it, and our analyzing the issues (Rachman & Wolf, 1999).

Peers as curative agents

Alexander Wolf made another important contribution to my personal growth and analytic education with his idea of the alternate session. He introduced this controversial technique in 1938 and was later described in his pioneering book on group analysis (Wolf & Schwartz, 1960b) and in a journal (Wolf & Schwartz, 1960a). An alternate session involves the scheduled meeting of the members of a therapeutic group without the presence of the analyst. Such sessions alternate with sessions when the analyst is present. The purpose of the alternate session is to facilitate emotional interactions in the absence of the analyst. In the previously cited discussion of the silent group experience frustrated group members decided to meet for an alternate. Their meeting produced the lock-out session, and later, the discussion of the leader's countertransference. As I write this essay and integrate the associations which are flooding my brain, I realize how significant Al's ideas and clinical practice were towards understanding the meaning and power of peer relationships.

My need for empathy, affirmation and affection was also supplied by the peers. There was a particular group of peers at the Institute who spontaneously "gave me hugs" with their words, sharing of feelings, and affectionate gestures. Henry Kellerman, PhD, Robert Marshall, PhD and the late Harriet Pappenheim, CSW, were the heart of this peer group. We maintained a fifty-year relationship as we continue to meet regularly as friends and colleagues. Tragically, Harriet Pappenheim, who recently died of cancer, provided me with one of the most empathic moments of my professional life. After I had presented a talk about my career journey, including my difficulties with the Dean, Harriet gave me an "empathic gift" that was curative. In the discussion following my presentation, Harriet lovingly said to me:

> Arnold, didn't you ever realize that the Dean was jealous of you? That's why he picked on you to reduce your attractiveness. You're tall, attractive. People like you. He exercised his power and control over you to make you less attractive. The Dean was small, fat, unattractive and some people hated him.
>
> (Rachman, 2006)

While I was in the throes of a Confusion of Tongues trauma, as a result of my abusive relationship with the Dean, I never entertained Harriet's wonderful empathic-laden interpretation. As trauma survivors know, abusive relationship invert your sense of reality. As you are preoccupied with your hurt, you lose the capacity to become aware that your abuser is at fault for your pain. As Harriet so beautifully pointed out to me, the Dean's perspective was one of power and control, which was not only a reflection of his personality but of his analytic orientation. After Harriet's comment, I remembered that during our training, he told candidates that an analysis could be conducted, in almost total silence, or minimum verbal/emotional/interpersonal contact between analyst and analysand. This theoretical was referenced in the work of Karl Menniger (1958). What the Dean's belief in clinical technique revealed to me was that the analyst was in control of the analytic encounter, where empathy, responsiveness and affection were deemed to be unnecessary. What is more, there was no need for the analyst to examine his contribution to the therapeutic relationship. The analyst determines the relationship and the analysand is not a partner in the therapeutic relationship.

Establishing an identity as a psychoanalyst and psychohistorian

Analytic role model

Researching Ferenczi's life and work naturally lead to my learning about the early history and politics of psychoanalysis. I became acquainted with pioneering analysts, the personal issues between Freud, Ferenczi, Jones and other analysts who were also never mentioned in any of my education or training. I developed relationships with psychohistorians, like the late Esther Menaker and Paul Roazen as well as Jeffery M. Masson, with whom I am still in contact. They introduced me to information from their research and personal experiences, accepted me as a bona fide researcher of psychoanalysis, and encouraged and supported my research on Ferenczi. These three scholarly role models helped me develop an attitude for unearthing forgotten and unappreciated analytic contributors from a respectful dissident perspective (Masson, 1984; Menaker, 1982, 1996; Roazen, 1975). Esther regularly invited me into the comfort of her large, comfortable, old-world apartment on the Upper West Side of Manhattan, where many of the early psychoanalysts held their clinical practices. Over dinner, she would regale me with stories about her analysis with Anna Freud. Paul Roazen and Jeffrey M. Masson, whose writings about the history and meaning of psychoanalyses helped me understand that Ferenczi's ideas were deliberately removed from psychoanalysis and he was denigrated as an emotionally disturbed analyst. They also helped me to find my "dissident voice" in psychoanalysis. I began to feel comfortable and authoritative in expressing my critique of psychoanalysis. Esther and I put these thoughts into print (Rachman, 1999).

Sándor Lorand, a Ferenczi analysand

I had come close to "a living Ferenczi" through contact with one of his analysands, Sándor Lorand, in the 1980s. I became aware that Sándor Lorand, MD had his office on Central Park South. To my delight, he was happy to hear from me and agreed to meet. So began a walk back into the time of Freud, Ferenczi and the analytical pioneers. Sándor Lorand was the first European-trained analyst to immigrate to the United States, arriving in 1927. Lorand had seen Ferenczi for psychoanalysis in Budapest. Once in the U.S., Lorand became a leader in analytic circles, becoming Head of Psychiatric Education at Downstate Medical Center (Lorand 1975–76). Lorand was the first analyst to endorse a three times a week analysis which was revolutionary in the 1930s (Lorand, 1966). His office was furnished as if it was Freud's office, e.g. analytic couch, Persian rug, books and statues everywhere. I imagined being in Budapest in the time of Ferenczi.

Our first contact involved my interviewing him. Lorand had a very thick Hungarian accent. Most of the time I was able to decipher what he was saying even if I was not entirely sure what he was saying. One session was very difficult. I was presenting a case, "Oedipus from Brooklyn" (OFB), which I had written about through the years (Rachman, 2003a, 2003b). In my analysis of OFB, I had introduced a variety of non-interpretative active measures to analyze what I thought was a trauma survivor. I was eager to know if Lorand through my activity was in the Ferenczian tradition and if he, as an analyst, could endorse it. Lorand was very complimentary about my work. He said the basic test of an intervention was: "if it helps the patients, that's all that matter."

In order to illustrate his own use of Ferenczi's technique (Lorand, 1966), Lorand surprised me with an illustration of his own functioning. He began his clinical illustration with the following: "A man is on the couch: he does not speak to me. He remains silent. I say, make believe you are a *ventral-lock-wus*." For the life of me, I did not understand what he was saying. I stopped him to ask him for clarification. "Dr. Lorand, I'm sorry but, *ventral-lock-wus*? I'm afraid I don't understand." Lorand became frustrated and angry at me for not understanding him. He began repeating the phrase, over and over again as if the repetition would be clarifying: "Ventral-lock-wus! Ventral-lock-wus! Ventral-lock-wus!" Now, I was getting irritated. All of a sudden, it came to me. Lorand was saying "ventriloquist" in his thick Hungarian accent. I then shared my new understanding with Lorand: "Do you mean ventriloquist?" Lorand smiled and answered, "Yes! '*Ventral-lock-wus*."

Finding my analytic voice: presentation, papers and books

By now, it has been 42 years since I discovered Ferenczi, which has presented me with a career as a psychoanalyst and psychohistorian. My body of work about Ferenczi, which includes presentations at national and overseas conferences, published journal articles and books, has given me recognition in the analytic community as a Ferenczi scholar. As the noted Ferenczi scholar and feminist thinker, Adrienne Harris, PhD has noted:

> Arnold Rachman has been the heart and soul of the American psychoanalytic community working to rediscover Sándor Ferenczi. He has been a meticulous historian, archivist, and analyst of Ferenczi's work.
>
> (Harris, 2017)

Joseph Lichtenberg: a mentor

I have had the particular good fortune in establishing a relationship with Joseph Lichtenberg, MD. In his role as the editor-in-chief of

Psychoanalytic Inquiry and the *Psychoanalytic Inquiry Book Series*, he has taken a special interest in my work on Ferenczi. He has encouraged me to publish three special issues of *Psychoanalytic Inquiry* focusing on Ferenczi and the Budapest School of Psychoanalysis, and several books under the *Psychoanalytic Inquirer Book Series*, on Ferenczi's analysand, Elizabeth Severn, and Psychoanalysis' and Society's Neglect of Sexual Abuse. For me, he epitomizes a contemporary example of a kind, caring, empathic human being who happens to be a renowned psychoanalyst and leader.

Are Adrienne Harris and Joe Lichtenberg talking about the same person, who the Dean of the Institute, in the first few days of training, shouted at me:

Young man, you are a psychopath.

I believe my analytic journey describes my personal as well as my intellectual and interpersonal growth. My experiences at the University of Buffalo and the University of Chicago provided me with a democratic and liberal intellectual and humanistic interpersonal attitude. I learned to expect authorities to treat me in a positive, concerned and helpful manner. In my undergraduate and graduate interactions with faculty and department chairmen, I never had anyone mistreat me like the Dean had done. Academicians and Psychoanalysts are individuals who value and adhere to democratic and person-centered values. Unfortunately, the Dean acted like an autocratic who used his analytic skills like a laser knife to offer *interpretations without empathy*, which hurt rather than soothed or provided insight. I was not permanently traumatized from this experience because there were affirming and empathic authorities such as teachers, supervisors, colleagues, peers and my analyst who provided the necessary affirmation and empathy. I also was able to become acquainted with: "the most loving analyst of the pioneering analysts," as Phyllis Grosskurth had called Sándor Ferenczi (Grosskurth, 1988). I am proud to say that Betty Feldman chose me to be her analysand and became a nourishing, loving mother figure for me. I was able to transform an initial antagonistic interaction with a supervisor, Alice Hampshire, into a loving friendship. Another highlight of my training experience was being able to transform a teacher/student relationship with Alexander Wolf into one of being colleagues, collaborators and friends. He also became a loving father figure for me.

The final trauma

In my last year of training, I was involved in another and final difficult experience with the Dean. I presented to him a case of a young man who was struggling with his gay feelings. The Dean felt I was not being assertive enough in my interaction with this individual, insinuating I was contributing to his ambivalence about his homosexuality because I was not providing a good enough male role model. I was hurt by his interpretation, feeling he was calling me a "sissy" who did have the capacity to be a strong male analyst who could be a role model for a man struggling with his homosexual feelings. But, I did find the courage to challenge him, telling him my person-centered orientation, which I began to realize after my Ferenczi research and becoming part of the analytic community could be integrated into a relational perspective to psychoanalysis (Rachman, 2007). As I continued my presentation of the case, I emphasized being a co-creator with the analysand of the therapeutic encounter. I used the analogy that I was walking side by side with this individual, attuning to his subjective experience to guide my therapeutic behavior. The Dean's response became the last stage in the Confusion of Tongues trauma. His response to my analogy was:

> You sound like an Arab woman, who makes sure to walk behind her man!

I became full of rage and rejection. When he finally saw that I was unresponsive he added:

> Arnold, you are a very good analyst. I am being hard on you, because I want you to be a great analyst. You could be as good an analyst as I am.

Is there any more to say about this experience? I think I've said enough for now. I'm sure I will write about it again. I still find it difficult to say that the Dean helped me. It's very difficult to attribute goodness to an abuser.

References

Bach, G.R. (1966). The Marathon group: intensive practice of intimate interaction. *Psychological Reports*, 18, 995–1005.

Farber, M. (2006). *The foundation of phenomenology: Edmund Husserl and a quest for a rigorous science.* New York: Albany State University of New York Press.

Ferenczi, S. (1920). The further development of the active therapy in psychoanalysis. In *Further contributions to the theory and technique of psychoanalysis*, vol. 2, pp. 193–217. New York: Bruner/Mazel.

Ferenczi, S. (1933). The confusion of tongues between adults and children: the language of tenderness and passion. In *Final contributions to the problem and method of psycho-analysis*, vol. 3, pp. 156–167. New York: Bruner/Mazel [1955].

Ferenczi, S. (1950). *First contributions to the theory and technique of psychoanalysis*, vol. 1, E. Jones (Ed.). New York: Bruner/Mazel [1980].

Ferenczi, S. (1952). *Further contributions to the theory and technique of psychoanalysis*, vol. 2, J. Rickman (Ed.). New York: Bruner/Mazel [1980].

Ferenczi, S. (1955). *Final contributions to the theory and technique of psychoanalysis*, vol. 3, M. Balint (Ed.). New York: Bruner/Mazel [1980].

Ferenczi, S. (1988). *The clinical diary of Sándor Ferenczi*, J. Dupont (Ed.), Trans. M. Balint & N.Z. Jackson. Cambridge, MA: Harvard University Press.

Freud, S. (1919[1918]). Lines of advance in psychoanalytic therapy. *Standard Edition*, 17: 157–168

Gendlin, E. (1962) *The creation of meaning.* Evanston, IL: Northwestern University Press.

Grosskurth, P. (1988). The loveable analyst – the clinical diary Sándor Ferenczi. *The New York Review of Books*, December 8, pp. 45–47.

Harris, A. (2017). Endorsement/back cover. In Rachman, A.W., *Elizabeth Severn, the evil genius of psychoanalysis.* London: Routledge Press.

Jones, E. (1955). *The life and work of Sigmund Freud: vol. 2, years of maturity.* New York: Basic Books.

Lorand, S. (1966). Sándor Ferenczi 1873–1933: pioneer of pioneers. In *Psychoanalytic pioneers*, F. Alexander, S. Einsenstein, & M. Grotjahn (Eds.), pp. 14–35. New York: Basic Books.

Lorand, S. (1975–76). The founding of the Psychoanalytic Institute of the State University of New York Downstate Medical Center: an autobiographical history. *Psychoanalytic Review*, 62(4): 677–714.

Masson, J.M. (1984). *The assault on truth: Freud's suppression of the seduction theory.* New York: Farrar, Straus & Giroux.

Meachem, J. (2006). *History of Department of Psychology State University of New York Buffalo.* New York: Research Gate, University of Buffalo.

McDermott, J.J. (1977). *The writings of William James: A comprehensive edition*. Chicago: The University of Chicago Press.

McDermott, J.J. (1981). *The philosophy of John Dewey*. Chicago: University of Chicago Press.

Mead, G. H. (1934). *Mind, self and society*. Chicago: University of Chicago Press.

Menaker, E. (1982). *Otto Rank: a rediscovered legacy*. New York: Columbia University Press.

Menaker, E. (1996). *Separation, will and creativity*. Northvale, NJ: Aronson.

Menniger, K. (1958). *Theory of psychoanalytic technique*. New York: Basic Books.

Mintz, E.E. (1971). *Marathon groups: Reality and symbol*. New York: Appleton-Century-Crofts.

Rachman, A.W. (1969). *Life-saving fantasy* (unpublished).

Rachman, A.W. (1970). Marathon group psychotherapy: Its origins, significance and direction. *Journal of Group Psychoanalysis and Process* 2(2): 57–74.

Rachman, A.W. (1989). Ferenczi's contributions to the evolution of a self-psychology framework in psychoanalysis. In *Self psychology: Comparison and contrast*, D.W. Detrick and S.P. Detrick, (Eds.), pp. 21–41. Hillsdale, NJ: Analytic Press.

Rachman, A.W. (1994). The confusion of tongues theory: Ferenczi's legacy to psychoanalysis. In A. Haynal & E. Falzeder (Eds.), *100 years of psychoanalysis*, pp. 235–255. London: Karnac.

Rachman, A.W. (1997a). The suppression and censorship of Ferenczi's Confusion of Tongues paper. *Psychoanalytic Inquiry*, 17(4): 459–485.

Rachman, A.W. (1997b). *Sándor Ferenczi: The psychotherapist of tenderness and passion*. Northvale, NJ: Aronson.

Rachman, A.W. (1999). Ferenczi's "Confusion of Tongues" theory and the analysis of the incest trauma. *Psychoanalytic Social Work*, 7(1): 27–53.

Rachman, A.W. (2003a). Oedipus from Brooklyn (OFB): a Ferenczian analysis. In *Psychotherapy of difficult cases*, chapter 2, pp. 45–113. Madison, CT: Psychosocial Press.

Rachman, A.W. (2003b). *Psychotherapy of difficult cases*, pp. 45–113. Madison, CT: Psychosocial Press.

Rachman, A.W. (2006). Finding Ferenczi: A personal odyssey. Invited lectures, Psychoanalytic Society, Postgrad Psychoanalytic Society, Baruch College New Library. Oak Room, 147 East 22nd Street, New York City, December 8.

Rachman, A.W. (2007). Sándor Ferenczi's contributions to the evolution of psychoanalysis. *Psychoanalytic Psychology*, 24(1): 74–96.

Rachman, A.W. (Ed.) (2016). *The Budapest School of Psychoanalysis.* London: Routledge.

Rachman, A.W. (2018). *Elizabeth Severn, the "evil" genius of psychoanalysis.* London: Routledge.

Rachman, A.W. and Wolf, A. (1999). An experimental group experience with a silent group leader. *Issues: Journal of Postgraduate for Mental Health Group Therapy Alumni Association*, 13: 15–31.

Roazen, P. (1975). *Freud and his followers.* New York: Alfred A. Knopf.

Rogers, C.R. (1959). A theory of therapy, personality and the alternative session. *American Image*, 17(1): 101–108.

Stoller, F.H. (1967). Face to face with the drug addict: an account of intense group experience. *Federal Probation*, 31(2): 2–47.

Wolf, A. and Schwartz, E.K. (1960a). Psychoanalysis in groups, interpersonal relationships as developed in the client-centered framework. In S. Koch (Ed.), *Psychology: A study of science*, Vol. 3, pp. 184–256. New York: McGraw-Hill.

Wolf, A. and Schwartz, E.K. (1960b). *Psychoanalysis in groups.* New York: Grune & Stratton.

Chapter 2

Comprehending

Harnessing oblique defiance in the formation of an analyst

Fergal Brady

9/11

Everybody remembers where they were on nine eleven. That's an easy one for me. I was a patient in hospital. I got a text message from my brother that morning saying 'Turn on BBC.' I went out of my hospital room to the public part of the ward and turned on the television and watched with the rest of the ward, the rest of the world, as the horror of the terror attacks of September 11th, 2001 unfolded in front of us.

The mood was one of disbelief. I spent much of the next few days talking over what was going on in the world with a friend and fellow in-patient. He was older than me, wise and educated and philosophical. Together we talked it over for the next number of days.

He remembered a trip he had been on to New York, a business trip, no expense spared. Flights on Concorde and a tour of the Twin Towers. The Paris Concorde crash had been the year before and the planes remained grounded. 'What odds,' he joked, 'would you have gotten if you bet on me outliving both Concorde and the Twin Towers?' You see, the hospital we were both in at that time was St Patrick's, Dublin. The oldest psychiatric hospital in Ireland.

There I learned the first of what would be many lessons about mental health and how the mind, my mind, works. There I attended my first talks about mental health. There I learned the first lessons about healing. And there I suppose I began a new journey, a quest for understanding, that I am still enjoying today. I made a Freudian slip. I typed mond just now instead of mind. 'How the mond works, how my mond works.' Simple free association takes me from 'mond' to 'monde' and changes it to 'How the world works and how my world works.' And I guess that's about right.

I was coming to the end of my first stay there, I would spend – I want to say *serve* – another period of time as an in-patient.

I was in the middle of a long nervous breakdown of some sort; my psychiatrist called it an existential crisis. As it felt like the external world was falling apart with 9/11 and all that followed so it was with my internal world which was in some sort of state of crash or crisis.

Those two hospital stays represent a kind of midpoint of my life; they were the beginning of a long, slow, turning point. Let me go back a little and tell a couple of stories about how I got to that point. And then I will try to describe how I plotted a course out of it, which I suppose is the purpose of this paper.

1976 and 221B. The flow of the Wad River

When I was a boy there was a field behind the houses opposite our house. We called it, rather unimaginatively, the back field. The back field was a great place to play. There were lots of tracks with little jumps which were so much fun to race around on your bike. Back in those days we went everywhere on our bikes.

You weren't allowed to go there. It was muddy and, we were told, there were rats there. I wasn't afraid of rats. In fact, I was excited at the prospect of seeing some. I enjoyed many hours in solitary contemplation there, away from it all.

There was a river there, the Wad River. It was a small river, but I loved it. In summer or in dry spells the flow would reduce to not much more than a stream. But when it rained you got a great rushing flow that washed down branches and leaves and other detritus from further upstream. Shortly after our little stretch of the river bank it went underground, which only increased the mystique of the river for me. I loved it. It was to become a metaphor.

One day when I was riding around the back field on my bike, I met a man with a digger. I was concerned so I went over to him and asked him what he was digging. I didn't want anything to destroy our bicycle scrambling track. He told me they were digging the foundations for a library. That was to be one of the most exciting things I had ever heard. I couldn't believe that we were going to get a library. In the back field. If you wanted to do a grown-up analysis of it you night say that I was ready to leave my bicycling days behind and become a little more cerebral.

Anyway, in what seemed like no time at all the library was built and open and I was certainly one of their first customers. There was a children's section which I felt, at the tender age of 12, that I had mostly out grown. There was some sort of 'in between children and adult' section which I settled on and there I found a 12-volume set of the complete Sherlock Holmes. I excitedly borrowed the first volume and there began a love affair with libraries, with books and with mysteries; the more obscure the puzzle, the more theatrical the elucidation, the better.

Holmes was perfect and I read them all and then began at the beginning and read them all again. Years later, when illustrating how identifications work in learning, I made the comparison which exists in my mind between Holmes and Freud. For me, there is a permanent and unmistakable link between 221B Baker Street and 19 Bergasse. A friend and colleague reminded me recently that Sherlock Holmes is not real, he is a fictional character.

You see, in my way of looking at things it hardly matters if Holmes is real and Freud fiction or the other way around, whichever it is. They are part of the narratives we hear and what we understand of them. Stories we are told which we believe. Or believe in. Stories we symbolically transform in our own minds. Therein lies the heart of the matter for me. The reason for my breakdown and the direction of the transformation of my recovery, via the Wad River.

One true. Belief systems

I was raised in a world where I believed everything I was told. The world was straightforward enough. My family was a good family. We were lucky enough to live in the most beautiful country in the world. There was a God, He looked over us and as long as we kept our noses clean and obeyed the rules, we'd enjoy eternal life in Heaven. It wasn't easy, there were rules to obey and we would be tempted to break them, but it was the one true faith and we were the ones who were on the right path.

My father was involved in politics. My mother's family were too, they served in parliament. Once again, we were in luck here. Ours was the party of government, a convenient addition to our membership of the one true faith, we were spiritually and politically on the winning teams.

We had a football team too, our birth right, they were winning too. You didn't so much choose these things; you were born into them. I was born lucky, that's what I was told, and I saw no reason not to believe it.

I didn't know it then, but in these certainties were the fault lines which would lead to my later nervous breakdown.

Rat Trap

By the winter of 1978 things had taken a bit of a turn. I was beginning, just beginning, to feel a little disenfranchised, a little cut off from the perfect world of my earlier childhood. One event from that time stands out from all others in my memory of it.

I was sitting on the couch at home, one Thursday evening watching *Top of the Pops* from the BBC. Everybody watched *Top of the Pops* every Thursday. It had been a grim summer and autumn music-wise for me and my friends. The movie *Grease* had been released and the soundtrack was dominating the charts. This came to represent the epitome of our disenfranchisement and disenchantment with the world. For us, the film was the antithesis of cool. I know that it was a very well-received film, but for us, at that time, it was awful. Just not cool. And John Travolta, now regarded as cool I will grant you, and his co-star Olivia Newton John spent a total of 16 weeks at number one in the singles charts with two successive hit singles.

Then along came the Boomtown Rats. They were the very epitome of cool. And they made it to number one in the charts with their song *Rat Trap*. Their appearance on *Top of the Pops* began with their holding up pictures of Travolta to camera and then proceeding to tear them up with a snarl. My mother, beside me on the couch, said 'There was no need for him to do that.'

I, on the other hand, was transfixed. I could not believe what I had just seen. It was *our* music. They were *our* band. They were from *our* town. They went on the revered *Top of the Pops*, with the whole of Ireland watching, and they ripped up pictures of the very people who seemed to stand for the very opposite of what we stood for. I couldn't quite believe it. I couldn't believe that there was someone else out there who felt the way I felt. It was like he could see inside my head. It was amazing and cemented in my mind an appreciation for the importance of musical expression which I hold to this day.

I didn't become a punk rocker even though I loved it. I loved it and was afraid of its destructive power. I enjoyed it from the safety of my perfect suburban life. I remained a closet iconoclast. Enjoying the wish to destroy although leaving the heavy lifting of the struggle to others.

In our perfect suburban world, you left school and got a job, a permanent and pensionable job. That's what I was told to do and that's what I did. And, I can't believe I am about to type this: I got a permanent and pensionable job and stayed in it for 28 years. It wasn't a straight trajectory, however. I only really lasted 18 years and then it all started to fall apart. Only then in the telling of what happened after that am I addressing the real purpose of this essay. I am sorry it is taking me so long to get to the point, and thanks for sticking with it so far. I hope to be able to make sense of the back field and the library and the Boomtown Rats for you as we proceed. We have to talk about Joey Dunlop first.

Heading in the wrong direction

Joey Dunlop was a motorcycle racer. A working-class hero, a modest and shy man, he was the greatest motor bike racer in road racing, the bravest of the brave. Fearless, at one with his bike. His legend grew around him, he took apart whatever latest bike the factory delivered to him and put it back together himself. He knew every washer.

I was a Joey Dunlop fan in the same way I was a punk rocker, from the safety of my perfect suburban life. In the summer of 2000 Joey died and a little bit of me died with him. By this time, I was a married man, with two children, working as assistant manager in the bank.

The morning of Joey's funeral, which was carried live on television, I was commuting to work by car in the same way I did every other day. As I drove south from my home towards Dublin, I passed numbers of motorcyclists heading north for Joey's funeral. Fifty thousand people attended Joey's funeral, many travelling by bike from Ireland, Britain and beyond. I wasn't going.

As I sat at a set of traffic lights, waiting for the green light, I was passed again by another group of bikers heading north. 'I am heading in the wrong direction,' I thought to myself, and I was overcome. I pulled over to the side of the road and sobbed. I sobbed uncontrollably for several minutes and had difficulty pulling myself together to face the working day. I did, but a little piece of me had died. I carried an awful weight with me for the following months, a growing feeling of dread which I did not understand. A secret. Most of my friends or family wouldn't have known or understood how Joey's death had affected me. I was, as I said, a closet motorbike fan. A closet punk rocker. On the outside I wore a suit and made loan agreements.

Breakdown

Somewhere over that winter, following Joey's funeral, and it is no coincidence that it happened for me on the same stretch of road that I stopped to cry that day, I could go no further. One day I pulled the car over to the side of the road. I didn't cry. I couldn't cry. But I could go no further. I turned the car around and went back home. Unable to explain what was wrong with me I went to the doctor and he gave me a cert for chest pains to excuse me from work for a few days. I tried to go back to work a week or two later but I couldn't hack it. I was incoherent. I had no idea what was wrong with me. I couldn't form a sentence about it. I didn't know where to begin.

Much of the next two years is a blur to me. That is how long it took me to get back to some version of myself. I had a complete nervous breakdown. A deep, treatment-resistant depression. I was in a fog. I felt no pleasure. Nor did I feel much pain really. I often thought it would help to have a good cry, to let it all out. But I couldn't cry no matter how I tried. I felt nothing.

Anhedonia. I love that word. It would make a great name for a heavy metal album. I felt nothing. I was off work for months and eventually I was referred by my psychiatrist to St Patrick's hospital as an in-patient. I was lucky that because of my job I had private medical insurance and was in hospital a total of 14 weeks in two separate admissions. I was on a variety of antidepressant drugs. None of them made a blind bit of difference.

I accepted my treatment stoically. I was a willing patient, believing in my doctors and the help and treatment they gave. I believed the same way I had been believing all my life. I didn't realise it yet, but that was the problem.

During the second in-patient stay I had in St Patrick's, I was offered and accepted a course of treatment of ECT. Electroconvulsive therapy.

It is controversial, I know. I was, as I said, a willing, compliant patient. I can't remember exactly but I think I had six treatments.

It is likely that, in view of my current position in life, I will be asked for an opinion on ECT. I don't really have an opinion of it. I was in such a fog of not feeling at that time that I would have agreed to any treatment that was offered.

It had no effect on my depression. If anything, I would say that the only lasting effect of the ECT is a feeling that I was never as good at spelling afterwards. I was always a good speller. And since then I don't spell quite as well as I did. I have no proof of that.

I was discharged and after a row at home I had a brief, third in-patient admission. Then I had a conversation with a counsellor that was the beginning of turning things around. I say conversation; it wasn't a session. I met with the counsellor to talk about setting up some sessions. As part of that conversation she said 'You're not a banker, you're a social worker.' A touch paper of some sort was lit. it referenced the way I was about my banking career, if you could call it a career. Whatever you think of when you hear 'banker,' that was not what I was. Those were the days, I started in banking in the 1980s, of old-fashioned relationship banking.

Customers mattered, honour mattered, loyalty mattered. As the world changed, and I didn't, these things mattered less. Credit scoring and cost-cutting and standardisation and centralisation of decision making mattered more. The world I had belonged to was crumbling around me and all my belief systems were failing me. Things that mattered to me, that defined me, didn't matter anymore.

From somewhere, in that moment, I saw a glimpse of something. I didn't know exactly what, but it was the changing point of my life. In the bookshop in the hospital I bought a book, *Night Classes in Dublin 2001*. I looked through for anything to do with social work and I found a course. It was a National Higher Certificate in Social Studies and Counselling Studies. I thought the social studies together with the counselling studies was a nice fit following my recent experience with the counselling profession. I was discharged after a couple of days. On the way home from the hospital I rang the college, Dublin Business School (DBS), and enquired about applying for the course. I was in luck, but there wasn't much time. They could grant me an interview that Friday. So, I went to the college that Friday afternoon not really knowing what I was getting into or even if I would be considered a suitable candidate, especially in light of my recent psychiatric history. All I remember of the interview is that I wrote a cheque before it finished and the young woman in admissions told me that the course began that evening in a building around the corner. I went and I met some people that night who I would become very close to as we journeyed together for the following four years.

The first class on the Friday evening was followed by a full day of lectures on the Saturday. I had never been to college; I was 37 years of age. That first Saturday morning I met a man called Domhnall Casey who played an unwitting part in the direction my life would take from then on.

Firstly, Domhnall lectured on 'Contemporary issues' and began with a brief history of psychoanalysis and read a piece from Freud. I was hooked. Immediately. I am still hooked. I remember the excitement I felt, how refreshing it felt, to hear psychoanalysis and to hear Freud. I can't say I understood it all, I just know that it spoke to me. Here, somehow, was the key to unlocking something that I didn't yet even begin to understand.

As things developed and I got to know Domhnall better he explained that he was a member of the Irish Psycho-Analytical Association. He couldn't take me as a client because he was my tutor, but he recommended Mitch Elliott, then President of the Association, who would become my analyst.

Becoming

I'm sorry it has taken me 3000 words to get to the start of my task. My analysis represents the real beginning of my formation as an analyst. I remember Mitch the first day I met him. Tall, American, kindly, formal, polite. He took the intake very seriously I remember and I can recall how meticulous he was about details of my family history. And off we began.

There were aspects of the theatre of psychoanalysis that I really enjoyed. I liked the discipline of the couch.

I also liked the way you (I) could lie on the couch and think and not say anything and follow a line of thought and then say a bit of it and follow it and see where it goes and that Mitch would often sit and listen to lots of this and not say anything at all.

When he did speak, he had that ability that I was familiar with from Sherlock Holmes of being able to see a pattern or a thread or a theme in the middle of a muddle which I could not see at all. It was eye-opening and I had a thirst for more of it. I just couldn't get enough of psychoanalysis. I still can't.

My studies continued, Domhnall was tutor for what was called Counselling Theory and Practice, during which he taught me some things I haven't forgotten. His part of the course was brief, just an introduction, but he influences me to this day.

One of the first learnings I remember is that of hypothesising. Don't fool yourselves that you are not hypothesising about a client from before you even meet them, from the first contact by phone, from their appearance and demeanour when you meet. Don't fool yourself that you do it, so be in touch with your hypothesis from the start. Don't marry it, be prepared to be wrong. Largely, I think the way I work today is a variety of this whereby I hypothesise out loud in partnership with the client or patient or whatever you want to call them.

I hypothesise out loud, a kind of interpretation, I guess, and every week or with every new level of understanding reached we tweak the hypothesis and see where that goes.

Not being afraid to be wrong was incredibly refreshing. That was the complete opposite to the way of being in every version of the world I had operated in until then.

After a couple of years in psychoanalysis Mitch invited me to the Saturday Night Group. It represented an introduction to the next level of my training, although I didn't know it at the time.

The Saturday Night Group

The Saturday Night Group of the Irish Psycho-Analytical Association is a unique kind of meeting. Having its origins in the 1930s nobody living is sure exactly when it began. Based loosely on Freud's Wednesday Psychological Society, it was run every Saturday Night in one of the houses of the analysts, in rotation. A supper was served. This was said to be an important factor during wartime. There was a talk every

Saturday Night by Jonathan Hanaghan, founder and President of the Irish Psycho-Analytical Association.

Jonty, as he was known, died in 1967 and I never met him. In my time going to the group the talks were delivered in rotation by Mitch Elliott, my analyst and by John Cameron, who was the other senior analyst at the time. The topics ranged widely but were always psychoanalytic leanings on various aspects of life and love.

I say I didn't realise at the time that it represented part of my training because the training at the Irish Association was based on an old-fashioned kind of system whereby candidates were identified as part of their analysis and then brought up through a system of meetings, seminars, reading groups and the Saturday night group.

Mitch identified me as a candidate for full membership around about 2004 and thus began my informal, to begin with, training as a psychoanalyst.

The college course I had begun in Dublin had a two-year term and then I went on to do another two years and complete an honours degree in Counselling and Psychotherapy. There were lots of experiential learning modules in the course. Group Analytic Practice was key to this. It was a full analytic group which we were thrown into, unknown and unknowing in the first week of college. No explanation was given for the purpose of the group. The best answer we could get from the analytic facilitator was that 'the purpose of the group is to be a group'. It was a great experience. I was lucky with that group. I have had lots of group experiences since but nothing matched that first group.

What was special about it – rare, I would say now – was that it was a group of people who supported each other. There were no rivalries, there was a lot of respect and no little affection. We helped each other through.

There were other groups I experienced as part of my training where I learned more about the negative aspects of human nature, and the corrosive effect that has on learning and creativity.

I was in group supervision experiences that were very openly hostile and you had to learn how to keep your head down and be cautious about what you said for fear of being attacked.

I had a group experience where the group leader, a member of the course team, was prone to turning on a student and I had the very uncomfortable experience of being on the receiving end of her wrath. It was the antithesis of what I had learned from Domhnall and what I experienced in that first Analytic Group.

Now I know that in order for any learning or growth to happen in this work there has to be the ability to be open and honest about one's own process in group without fear of attack or nothing good can happen. When I say attack, I mean undue criticism as opposed to anything constructive. Jealousy seems to play an important part in this. I would find resonances of this much later in my training when I came across the story of Sándor Ferenczi and how his legacy was treated in particular.

Formal training. And metapsychology

The Saturday Night Group meetings continued, and continue to this day, and I learned a great deal there. Through regular attendance there I became steeped in a psychoanalytic way of thinking. It was wonderful.

After I graduated from DBS School of Arts with my honours degree in Counselling and Psychotherapy, Mitch and the Officers of the Association laid out a formal training programme for the candidates; there were four of us. We did a Masters in Psychoanalytic Studies at the University of Sheffield.

The Masters Programme in Sheffield was well designed and well run. There was the same supportive creative environment that I had experienced in the first Group in DBS. This included a great dynamic between fellow students and between students and lecturers. It was a dynamic environment conducive to learning.

There were heavy modules on the basic Freudian papers. I am grateful to this day for the very thorough grounding I got in those times in the fundamental tenets of psychoanalysis. As I write I have my well-thumbed copy of volume 11 of the Penguin Freud Library beside me. I spent a lot of time lost in its pages. A lot of time.

I studied Freud's 1915 paper 'The Unconscious' at great length, spending many hours in the library poring over the details and trying to comprehend Freud's topographical model of the psyche. It was unusual to spend so much time on a course of study that didn't have an immediate end. That is, there was no assignment I was preparing for in studying this text. I just wanted to give myself the best understanding possible for the *Unconscious* and what it meant and how the processes worked.

At the same time as I was studying this in University, I had begun to attend the Reading Group of the Association. We were working on a project – it is fairer to say witnessing a project – lead by Mitch Elliott whereby he wrote a long paper called the anatomy of depression (Elliott, 2009). It was never published, but the Reading Group spent four or five years studying various texts with Mitch regularly updating and circulating the latest updated version of his paper.

We read *Mourning and Melancholia* (Freud, 1917). Mitch read it. It was another of those great psychoanalytic experiences, meeting on the first Saturday of every month in the basement of the building in Glasthule, Dublin where Domhnall worked. Again, like the paper 'The Unconscious', which is in the same volume of the old Penguin Freud, I spent many, many hours reading over that text trying to understand every detail and nuance of it. I loved the 'Shadow of the Object' and could even cope with learning that the topography that I was spending so long studying was later replaced by a revised version.

Following *Mourning and Melancholia* we read *The Drama of Being a Child* by Alice Miller (1995). We spent some time on *The Dead Mother Syndrome and Blank Mourning* by Andre Green (2003). We studied what was called the Colchester model of the Superego, incorporating phylogenetic parts of the superego to add to separate maternal and paternal parts. This was under the influence of Mitch's liaison with Karl Figlio at the Psychoanalytic Studies Department University of Essex at Colchester.

We spent some time too on Bjorn Killingmo and his comparative study of conflict versus deficit pathology (Killingmo, 1989).

It was a really world-class and vibrant reading group experience and I am very grateful for the grounding it gave me and the comprehension of complex psychoanalytic concepts. Over those years I became steeped in psychoanalysis and in study. I couldn't get enough of it. It was, and remains, as much a hobby for me as a scholarly or professional pursuit.

Analysis. The new couch

My analysis continued through these years. I learned so much from Mitch. So much of it by osmosis, by identification with him and copying his style and technique. I spent little or no time really talking about my breakdown – he said it was all right to call it a breakdown rather than using any more technical term – I liked that. I talked about all sorts of thing, getting better at just talking in a free associative style. I learned my craft really in those times and in that way. I learned to trust the process of a psychoanalysis. Just talk without censor. Don't try to make sense, don't be in too much of a hurry to find meaning. For me, it was not about great 'lightbulb' moments of great insight. It was a long, slow journey of rediscovery through my past during which I got the impression of turning back into myself. Mitch encouraged me to trust and rediscover the spirit of discovery and adventure of the boy on the bike in the back field.

Mitch wasn't greatly impressed with the River Wad and its minor tributary status. He recalled the Hudson River of his childhood and asked me to imagine a mile-wide river rather than my little stream. I didn't like his disrespecting my river, but I never said. I knew what he was trying to do.

One day, after about five years of analysis, I turned up as normal to find a new couch in his room. I lay on it and admired it. 'I like the new couch', I said. Mitch, being a wise old fellow, asked me to say what it was that I didn't like about the old couch. 'It was wicker', I replied, 'you always got the feeling that it was a little shaky'. When he asked what I liked about the new couch I had no problem in heaping praise in its solidity, complementing him on his choice of mahogany as a firm and solid frame to lie on.

He didn't say anything for a minute or two as we both basked in the enjoyment of the new solid frame. After a little time had elapsed, he said

It might surprise you to know that the couch you are lying on is 20 years old, I bought it in the winter sale in Arnott's Department Store sometime around 1994. It is the same couch you have been laying on these past five years.

Well, I was completely stumped. Though Mitch wasn't. He understood straight away that the feeling I was expressing, indeed projecting onto the couch, was in fact about the new-found solidity of my own psyche.

Oral and anal phases

We spent a great deal of time going over my potty-training experiences as a child. It was not a good experience for me. I know that anal phase ways of looking at things is out of fashion in psychoanalysis, but it seems likely that a certain stubbornness about my character developed, or was honed, during the time when I resisted my parents' attempts to control when and where I defecated or urinated. It is an art, potty training, and my parents were old-school, 'You will do what you are told as long as you are in this house' types. The same regime applied when it came to food. You finished your dinner, there was no debate about it. You were reminded of the starving children in Africa who would be glad to have such a dinner. These things were really awful battles of will during which I refused to bend. I could not assert myself in the face of the overwhelming control of my parents so I retreated somewhat into my inner world, in my own head. I became a funny mix of angry defiant yet introverted compliant little boy. I stayed that way and it became the template for my adult personality. I remember later spending hours reading Melanie Klein's 'Our Adult World and its Roots in Infancy' (2017) and reflecting on my own experiences as a child. Again, that paper remains a favourite, I remember where I was when I read it first. And like 'The Unconscious', it was a paper I read and re-read and studied and made notes in the margin despite not having the immediacy of having to produce an assignment on it.

Mitch said, in relation to this stubborn compliance, that when I said something, even something important to me, I often said it obliquely. He was so right about that and I know I still do it. Something about having others assert themselves over me left me reluctant to assert myself over someone else. I don't value or respect it as a way of achieving anything. It can be a blind spot – more of that later – and it also had a role in the development of my depression.

Telling the story out of sequence, when I finally concluded my analysis, I felt robust and strong, capable of taking whatever slings and arrows life would throw at me and confident in my ability to cope.

However, when I took a look at myself in the years immediately following the ending of my analysis, I saw a fat, unhealthy, middle-aged man approaching 50 years of age. I knew I had to make some lifestyle changes or begin to suffer ill health. I smoked, I drank – probably a little too much – and I weighed 270 pounds. I felt an inauthentic authority on mental health, or any other kind of health for that matter. I felt that I lacked authority to speak with clients on issues that I was so obviously ignoring or repressing in myself.

In another of those important visions of a future that happen from time to time I decided to do some more work on myself, by myself and gradually make some changes. It took about four years all told to get to where I wanted to go and, in that time, I stopped smoking, stopped drinking alcohol and lost 100 pounds.

A great deal of the motivation for doing this came from my remarriage following divorce and also in my work with clients and ongoing learning in that way.

I began to understand the importance of mirroring. And the effect of a lack of it. I understand addiction, the oral phase addictions, as being relational in origin. I had developed a better relationship with myself as a surprising by-product of whatever process it was that I had been on for 15 years by this time.

I mentioned divorce. There's hardly any need to say too much about it here – out of respect for the others involved as much as any other reason. I learned, gradually, that I had been in some kind of Bollas state of mind for the previous 15 years. A combination of some kind of Normotic Illness and an Unthought Known had led me into the fog of my depression. When it came time to finish my first marriage it was all done respectfully. Any feeling or loss had long since been dealt with, without talking about it, and it was – I wouldn't say amicable – but business-like, devoid of any acrimony. Devoid is a good word to sum the whole thing up actually. *Ça va.*

Clients and research and sexual abuse

I developed a specialty – quite by accident – in the first years of working with clients. Some simple questions presented themselves through working with clients who had been sexually abused. I was all about comprehending. I need to understand. I valued the process of understanding and the power of change that could be brought about by sufficient understanding – worked out collaboratively – in psychoanalytic psychotherapy. I didn't yet have the theatrical elucidations of the Sherlock Holmes of my youth or the Sigmund Freud of my studies.

What I did have was a stubborn refusal to accept not being able to figure out what was lying hidden in the story of how people behaved. I knew that in psychoanalysis I had the tool to facilitate opening up understanding of these things and through my love of a good library and the love of a good book I valued original sources rather than trusting someone else's commentary or technical recommendations. I sat with patients and wondered with them, for example, what a mother might have known about the sexual abuse of her daughter by the father. Wondered about the position of really often quite pitiful alpha male figures who asserted their dominance in part through exercising sexual control over their children's lives. A code of secrecy and perverted loyalties was at play in some of the murkier parts of this. It is expressed in analysis with patients and I and they began to find ourselves asking questions and trying to understand what structures were at play in the psyche, in particular a group psyche in this regard.

This became the subject of my research at the University of Sheffield in a dissertation that I would eventually title 'The Phylogenetic Structure of Child Sexual Abuse'. I interviewed analysts and asked them about their experiences of working with patients who had been sexually abused. It remains my principal area of study and I continue to work on papers for conferences. I hope a paper of mine on this subject will be published soon.

During my researches in this area at Sheffield I came across the work of Sándor Ferenczi for the first time. It was a turn which would influence the future direction of my work. There were a couple of things that took my interest in the first instance. The first was the paper 'The Confusion of Tongues' (1933). Ferenczi's descriptions of the identification processes, the transmission of guilt and the confusion of tongues itself as he outlines it are beyond compare in the literature. The fact that this was written in 1933 and largely overlooked for many years only increased my interest in him and the whole story of the Budapest School. I had had an interest in Michael Balint as part of our study of object relations at DBS in Dublin, but I hadn't known of the connection between them.

The second keen interest of mine from my work with patients was about the effects of trauma, specifically sexual abuse, on memory. In his Clinical Diary (Dupont, 1985), Sándor Ferenczi outlines some of the very traumatic experiences of his client RN during her childhood.

I wondered how he worked with that. I wondered how he, in collaboration with his patient, worked out what was true and what was not.

I had one case in particular at that time where this kind of thing was a feature. There seemed to be three classes of memories. The first of these were things that the patient could say definitely happened. There was a category of 'memory' which were parts of what I came to understand as a process of the psyche trying to work things out, a sort of bargaining or 'what if' process where there were 'memories' of events which probably hadn't actually happened. And then there was a third category, somewhere in between, flashes or snippets of things or traces of memory where a part of a story is missing, the key part, with a before and after memory of what was clearly a traumatic real event but with big pieces missing. Within the second category in particular, but in all three, there were large areas of indistinct recall that the client couldn't be sure of.

These aspects of memory in abuse made the relationship between the clinical and the outside world more difficult because we were now operating in a climate of statutory reporting of child protection concerns where child sexual abuse was present. In the main, such cases were straightforward enough as there were distinct traumatic abuses that could be reported without fear of contradiction. It didn't help though that there is a whole area of 'memory', which I don't think should correctly be called memory as it belongs to a function of the psyche which forms part of a process of coming to terms with trauma. I hope to have the opportunity to continue to work in this area and wrote a fuller account of it in time.

Project psychoanalysis

There was another aspect to my training which sent me off on this individual path of study and lead me to the Budapest School, in the process raising me to levels I never would have dreamed possible.

Mitch was fond of describing psychoanalysis as a project. He had a little talk about it which often served as his preamble to a Reading Group or when a new member was in attendance. Begun by Freud in 1896, Psychoanalysis was a body of study on the mind, so the story went, that was as yet unfinished. Describing Freud as a 'man, with blind spots', he would say that we don't think of him like a guru or someone who we blindly follow and defend. In the way Mitch outlined this history of psychoanalysis the project was added to by various others who had learned it and worked using its methods in the intervening years. Each one of us who followed had a right, a responsibility even, to seek out new understandings of things and report from our work with patients back to colleagues. Every one of us, I learned to believe, has an equal right to make a contribution to the body of psychoanalytic knowledge in this way.

It's a funny thing that, because the effect it had on me was to set me off on my psychoanalytic career with patients in a mode of enquiry and feeling that I had a responsibility to bring back to the group what I learned. It is quite an inspiring way to look at it. I have to say that Mitch and his colleague John Cameron were always very open, receptive and generous with my contributions to the Saturday Night Group in particular over the years.

I enjoyed the close contact with the senior members of the Association and to their thinking that was afforded to me as part of my training. I lapped up their insights, their knowledge of theory and their differing clinical experiences. During all this time I was studying part-time and still working full-time at the bank. These were, paradoxically, my happiest years at the bank as I increasingly bridged the gap between these two very different worlds, not knowing how exactly I was going to be able to bridge the gap further and make the leap from the financial world into psychoanalysis full time.

The opportunity did come eventually; I wasn't finished with my psychoanalytic training but I had my counselling and psychotherapy accreditation and began to work full-time in clinical practice. I set up a therapy centre in Dundalk in partnership with the woman who would later become my wife. There were some financial hardships going from salaried work in finance to self-employed therapist, but the freedom of it was fantastic and the increased growth through full-time practice was beyond my expectations.

With regard to one of the questions that had informed my research, that of memory, a kind of answer came to me in the course of my work. The best explanation of it I can give is to describe it as a 'kind of knowing' that seems to come from the shared unconscious space between analyst and patient. It is a way of working that is largely informed by countertransference and brought me further into the work of Ferenczi and the large international community of psychoanalysts working, researching and writing on contemporary Ferenczian lines of thought. This group attracted me and drew me in and it was here that I had the good fortune to meet Arnold Rachman.

I met Arnold in Florence in 2017 at the Ferenczi Summer Course organised by Carlo Bonomi. Arnold and I got talking one day over coffee. I was just this guy from Ireland with this story to tell and he was presenting at the Summer School the ongoing research he was doing into Ferenczi's work with Elizabeth Severn, having secured her papers. He was very interested in my work and was very generous with his time, arranging a meeting with me where I could tell him about my work around sexual trauma and the role I felt fantasy played.

Over the next couple of days, it became clear that there wasn't going to be time in the daily schedule to hear the clinical vignettes I had prepared. And then Arnold made an extraordinarily generous gesture. He cut his presentation short and devoted 90 minutes of the time allotted to him to give me an opportunity to present my paper. It was, as I've said, a very generous thing to do. He introduced me with the minimum of fuss and didn't want to be thanked really and treated it like the most normal thing to do. I've never met anyone quite like him.

At that time, Carlo Bonomi had just published the second volume of his book, *The Cut and the Building of Psychoanalysis* (Bonomi, 2018). His is a fantastic and creative theory. Like Arnold, he operated modestly and with a minimum of fuss. He came to me after my presentation and made some suggestions about my work with my client. His intervention was very important and sent me on a further area of study within the Ferenczi school discovering Carlo's theories around the effects and denials of circumcision.

This had a direct influence on my work and the direction I took and together with my liaison with Arnold lead to me proposing and then organising a conference in Dublin. That would take another couple of years to come to fruition.

Cello and countertransference

I always valued music. There is a short paper of Sándor Ferenczi's which is a favourite of mine, 'On the Interpretation of Tunes that Come into One's Head' (from about 1909). In it, he talks about the experience which we are all familiar with, I guess, of finding a song stuck in your head. He outlines how he initially followed a free associative path in trying to understand possible meanings for a particular song which might become lodged in our mind. The 'Interpretation of Dreams' was recent and he was keen to use the word association technique to reveal unconscious meaning. What he found, when he realised what the song in his head was, Mendelsohn, *Song without words* – was very simply that the mood elicited by the melody was perhaps of most importance in these matters.

So it goes for the way in which I have allowed myself to be informed, by and within my work. I heard music sometimes and sometimes related it to a particular client.

I had an experience close to the one Ferenczi describes. I had a piece of music stuck in my head. My free associations associated it with one particular patient. From my psyche came the image of me as a musical instrument. The patient was playing a tune. On me. I had to try to tune in to this tune to understand something of his experience. If I could bear it.

Before I lost the weight, I was a double bass. Now, the cello was more appropriate. I had a piece of cello music playing which I had no conscious memory of. Bach's cello suite is well known and a favourite. This, however, was something different, something darker. It was Vivaldi. If you had asked me, I wouldn't have associated Vivaldi with the cello but there you go. I looked it up and there it was. Largo, a slow mournful air, followed by a play with a quicker allegro piece.

What I learned was that there was something about this client's presentation that I didn't like and that it was difficult for me to bear. I realised too that he was communicating to me that he found it difficult to bear too. So, I guess what I was called on to do was to learn to bear it with him.

You can't find evidence for this kind of thing. It is at best beyond words, a way of working whereby an unconscious to unconscious communication takes place and if both parties are for a time on the same frequency then some movement or even some healing can happen.

More and more with practice I have come to work in this way. I have come to trust in it. The key seems to be to check that the frequency you are tuned to is in fact the patient's and not coming from somewhere else. It is one of those things you have to experience to really believe.

It relies on the bond between the analyst on the one part and the client on the other. It seems that there needs to be a bond of trust in place before this line of communication can open. It is a level of communication that has a kind of purity in it. An intimacy that feels like a privilege to be part of. It seems to me that there is something about this that finds its best home with Ferenczi and what has become known as the Budapest School.

I have increasingly found resonance in this regard with the writings of Michael Balint and Enid Balint. I am playing with Balint's third area of the mind, that of creativity. Here, he says, there are no objects. It has taken me somewhere close to 18 years study and over 50 years of life to begin to master this. And to find an object out of it.

I have increasingly found resonance in this regard with the writings of Michael Balint and Enid Balint. I am playing with Balint's third area of the mind, that of creativity. Here, he says, there are no objects. It has taken me somewhere close to 18 years study and over 50 years of life to begin to master this. And to find an object out of it. I read with interest *The Basic Fault* (Balint, 1968), *Thrills and Regressions* (Balint, 1957), *Problems of Human Pleasure and Behaviour* (Balint, 1957) and Enid Balint's *Before I was I* (E. Balint, 1993).

I don't have time here to trace out the entirety of my thinking on this. That will have to wait for another paper some other time. See what I am doing? That was a favourite narrative tool of Arthur Conan Doyle's. Watson would refer to a case from his diary and he and Holmes would both agree that it was far too sensitive to make public just yet. And you'd have to wait to find out. I am playing with you now. That is what I have learned how to do. Psychoanalytically.

Endings, graduations, Orpheus, symbolism and beyond

Our psychoanalytic training came to an end. It wasn't entirely smooth towards the end and, as the student cohort gradually attained the necessary knowledge and experience and the closer it got to the end of the training, things became a little fraught. There was a brief standoff between us students and the course team. It felt to us like they were reluctant to let us go, reluctant to allow us take our place as fully formed analysts beside them. There were some representations made and, in their defence, the course team resolved matters between themselves and there was no need to set up any kind of dialogue between two sides in a dispute situation.

I finished my personal analysis shortly afterwards. It was the place, above all others, over those seven and a half years where I could be my complete self and explore the limits of what I might be capable of. It was such an important holding space for those critical years where the direction of my life changes completely. There, I learned for the first time to think the unthinkable. Then to begin to say the unsayable. Finally, to begin to do some of what I had begun to think and begun to say. It was great, I loved it.

I remember Mitch as being this incredibly intelligent, wise and gentle spirit. At times, he could be idealistic, at times he talked a lot, for an analyst, he told stories. And at times, maybe when I had needed it the most, he was just kind.

I began to take on a more active role in the affairs of the Association over the next few years. I was part of a rotation of speakers at the Saturday Night Group. I couldn't have believed that a few years before. Domhnall was the lead of the Reading Group, but he became ill and I began to coordinate that group's meetings.

I had always had a penchant for poetry and for music. I thought they were both important. I wouldn't have relegated them to only belonging to the area of 'the Arts'. As part of our graduation process from the training we had to deliver a talk to the officers of the Association on a topic of our choice. I had enjoyed the study of Psychoanalysis and the Arts at Sheffield. I had this interest and then I had this idea.

It came to me one evening when I was driving home from the clinic. I was listening absentmindedly to BBC Radio 4 when I heard a reference to something Seamus Heaney said as part of his introduction to his translation of *Beowulf* (Heaney, 1999). Heaney initially struggled with the task of translating the poem. Then he began to get an insight into how he might achieve it and a further insight to the cause of the blockage, inside himself. He writes:

the Irish/English duality, the Celtic/Saxon antithesis were momentarily collapsed and in the resulting etymological eddy a gleam of recognition flashed through the synapses and I glimpsed an elsewhere of potential that seemed at the same time to be a somewhere being remembered ... a place where the spirit might find a loophole, an escape route from what John Montague has called 'the partitioned intellect', away into some unpartitioned linguistic country, a region where one's language would not be simply a badge of ethnicity or a matter of cultural preference or an official imposition, but an entry into further language.

(Heaney, 1999, p. xxv)

This was ringing bells in my head with regard to my own process and my analysis. In a wider way, with a little help from Plato and Freud, I managed to weave it all into a 7000-word essay which formed a kind of grand statement of my philosophy on the occasion of my becoming a full member of the Association.

Mostly, I recognised in Heaney's description resonances of my own moments of insight where I glimpsed an elsewhere of my own potential. I was now able to put that into words and into action.

Orpheus played a surprising role in my essay with regard to looking back and not looking back and the practice of psychoanalysis. I was becoming increasingly becoming familiar and comfortable with the language of symbolism as expressed in folklore and myth. I was joining together modes of thought that seemed capable of reaching down into the depths of the unconscious, mine and my clients' and, indeed, a societal unconscious. Over the years I had developed a confident and robust faith in the language, process, theories and frankly the play of psychoanalysis. My treatise was very well received, Mitch describing it to me later as having exceeded the highest expectations, which was generous praise indeed.

Helen and Aphrodite

Over these years too I had been enjoying an interest in Helen of Troy. I was fascinated by her and, like a lot of my experiences with these things, I don't think I had a good enough understanding about her and what, frankly, the whole fuss was about.

One day a beautiful young woman came to my office and told me the sad story of a turn that had been taken in her love life. How her family had reacted to her leaving her long-time boyfriend. Representations were being made on his behalf to her father. The story seemed unbelievable in the twenty-first century and I watched, transfixed and at times horrified, as the story of Helen played out in front of me over the following months. I'm glad to say there was a satisfactory outcome for my contemporary Helen, but I could not quite believe the similarities there were between the two stories, hers and the Helen of Myth. In the process I began to better understand sex, sexuality and the feminine in particular.

This modern-day Aphrodite seemed genuinely unaware of the power she held and the madness men were capable of in its service. Her modesty was part of the attraction that drove men mad. It was one of many cases where I learned more of the power of sex and sexuality and together with my work on sexual trauma and abuse and my casework following Carlo's thesis, I was beginning to form a joined-up theory of humankind and its primitive psyche.

Dublin, Budapest and the River Wad

In November 2018 at the annual general meeting of the Irish Psycho-Analytical Association I was elected President. Mitch had had a hip replacement was taking a step back from his active role in the Association. He was gracious and generous and proposed me to replace him.

Over the coming months I organised a conference in Dublin, with Arnold and Judit Meszaros as speakers. The conference was called 'The Budapest School of Psychoanalysis: Ferenczi, the Balints and Beyond'. It was a success.

In the months following the ending of my analysis the River Wad went into flood. The river of the back field of my childhood went into flood. Or, it would have gone into flood if there was a plane for it to flood. Because of development the back field was no longer a field, and where there had been various streams and rivulets there was now housing and other development. Much of the course of my river was now underground. In a wee pipe. If they had asked me when they were putting it in, I could have told them that the pipe was not big enough. A small pipe could take the flow of the river most of the time. But from time to time, and I had witnessed it as a child, our modest little river went into a roaring, proud flow.

And so it happened. The tiny, underestimated river found ways to flow around and over and through the concrete that had encased it.

Shores on the main road were breached, their heavy iron cast aside as the flow found full expression. Huge cracks appeared along the main road and traffic was reduced to one lane. There was an apocalyptic air of climate change-induced terror in the denizens of my former neighbourhood.

I can't tell you how happy I was at this turn of events. I was so happy to see the river in full flow again. I parked up at the side of the road for a while and watched it and listened to its flow. Not far back up the road I had pulled in to have a cry on the day of Joey's funeral. I thought of the Boomtown Rats, tearing it up in 1978.

I looked at the library, my library, still there with the old river flowing around it. There was no need to feel afraid of the river's destructive power. It was renewing.

I thought of Sherlock Holmes and of Sigmund Freud. I laughed as I enjoyed the conflation of the two characters in myth and in unconscious, and of their occasional theatricality. I thought of Orpheus, the Underworld. Of Eurydice, Helen and Aphrodite and all the other women. I laughed out loud. I knew that everything would be all right and I drove on.

References

Balint, E. (1993). *Before I was I. Psychoanalysis and the imagination*. London: Free Association Books.

Balint, M. (1957). *Problems of human pleasure and behaviour*. London: Maresfield Library.

Balint, M. (1957). *Thrills and regressions*. London: Maresfield Library.

Balint, M. (1968). *The basic fault. Therapeutic aspects of regression*. London: Routledge.

Bonomi, C. (2018). *The cut and the building of psychoanalysis, Volume II. Sigmund Freud and Sandor Ferenczi*. London: Routledge.

Dupont, J., ed. (1985). *The clinical diary of Sandor Ferenczi*. Cambridge, MA: Harvard University Press.

Elliott, M. (2009). *The anatomy of depression*. Unpublished.

Ferenczi, S. (1933). *The confusion of tongues. Final contributions to the problems and methods of psycho-analysis*. London: Karnac.

Freud, S. (1917). *Mourning and melancholia. The standard edition of the complete psychological works of Sigmund Freud. Volume XIV*. London: Vintage.

Heaney, S. (1999). *Beowulf*. London: Faber and Faber.

Killingmo, B. (1989). Conflict and deficit: implications for technique. *The International Journal of Psychoanalysis*, 70(Pt 1): 65–79.

Klein, M. (2017). Our adult work and its roots in infancy. In *Envy and gratitude and other works. The collected works of Melanie Klein*, Vol. III. London: Karnac, pp. 247–263.

Miller, A. (1995). *The drama of being a child: The search for the true self*. London: Virago.

Chapter 3

Family gifts and the artful practitioner

A journey of personal, professional and artistic growth

Alan D. Entin

All families have secrets. I discovered mine at a young age, in a box or paper bag, I don't remember which, in the closet. I knew even then it was a secret, an important secret. No one in my family wanted to talk about my prescient treasure: there were letters and there were photographs. I was too young to read the letters and did not know who were in the pictures. Among the few photographs, the two that stood out were my Uncle Bernie, the union organizer, the activist. They were taken at union strikes of department stores in New York. In one he was standing next to a person wearing a large animal mask and costume. I was so afraid I might forget who it was in the picture that I printed, with a colored pencil or crayon, "Bernie Pops Brother" on them so I would not forget. The letters were those my Uncle wrote to his mother and my parents about his feelings and reactions about the family and his thoughts about going to Spain to fight fascism in "not a civil war, but an international war" (Entin, B., July 15, 1937), a term many now think more accurately describes the Spanish Civil War and characterize as the first battle of World War II.

And from that first discovery, I kept the photographs and letters throughout my life, somehow realizing their importance, if only because they were a secret. It was only after the death of my parents that an older family cousin, Muriel Sholin Miller, was willing to talk about my uncle Bernie. Thus began my lifelong interest in family photographs and the secrets they contain. Their secretiveness was wrapped in a mystery that set off my curiosity about what was so important, so emotionally charged, that my family did not dare speak about it. I did not realize that this secret would become a gift, the engine that would be the driving force in my life's unique journey as a family psychologist: learning about my family's history and helping others to learn their family's secrets and history.

My interest in family photographs continued. In the beginning there were photographs of my family, people I have never met, people whose existence preceded mine, people I know only through photographs and some people only through stories and photographs. Next came a few pictures of my grandparents, parents and their friends, me and then my brother and me. Then I began to take pictures, pictures of my family, images that would be passed down as heirlooms, precious icons of the family, which would one day be seen by generations whose existence I preceded. I became the family photographer, historian and genealogist as a child and adolescent.

I still have my first Brownie camera and a gift that my Uncle Jay gave me at age 12, the book, *This is Photography* (Miller & Brummitt, 1952), with the inscription "May this hobby lead to bigger things." The bigger things, I came to realize, from my uncle who would create elaborate stories about "Velvul the Vulf" for us, would include sparking my mind, my use of fantasy and imagination, the value of play, and propel me into the world of creativity. This was another prescient gift that would shape my passion and journey as a photographer as profoundly as the gift from Uncle Bernie.

These twin gifts from my uncles, one, expressed as my professional passion, the other, as my personal passion, coalesced into an unusual journey— a journey combining family psychology and photography, namely, the use of photographs and family albums to understand family relationships.

Exploring personal and professional history

I grew up in Brooklyn in a working-class family, with my parents and a younger brother. My father's mother, who had series of strokes after she learned that Bernie went off to Spain, lived with us in our small apartment and cared for my brother and me when my mother returned to work after my brother's birth. My father had several jobs and on the eve of the Korean War he got a job in Chicago, selling and delivering cookies. I took a test for admission to Brooklyn Technical High School because the school guidance counselor said it would "help me think," even though I was not a stellar student. To everyone's surprise, the boy voted class clown—me— got admitted to this highly competitive school. A year later my family joined my father when we moved to Chicago. I continued by going to a technical high school, where I concentrated in college preparatory courses. Upon graduation I attended the University of Chicago.

At the University I majored in the interdisciplinary studies program of Human Development and earned an AB, MA and PhD, with an emphasis in Clinical Psychology. The program taught me to think in a more holistic and inclusive manner, incorporating diverse views and interdisciplinary approaches, which I try to implement in all my endeavors. One of the bedrocks of the program was the theoretical concepts of Erik Erikson (1950), describing psychosocial stages of development from infancy to old age. I suggested to William E. Henry, PhD, that I wanted to use Erikson's concepts to study personality development and adjustment in young children for my dissertation. The stumbling block was that the theory had never been operationalized, or extended to the techniques of observations of children, the Draw-A-Person Test, and teacher's ratings. I returned the following week with ideas how to operationalize the theory, he liked what he heard, we submitted and received a grant from the National Institute of Mental Health (NIMH) to carry out the research project and I earned my PhD in 1967.

Afterwards I continued my training with a postdoctoral fellowship at the University of Wisconsin in Madison in the Department of Psychiatry, where I focused on the dual specialties of child and family psychiatry. I worked with the legendary Carl Whitaker, MD. He was brilliant, analytical, charismatic, and intuitive. His approach was largely based on his own personality and intuition. It was impossible to duplicate, although all the trainees attempted to be junior Carl Whitakers and spouted Whitakerisms constantly.

The first day I arrived there was a guest expert: Murray Bowen, MD, another founder of family psychiatry, but with a systems theoretical framework. In the course of my training that year, I learned that it was more effective to treat the heads of the families for symptoms that developed in the children than to treat the children, and I shifted my interests to working with the family.

When it came time for me to leave Wisconsin, Whitaker had me contact Bowen. Through my readings and exposure to different prominent family psychiatrists that year, I thought that Bowen's Family Systems approach, focusing on "the family as a unit of study," had the most to offer. It was a ground-breaking approach, and replicable, because it was grounded in a solid theoretical system. I thought it offered a new way to treat individuals and families experiencing a wide variety of emotional, physical, and learning problems. I wanted to learn more about it and joined the faculty in the newly created Virginia Commonwealth University (VCU), Department of Psychiatry, Division of Psychology where Bowen was to head the teaching program in family psychiatry. He came monthly for a number of years, although his plans to move to Richmond full-time never materialized.

A central feature of the program was Bowen's interview of a family. When it was my turn to bring in a family for him to interview, I surprised Bowen when I introduced him to the family—my parents. The interview was bland and non-revealing. Just when I thought the interview was about to end, Bowen hit on a family secret: the conflictual relationship between my mother and grandmother and an incident which led to my parents' almost getting a divorce. It highlighted my mother's major dynamics—"£peace at any price." She did not speak about her negative feelings or voice disagreement. She acted as if she liked everyone, and she wanted to be loved by all. She rarely spoke up for herself. She was conflict-avoidant.

Likewise, my father did not talk about his feelings. He once said that a salesman approached him and asked if he had a relative named "Bernard," and he passed out. I could not get beneath his denial to elicit any more information, though I spent my professional life talking with families about their intimate experiences. I had hoped that Bowen would be better able to penetrate their defenses and unlock more family. It was a fertile background for a future family psychologist and illustrated the difficulties involved in getting below the surface to know one's own parents as people. The topic of Bernie never came up. And my parents did not talk about the interview with Dr. Bowen.

After seven years on the faculty, I left VCU for the same reason I was hired: I was interested in Bowen Family Systems Therapy, and the Department of Psychiatry wanted to emphasize the biological basis and treatment of mental illness. Years later I discovered that the real reason I was hired was the then Chair of the Department hoped I would operationalize Bowen's Theory of Family Systems

Therapy, much as I had done with Erikson's concepts of personality development.

The transition into independent practice was both daunting, very challenging, and exciting. It was before insurance would cover a psychologist's services. I joined a psychological organization for private practitioners that evolved into the Division of Independent Practice (Div 42), of the American Psychological Association (APA). I became active in their leadership and other APA divisions, which amplified my opportunities to present my research about photographs and their uses in psychotherapy. The richness of my life was enhanced by becoming involved with these communities of practice that also resulted in life-long friendships.

Bowen Family Systems Theory

I see individuals or couples for therapy using the Bowen Family Systems Theory approach (Bowen, 1971, 1972, 1976,1978; Kerr & Bowen, 1981). If patients ask for "homework" or something to read, I suggest several books based on Bowen theory written for general audiences (Bryan, 1999; Gilbert, 1992, 2004; Hendrix & Hunt, 2019; Lerner, 1990, 2014).

Bowen Family Systems Theory is a way of thinking about and dealing with emotional problems in families. Emotional disorders are conceived as a dysfunction in the family emotional system, and treatment is directed toward a modification of the relationship system between the most important members of the family, usually the spouse or parents. If an individual is to change, the context in which they live must also change, and if one individual in the family is symptomatic, all the members of the family are involved in the problem. It is a family problem.

While I am gathering information about what brings the patient(s) to therapy, and the problems they are experiencing, I am recording the information on a family genogram, a family tree. I am interested in obtaining information about the important people and relationships in their lives (children, parents, grandparents, significant others, previous marriages, etc.). I am also seeking information about stress areas, "which are marital conflict, illness or other dysfunction, and projection to a child. A change in stress symptoms might be related to internal

dynamics or external events. The dates of changes are important"
(Bowen, 1978, p. 171). This overview can be obtained fairly quickly
initially, but the elaboration of details of functioning within the family
is an ongoing process throughout therapy.

Two of the most important observations I can make based on my
experience with families is that emotional problems can best be understood by placing them in the context of a three-generational emotional process. Thus, the extended family system of an individual,
parents and grandparents are prime resources in the resolution of
conflicts and stress within the nuclear family. Symptoms that develop
in individuals can best be alleviated by helping the individuals "work
on their family" to resolve their "mirror image" patterns of repeating difficulties and longstanding issues that have "funneled down" the
"emotional hereditary" axis from the parents and grandparents. To
accomplish this, an individual has to understand the structural and
functional laws of family process, become an expert about their family
system, the part they play in the emotional process and the triangular processes that lead to the stabilization of emotional dysfunction,
and changing their part by working towards the development of the
person-to-person relationships with their parents and other important
individuals within the family system. It means finding out about the
family and how it got to be programmed through the generations, and
their various mythologies, labels and rules of how men and women
and boys and girls should be and behave in the family.

Getting to know one's family is best accomplished through family
visits in which the goal is to differentiate from and/or revive stale or
dysfunctional relationships with middle-aged and elderly grandparents. In relating, it means talking about self, being open about your
shortcomings first, not criticizing the other person, and allowing the
other person the opportunity to talk about themselves. It means not
labeling or blaming parents and grandparents, to get to the "person."
It makes the past real and bridges the generation gap, restores a sense
of continuity with the past. It takes many attempts to talk in a non-
defensive, non-blaming manner, and real change takes a long time
to achieve. Bowen (1978, p. 247) describes the process of taking an
"I position" and getting to know one's own family of origin for the
"differentiation of the self," through the establishment of person-to-
person adult relationships within the family system, as "growing up."

I encourage them to visit with their family and talk individually to people, to develop individual adult-to-adult relationships with each person. If they talk about the resistance they are likely to meet, or if the relatives might be emotionally reactive or deniers, I suggest the use of photographs can be invaluable. By teaching them to "think systems," they can then apply those concepts, when talking with their family, about the people and events in the pictures. For example, a rebellious, non-conforming adolescent may not be included in a family photograph either because they or the family may not want to be defined as part of the family. Or, an individual is consistently marginalized and on the edge of the picture. Or, they may not be present at the family event. Only questioning the family may reveal the meaning or issues so overtly, yet covertly, expressed in the family photographs.

By using photographs in talking with their family, the pictures serve as a distancing mechanism, creating a triangle (discussed below), to function as a third leg in the triangle between them. That is, they are talking about a picture and not directly about themselves, about something that is in the past, not about them today. This sometimes makes it easier for them to enter into a discussion about the relationship. It involves asking about what the event was when the picture was taken, what happened before and afterward; essentially, who, what, where, when and why. Who is in the picture and who was not, all are revealing pieces of information about the family.

Exploring my family history: my search for Uncle Bernie

Exploring family history is central to my professional life, something I talk about with each of my patients and encourage them to do in the healing process. Because it was so difficult to find out about my own family history, I would like to describe my process in the voyage to unlock the mystery surrounding my Uncle Bernie. Turning the lens on my own family history is important to me as a family systems therapist; however, he is a man a few people know only from distant memories. Whatever happened to Bernie, son, brother, cousin and uncle? That question has puzzled, vexed, mystified, and frustrated me all my life. It was a topic that was not readily talked about or openly addressed. Like all secrets, it has its own mystique and legacy for future generations.

It is the kind of stuff that creates legends and myths—a ready-made fill-in-the-blanks history of what was and what might have been. It is a "meditation on ... memory and loss and of the simultaneous existence of the past and present" (Vecchi, 2005).

Growing up, I knew the outline, but not the details. Uncle Bernie, born March 1, 1915, was a union activist and organizer, implicated in a paternity suit, went to Spain to fight in the Spanish Civil War, and was never heard from again. I had the family photographs and the letters he wrote home from Spain, including a "petition to erect a memorial" (Veterans of the Abraham Lincoln Brigade, 1937), in memory of those killed in Spain, with his name on it. Yet, my family seemed unwilling to accept, or acknowledge, his death, with the same resistance and denial as to his life. I "Googled" Bernard Entin in 2005, expecting a futile search yielding nothing. He died so long ago—was young, an infantryman. As he was not an officer, not a leader in battle whose story would be immortalized, I did not think I would find any information. Nevertheless, I typed his name in the search engine, and to my surprise, his name popped up on the website of the "American–Israeli Cooperative Enterprise." The listing was for the *Jewish Virtual Library* and referenced Jews in the Spanish Civil War (Part 2) edited by Martin Sugarman. In a list of names there it was: Bernard Entin, KIA and Brunete (which I did not realize meant Killed in Action in battle at Brunete), the month and year of his death (July 25, 1937), and his family's address in Brooklyn, New York, when he left for Spain. This was more information than I ever had.

The second website on Google referred to an article by Harry Fisher in *The Volunteer, Journal of the Veterans of the Abraham Lincoln Brigade* (*VALB*, 2001, Spring, p. 16), and referenced what turned out to be on the third website, Fisher's book *Comrades* (1997), about his experiences in the Spanish Civil War. In the article, Fisher reports seeing Bernie wounded, for the last time just before he died. I got goosebumps reading the article. I was very excited that I hit pay-dirt and I did not think there would be another reference to Bernie. However, in those few minutes I learned a lot; first that there was an organization of the Abraham Lincoln Brigades Archive (ALBA) promoting the memory and legacy of the Lincolns, which I called first thing the next morning and spoke to Moe Fishman, a veteran and secretary of the organization, who was extremely knowledgeable about the members of the Lincoln Brigade and pointed me in the direction to find the missing pieces of my history.

I also discovered that my uncle had a "best friend," a friend I hoped might still be alive, someone who might be able to provide me with first-hand information about Bernie. And, thirdly, that Fisher had given his son the middle name Bernard, in honor of his close friend, my uncle. Unfortunately, Harry Fisher died several years before I began my family research, but Moe was able to give me the name of his son, John Bernard Fisher, and I was able to talk with him and his sister Wendy. Through Moe I was even able to locate people who knew Bernie and were able to provide personal accounts and insights (Jack Shafran, 2005, personal communication; Norman Berkowitz, 2005, personal communication). And with more Google searches I was able to locate information with lists, and references to books and articles which mention Bernie. Eventually I even found his date of birth. Gail Malmgren of the Abraham Lincoln Brigade Archive Collection, Tamiment Library, New York University, sent me a student's paper (Rowe, 2005), which cited two *New York Times* front page articles featuring labor strikes Bernie organized (1937, March 16, p. 1 and 1937, March 18, p. 1). As if by magic, once the search started, sources proliferated and came unexpectedly.

Moe invited me to attend a fundraising celebration for ALBA, where Pete Seeger sang; I took a photograph of my wife with his beloved banjo, a "selfie" with him, and met some vets and their families who had known Bernie. Before long my wife and I had tickets for Madrid to attend the 70th Anniversary Commemoration of the start of the Spanish Civil War, the first of a half a dozen such trips. My daughter accompanied me on my last trip to Valencia and Madrid, which commemorated the ending of the war. These "homenages" were crucial in revealing the psychology of the International Volunteers who came to defend the newly-elected democratic government of Spain that Franco was trying to overthrow. I also learned that many of the vets kept their experiences of going to Spain a secret, and did not talk about it after they returned.

On one trip I visited Brunete, the site of one of the bloodiest battles of the war—the battlefield where my Uncle died, I saw a rainbow in the morning sky. On a gate to the hallowed ground, the place where I was going to recite the Kaddish, the Memorial prayer for the dead, the gate was painted in the rainbow colors of the Spanish Republic. And in the setting sky, after a very emotional visit, as we left the consecrated ground, there was another *arc-de-ciel*. It was as if my Uncle Bernie sensed my presence and thanked me for honoring his memory.

At the outset of my research, information about Uncle Bernie was scant, only an index card with some basic demographic information from the VALB (1937) archives. After years of research compiling information and writing articles about Uncle Bernie, I donated my materials and the original, fragile copies of the letters he wrote home from Spain. There is now at Tamiment Library "a vertical file" on Bernard Entin, a venerable status designated to those volunteers whose files contain considerable material.

My internet searches, along with reading books and articles about the Spanish Civil War, plus research at Tamiment Library, and trips to Spain to visit the historic sites and battlefields (and meeting families of International Volunteers) yielded considerable insight into the young man who left his family in Brooklyn to fight for democracy in Spain. I learned that he was a bright student who was caught in the dilemma of pursuing his education for a career in a country in the midst of a depression with whose politics he increasingly disagreed; he was a visionary who followed his dreams to volunteer to fight for the working class, freedom, and equality. Never did I imagine that one day I would research my family history to uncover much about the man that the Spanish historian Juan Maria Gomez Ortiz (2006, personal communication) would describe as a figure much like Don Quixote. For those interested in Bernie's history, I wrote an article, which included his letters, for the *Volunteer* (Entin, 2006b).

My trying to understand my family, the relationship between my father and uncle, and my uncle and his parents, and my uncle's decision to go to Spain are a little clearer for me, but because my parents and uncle, and anyone who knew my uncle, are all deceased, I do not know if I will be able to obtain any more information. Uncle Bernie's gift triggered the journey, which launched my search for self and family.

What I have learned from this experience is the commanding strength of our psychological needs for family: to imagine what they might have experienced, and even to experience what they might have experienced, even to search for ones we did not know, and to walk the places they may have walked; and to photograph the sights they may have seen, know the people they may have known, and even share the honoring of their memory with others, honoring their loved ones and perhaps their ideals and values. Family history is a fulfillment of our insatiable psychological need for a sense of family, both as the scientist and as the artist in all of us.

My trips to Spain were all very interesting, informative and memorable, paying homage to all the International Brigadistas who volunteered to go to Spain, to "do the right thing." And those who knew Bernie, personally or by reputation, knew him to be a "hero," just as all those who volunteered to fight for the Republic against fascism were heroes. This was his legacy, to leave the world a better place, just one of the many important lessons I learned from him and which influence me to volunteer and "give back" to my community and my profession.

The use of photographs and family albums in psychotherapy

I have been interested in family photographs since I discovered the secret treasure trove of my family's photographs; thus I have been the family historian in preserving the visual archives through the family photo album and its oral equivalent, the family genogram (Entin, 1978, 1980). These interests merged in consideration of family sculpting techniques described by Peggy Papp et al. (1973) and the three-dimensional photographic sculptures of Dale Quarterman (1970). They are both converting emotional processes and relationships into a visual or pictorial image in space. From there it was only a short step to conceptualize the use of family photographs as a technique for facilitating, understanding, and mapping the relationship patterns of families and their applications in therapy.

I began to wonder how these photographs were related to my being a family psychologist, and how that piques my photographic interests and activities, and how photographs and albums can be used in family psychotherapy to help understand family dynamics. I remember the deafening silence about my uncle and his history whenever I tried to get some family history or information about the pictures of Bernie. However, when I became a family psychologist it opened the idea for me to use photographs to unlock family secrets and conflicts, and the trajectory started by the photographs I found as a child completely changed.

I discovered that family photographs are

> cherished, treasured possessions, irreplaceable reminders of family, friends and experiences. They are valued over and above the image and imbued with special meanings. Those photographs that take on significance as "favorite photographs" are treasured for their visual, metaphoric, symbolic representations and remembrances. They become elevated to the status of an icon.
>
> (Entin, 1983, p. 117)

They are the records that contain the individual and collective history of the family and its members, reflecting the movement through time and space of the family. They give striking evidence of ancestors and the traditions, values, and ideals of the family over the generations. The albums testify to a sense of continuity for the family as a visual record of ancestors whose existence preceded the present generation and images of family members that one day would be seen by generations who succeed the present generation.

Family photograph albums reflect how the family chooses to document its existence as a family: they can be studied to learn about what this particular family values and its commonalities and differences with other families; they are a form of communication addressing the question: what does it mean to be a man, a woman, a boy or a girl, in this family?; they are the richest sources of collected memories and traditions about the family; they are important not only for the individuals depicted in the photographs, but for the family as a whole, calling attention to important events in the life cycle of the family; they are signals of family life cycle ceremonies, rituals and traditions important for the development of the "identity" of the person involved and for the "family identity;" they are links from the family's past to the present, and an affirmation of the traditions and ideals for the future.

A touchpoint in my work on the use of family photographs came when I presented a photo-essay on the artwork of Tim Whitehead, an artist, poet and social worker at the Georgetown Symposium on Family Theory and Family Psychotherapy (Entin, 1977). The emphasis was on how his artwork changed after he visited his "family's old stomping grounds," in Ireland. In the Q and A afterwards, I was asked about using photographs to understand family relationships. I audaciously responded that I thought I could operationalize Bowen Theory and apply it to understanding family relationships. Six presentations and two years later, I returned to the Symposium to present an illustrated slide show, *The Differentiated Eye: The Use of Photographs in Family Psychotherapy* (1979a), demonstrating how the Bowen concepts, such as triangles, differentiation of self, and emotional cutoffs, could be translated into a visual language, and wrote a series of articles exploring the ways that the theory could be translated and demonstrated in a visual relationship (Entin, 1980, 1981, 1982, 1983).

The principle that guides my thinking is "How can the concepts of family systems theory be operationalized and conveyed visually?" The theory is a guide to think about the photographs. There are no direct translations or correspondences between the theory and the photographs. Looking at photographs and family photo albums

> provides family members with the opportunity to reestablish contact with close relatives that are distant (or with distant relatives), to learn family history, to deal with unresolved issues (often the source of current anxiety and problems), and the opportunity to take the responsibility for their part in the operation of the family systems.
>
> (Entin, 1983, p. 121)

While I conceptualize family relationships according to the Bowenian Family Systems model, I think other approaches and conceptualizations can equally be applied. It is essential for the therapist to have the prerequisite skills, knowledge, and training in the theoretical orientation before attempting to study family photographs. The applications of the theoretical concepts to the observation of family photos and albums are extensions of the theory. Once the concepts are understood, creative ideas for their interpretation and translation into visual images will suggest themselves to the therapist. The examinations, interpretations, and experiences of looking at photographs and discussing issues with family members become, in turn, the basis for changing their relationships with parents and other family members.

Theory is a guide to think about the photographs. I think in terms of Family Systems Theory; however, others can use different psychological theories to help them think about incorporating photographs in their therapeutic approaches. I would emphasize that it is essential that the therapist have a solid theoretical background and training in the field so as to be able to control their own anxiety and thinking. As Mike Kerr, MD, writes "keep(ing) the main emphasis on theory and the therapist's ability to avoid simplistic concepts and solutions to human problems" (1981, p. 226). Thus, I do not interpret photographs; I teach patients about concepts of family systems and then suggest that they visit with their families and use the photographs as a way to engage their family in a discussion of the relationship patterns guided by the theoretical concepts (Entin, 1980, 1982, 1983). Sometimes they bring in family photos and we discuss them using a family systems approach.

The field of phototherapy

My interests in using family photographs in therapy converged with others also interested in the therapeutic uses of photographs and photographic techniques (Entin, 1985). The emerging field became known as "phototherapy" and culminated in the book, *Phototherapy in Mental Health* (Krauss & Fryrear, 1983) and several conferences (Entin & Crocco, 1979; Entin, 1979b, Virginia Psychological Association), and a series of journals (*Photo Therapy Quarterly*, 1979–1982).

There are many diverse ways that photographs, family albums, and photographic techniques have been and could be used in individual and family psychotherapy. The multiplicity of creative approaches underscore the ubiquity of photographs and the profundity of visual images in our culture, perhaps in most cultures in our century, reflecting the tremendous technological advances in image making. It takes only a few seconds and, with study, "understanding your family can be a snap" (Fenjves, 1981, pp. 16–17). What distinguishes my approach from others is that it is theory-based.

A few examples from my clinical practice may be helpful to understand the process and reveal secrets that the patients learned while discussing their family photographs.

The concept of *triangles*, one of the most important, deals with the emotional closeness and distance between two individuals and the role of a third person, or issue or object, in that relationship. There are two insiders and one outsider. Triangles can be observed in pictures by studying spatial closeness and distance, which often mirror the emotional distance between people. And I caution not to overinterpret photos, as they may reflect only the mood of the moment, and pictures over a period of time have to be studied to differentiate between temporary alliances and patterns and more characteristic relationship patterns.

In one set of photographs, a successful woman executive brought in photographs taken when she was growing up. Each was a picture of her parents, older brother and herself. In each, her mother held her, her brother stood close, leaning towards them, while her father, dressed like "out of the bandbox" always in his three-piece suit with his hands in his pocket, stood isolated from the family. Through a veil of tears she discussed the emotional distance between her father and herself and the impossibility she felt of ever being able to get close to him or discuss important issues affecting her life with him. The secret revealed was the same triangular pattern of distance with her husband and his overinvolvement with their young daughter; it mirrored the pattern with which she grew up. One of the tasks in therapy is to help her change her relationship with her father, which should promote changes in her marriage.

An attractive young couple married a year was experiencing severe marital conflicts resulting in distance and a lack of intimacy and emotional involvement with each other. I suggested they bring in some family photos when I discovered that they were college sweethearts and this was the second marriage for each. I thought the photos might hold a clue as to the secrets of the relationship. They brought in three pictures from their marriage held at her parents' home. In what appeared to be a picture of the newlyweds, her daughter from a previous marriage was the central figure and they were relating to each other through their daughter, each holding the daughter's hand, forming a triangle. In the second photograph, at the bottom of the stairs leading to a guest bedroom, the couple was smiling gaily, even eagerly. But as the destination was approaching, the relationship pattern immediately emerged: she wants closeness and intimacy and he is distancing and pulling away from her. They are having a tug of war on the stairs. This pattern was to continue and culminate in the second termination of their relationship. Their verbal interpretation was consistent with the visual communication of the photograph. Interestingly, in his memory of the wedding photographs, he is positive there is a picture of his pulling her up the stairs. That picture, if it exists, however, is not included in their "official wedding album."

Joyous holiday visits can also be stressful, reviving family conflicts, with the pictures revealing secrets. After a Christmas visit from her older sister, a woman complained that her sister was closer to her husband than to her, a familiar old pattern of them being a close twosome and her the distant outsider. She brought in several pictures from the visit. In the first, she and her sister were sitting on a couch, with some space between them. She liked the picture because, despite their sitting apart, they were sitting at an angle and "at least our knees are close to each other." She wanted a picture of her husband with her sister. The picture she took proved it! She wanted to "include the Christmas tree," so instead of taking the picture frontally, as did her husband, she moved to the end of the couch to get the tree in the photograph. In so doing, however, not only did she get in the high end side of the couch and a number of throw pillows, the change in perspective shifted so that it looked like her husband and sister were sitting much closer than they actually were. The photograph revealed that she was the one putting up barriers to closeness in the relationship.

The concept of *differentiation of self* attempts to conceptualize all human functioning on a scale reflecting their ways of managing issues of thinking versus feeling, individuality versus togetherness. It is a concept of theoretical, rather than empirical, importance and difficult to operationalize in a photograph. A creative interpretation may permit the inference to this important concept in a family photograph— an anonymous portrait of Sigmund Freud and his five sisters and a brother. The caption published with the picture interprets his position and stance in the photograph as "the reserve and distance evident in the portrait are said to be consistent with Freud's later statements about his childhood" (Anonymous, 1979, p. 13). I would suggest an alternative explanation; namely, that Freud was less involved in the family togetherness and consequently able to achieve a more optimal level of differentiation, a level of well-defined individual functioning that would enable him to conceptualize about human development and psychological functioning in a creative new way. Although I do not "interpret photographs" on the basis of body language, this photograph is consistent with other family photographs, as published in *Sigmund Freud, His Life in Pictures and Words* (Freud, Freud, and

Grubrich-Simitis, 1978), the consistency adding more credence and authority to the interpretation.

Another example is of a photograph of a professional man at his son's wedding, on one knee, a seeming supplicant, his hand holding his mother's hand, with his mother in the center of the picture surrounded by the extended family, including his new (and third) wife. Emotional fusion was an obvious inference, supported by his current wife's statements of his emotional dependency on his mother, wanting to please her and prove to her that he was a "good boy."

The concept of *emotional cutoff* describes one way people deal with unresolved togetherness, emotional fusion, in their family. Typically this is done through emotionally cutting off from the family or through physical distance from the family, or the withdrawal or avoidance of emotionally charged issues while with the family. Its significance is in the importance of the re-establishment of viable contact between the generations, and not merely a simple matter of making a home visit. In looking at photographs and albums it is extremely important to ask about who is not in the picture, in addition to who is in the picture and their placement. What does a person's absence mean? Perhaps a "camera-shy" child or adolescent reflects an emotional upset or rebelliousness and not wanting to be included in the family or the family not wanting to include the non-conforming child. Or, an absent person, one who always took the picture and refuses to let any else take it, may be one who is emotionally cut off from the family and does not want to be included in the family portrait.

A vivid portrayal of a cutoff is when an individual is "cut off" by being "cut out" of the picture. While not meant to call attention to the missing person, the resulting photograph highlights the issue—people invariably ask about the "cut out" or missing person. This demonstrates that cutoffs, whether emotional or physical, do not "solve" problems; the "cut off" person, is still there, present by their absence, and, therefore, the cutoff continues to exist until the issues are resolved.

The artful practitioner: artist as psychologist

My two gifts from my two uncles, present and influencing my life since childhood, fully bloomed in adulthood—two parallel in expression—sometimes distinct and sometimes unified. My writings and presentations about the use of family photographs to understand family relationships (1980, 1982, 1983) resulted in considerable media coverage, including the *New York Times* (Brody, 1984, July 17, C1). These experiences burgeoned into my involvement with psychology and the media, a wonderful outlet for my creative impulses, and a counterpoint to the contemplative rhythm of a psychotherapy session.

In addition to my theoretical writing about photographs from a psychological perspective, my involvement as a photographer at APA began in 1985, when I was appointed the first Historian of the Division of Independent Practice. President Arthur Kovacs, PhD, president of the Division of Psychologists in Independent Practice, appointed me historian of the Division. He knew I loved taking pictures and always had my camera with me at APA meetings. Ever since, I have documented many APA events, including the ground-breaking ceremony for the second building (Entin 1992), Arlo Guthrie performing at the opening ceremony of the 2005 Convention (Entin, 2005), and the cover of the *Handbook of Research Methods in Clinical Psychology* (Roberts & Ilardi 2003).

The artful practitioner: psychologist as artist

I began using "toy cameras," plastic cameras with limited controls and poor lenses that allow for multiple exposures, light leaks, distortions and other happenstance effects, on a trip to Paris. In an exhibition of photographs from that trip, one reviewer, McLeod (2000, p. 31), wrote "Entin's scenes are of France: a cluster of boats moored near a bridge in Chambord that seem to be receiving a blessing … France is a place where magic constantly interferes with formality, as it does in Entin's photographs." Another review described my photograph of Chambord Castle as "the best pure photography of the show" (Humphrey, 2000). I thought it does not get any better than that, and I should quit while I was ahead. However, I am glad I did not. Since then, I have been in many solo and national juried exhibitions, my photographs have been widely published in books, magazines and catalogues, and are in private and public collections, such as the Embassy of Chile and Capital One Financial.

I think creativity is a process, a practice and a journey, an unusual journey, much like psychotherapy. It does not depend on technology.

It is about vision. I am often asked about the equipment, camera, lens or settings I use, as if knowing my secrets would enable the person to make amazing photos. I use cameras which enable me to create magical and dream-like impressionistic images that reflect my vision; cameras that allow me to produce multiple exposures to create in-camera photographic collages (layered images); photographs that can be read many times and in many ways to reveal the wealth of information they contain.

> Thus, I am able to break free from dependence on technology, precision, and sharpness to explore my inner world. I want my photographs to reflect my unique experience of time, place, and space and to stimulate questions in the viewers' mind as to why those pictures were taken and what thoughts and feelings they produced in the viewer.
>
> (Entin, 2004, p. 7)

In an interview about my art, Sandra Fowler wrote

> His aim was to create balance between brain and heart, body and soul. By combining thinking and feeling in the same image, Entin made this his personal vision. The viewer must think about it to understand it, giving it magical, haunting, and interactive qualities.
>
> (2006, p. 80)

Expressing my unique vision, telling my own story, makes my photographs art; it does not matter what camera or lens I use.

For my contributions to art and psychology I was awarded the 2008 Rosalee G Weiss Lecture for Outstanding Leaders in Psychology by the American Psychological Foundation and the APA Division of Psychologists in Independent Practice.

Reflections

My two uncles gave me profound yet completely different gifts: One was a deeply held family secret, and the other was an aspirational message; both profoundly altered the course of my life and my career. Little did I realize at the time that they would shape and guide my life choices and professional and creative sensibilities. My Uncle Bernie's gifts were indirect, a trove of photographs and letters, which, by their secretiveness, heightened my fascination and their importance, and whose meaning was not revealed for many decades. My Uncle Jay's inspirational message was more direct, that my interest in photographs would actualize in growth, "in bigger things," throughout my life. At the time I never realized that my interest in the use of family photographs to understand family dynamics might be a fulfillment of the twin inspirations of my uncles. And both, as were my parents, active volunteers in the community, giving back to others, and making the world a better place. Uncle Bernie volunteered to go to Spain and made the ultimate sacrifice. Uncle Jay volunteered with the soldiers on a kibbutz in his travels to Israel and was recognized for his volunteerism and philanthropy as "Person of the Year" at the Miami Jewish Home for the Aged where he lived for many years. All are important role models for my giving back to psychology and living a righteous life.

Concomitantly, as I began working on my self and my relationships with my family of origin, which is the cornerstone of Bowen Family Systems Theory "differentiation of self," my photography began to change, my "vision" became unique and individualistic. When I first entered photographs in exhibitions or juried competitions I was concerned about the reactions of others or the jurors; now I am more confident in my photographs as expressions of my own point of view, my own interpretation of a time, place or person. I use cameras that allow me the opportunity to create collage multiple-exposure photographs. And I enjoy creating "extended photographs" by hand painting or applying collage elements to my photographs. I bring creative thinking and sensibility to my work with families. The delicate, often precarious, balance between work and play, passion and profession, is an essential component in professional development, well-being and healing. We recognize the serious business of play for children, but seldom schedule leisure time activities for ourselves. As psychologists and psychotherapists, we are the potential victims of burnout, always giving and giving more than we receive, seldom replenishing our own resources. Photography serves as my source of balance, providing a restorative, healing power in my life. Creativity is a practice best performed daily. My twin passions of psychology and photography have enriched my journey.

As my two transformative gifts are linked, so are my art and psychology. My personal passions have traversed many unusual journeys

Le Penseur Rouge   Alan D. Entin

Figure 3.1 Le Penseur Rouge (2002) (original in color).

to help me develop into the family psychologist and artist I am today. A photo caption of me at an art opening quipped I "deal in psychology when not taking pictures" (Frost, 2003, p. 7). So, being a psychologist and artist, a psychologist as artist and artist as psychologist, my greatest thrill was at the nexus of the two: the cover of the *American Psychologist* (Entin, 2006a, January) (Figure 3.1).

References

Anonymous. (1979). Photo Psychology, *Innovations, American Institutes for Research, Palo Alto.*, Vol. 6, No. 3, p. 13.

Bowen, M. (1971). Family and Family Group Psychotherapy. In Kaplan, H. & Sadock, B. (Eds.) *Comprehensive Group Psychotherapy*. Baltimore, MD: Williams and Wilkins. Reprinted in Bowen, M. (1978). *Family Therapy in Clinical Practice*. Northvale, NJ: Jason Aronson, pp. 147–181.

Bowen, M. (1972). Toward the Differentiation of Self in One's Own Family. In Framo, J. (Ed.) *Family Interaction—A Dialogue Between Family Researchers and Family Therapists*. New York: Springer Publishing.

Bowen, M. (1976). Theory in the Practice of Psychotherapy. In Guerin, P. (Ed.) *Family Therapy: Theory and Practice*. New York: Gardner.

Bowen, M. (1978). *Family Therapy in Clinical Practice*. Northvale, NJ: Jason Aronson.

Brody, J.E. (1984, July 17). Photos speak volumes *about* relationships. *The Science Times, New York Times* (front page), New York, NY. C 1–2.

Bryan, M. (1999). *Codes of Love, How to Rethink Your Family and Remake Your Life*. New York: Pocket Books.

Entin, A. (1977). Time and Symbol in the Differentiated Self: One Man's Celtic World. *Photo-essay of the Paintings of Timothy Whitehead*, Georgetown Symposium on Family Theory and Family Psychotherapy, Washington, DC.

Entin, A. (1978). The Genogram: A Multigenerational Family Portrait. American Psychological Association Convention. *ERIC, Resources in Education*, ED 167 866, The School of Education, University of Michigan, Ann Arbor, Michigan, 48109.

Entin, A. (1979a). The Differentiated Eye: The Use of Photographs in Family Psychotherapy. Photo-essay. Georgetown University, Symposium on Family Psychotherapy, Washington, DC.

Entin, A. (1979b). Chair, Psychology and Photography Workshop, Virginia Psychological Association Fall Convention, Williamsburg, VA.

Entin, A. (1980). Photo Therapy: Family Albums and Multigenerational Portraits. *Camera Lucida*, 1(2), 39–51.

Entin, A. (1981). The Use of Photographs and Family Albums in Family Therapy. In Gurman, A. (Ed.) *Questions and Answers in the Practice of Family Psychotherapy*. New York: Brunner/Mazel, pp. 421–425.

Entin, A. (1982). Family Icons: Photographs in Family Therapy. In Abt, L.E. & Stuart, I.R. (Eds.) *The Newer Therapies: A Sourcebook*. New York: Van Nostrand, pp. 207–227.

Entin, A. (1983). The Family Photo Album as Icon: Photographs in Family Psychotherapy. In Krauss, D. & Fryrear, J. (Eds.) *Phototherapy in Mental Health.* Springfield, IL: Charles C. Thomas, pp. 117–132.

Entin, A. (1985). Phototherapy: The uses of photography in psychotherapy. *The Independent Practitioner, Newsletter of the Division of Independent Practice,* 5(1), 15–16.

Entin, A. (1992). Photograph. Groundbreaking Ceremony for the APA Building. In Evans, R., Sexton, V. & Cadwallader, T. (Eds.) *100 Years, The American Psychological Association.* APA: Washington, DC, p. 232.

Entin, A. (2004, Spring). Photography as media psychology. *The Amplifier, Newsletter of the Division of Media Psychology,* 1, 6–7.

Entin, A. (2005). *Arlo Guthrie Live at APA: My Peace.* CD Album Photographs. American Psychological Association CD, APA Music, Washington, DC.

Entin, A. (2006a, January). *Le Penseur Rouge* (2002). *American Psychologist,* 61(1), front cover.

Entin, A. (2006b, March). Salud, Bernie. *The Volunteer, Journal of the Veterans of the Abraham Lincoln Brigade,* XXVIII(1), 7–9.

Entin, A. & Crocco, R. (1979). *Photography and Psychotherapy: Toward a Psychology of Photography Conference.* The Delaware Humanities Forum, Wilmington, DE.

Entin, B. (1937, July 15). Unpublished Letters, The Tamiment Library/ Robert F Wagner Labor Archives, Elmer Bobst Library, York University Libraries, 70 Washington Square South, New York, NY, 10012.

Entin, B. (1937). Unpublished Letters, Collection of Alan Entin. Vertical File, The Tamiment Library/Robert F Wagner Labor Archives, Elmer Bobst Library, York University Libraries, 70 Washington Square South, New York, NY, 10012.

Erikson, E. (1950). *Childhood and Society.* New York: W.W. Norton & Co.

Fenjves, P.F. (1981, November 20). Understanding your family may be a snap. *Chicago Sun Times,* 16–17.

Fisher, H. (2001). Germans and Americans Facing Each Other Again. *The Volunteer, Journal of the Veterans of the Abraham Lincoln Brigade, 16.*

Fisher, H. (1997). *Comrades, Tales of a Brigadista in the Spanish Civil War.* Lincoln, NB and London: University of Nebraska Press.

Fowler, S. (2006). On The Cover Interview. *American Psychologist,* 61(1), 80.

Freud, E., Freud, L. & Grubrich-Simitis, I. (1978) *Sigmund Freud, His Life in Pictures and Words.* New York: W.W. Norton.

Frost, K. (2003, September). IMAGES, *Fifty Plus.* Richmond, VA, p. 7.

Gilbert, R. (1992). *Extraordinary Relationships, A New Way of Thinking About Human Interactions*. Minneapolis, MN: CHRONIMED Publishing.

Gilbert, R. (2004). *The Eight Concepts of Bowen Theory, A New Way of Taking About the Individual and the Group*. Falls Church, VA: Leading Systems Press.

Hendrix, H. & Hunt, H., (2019). *Getting the Love You Want, A Guide for Couples*. New York: St. Martin's Griffin.

Humphrey, T. (2000, October, 22). Cheap Shots: Artists and their "Toys." www.artzites.com/cheaprev.htm

Kerr, M. & Bowen, M. (1981). Family Systems Theory and Therapy. In Gurman, A. & Kniskern, D. (Eds.) *Handbook of Family Therapy*. New York: Brunner/Mazel.

Krauss, D. & Fryrear, J. (Eds.) (1983). *Phototherapy in Mental Health*. Springfield, IL: Charles C. Thomas.

Lerner, H. (2014). *Dance of Anger, A Women's Guide to Changing the Patterns of Intimate Relationships*. New York: HarperCollins.

Lerner, H. (1990), *Dance of Intimacy, A Women's Guide to Courageous Acts of Change in Key Relationships*. New York: HarperCollins.

McLeod, D. (2000, February 8). Cheap Shots: Fine Art Photography from Toy Cameras. *Style Magazine*, Art Review, Richmond, VA, p. 31.

Miller, T. & Brummitt, W. (1952) *This is Photography, Its Means and Ends*. Garden City, NY: Garden City Books.

New York Times. (1937, March 16). Fifth Store Joins Sit-In Strike: Parley Today May End Deadlock. New York, NY, front page, pp. 1, 8.

New York Times. (1937, March 18,). Woolworth Girls Strike In 2 Stores. New York: NY, front page, pp. 1, 4.

Papp, P., Silverstein, O. & Carter, E. (1973). Family Sculpting in Preventive Work with "Well Families." *Family Process*, 12(2), 197–212.

Photo Therapy Quarterly, An International, Multidisciplinary Journal. (1979–1982). The Official Publication of the International Phototherapy Association. I–III.

Quarterman, D. (1970). Photography Into Sculpture. Museum of Modern Art Exhibition, New York, NY.

Roberts, M. & Ilardi, S. (Eds.) (2003). *Handbook of Research Methods in Clinical Psychology*. Malden, MA: Blackwell Publishing. Jacket illustration.

Rowe, J. (2005). From The Picket Line to the Front Line: The New York City Department Store Workers' Union and the Fight for Spain. Unpublished Paper, The Tamiment Library/Robert F Wagner Labor Archives, Elmer

Bobst Library, New York University Libraries, 70 Washington Square South, New York, NY, 10012.

Vecchi, J. (2005, July 20). II Palazzo Guglielmi. *Photo-Eye Gallery Email Newsletter*, Online Gallery, 5.29.

Veterans of the Abraham Lincoln Brigade. (1937). 3×5" Index Card, Information filled out and maintained by the Friends of the Brigade on the eve of going to Spain.

Chapter 4

Imagining the impossible
Creativity in psychoanalytic practice

Dan Gilhooley

This chapter discusses the author's twin careers as a visual artist and psychoanalyst. As an artist, the author describes his imaginative process occurring in a dissociative trance. Art-making and being a psychoanalytic patient are related practices taking place in an altered state of consciousness and creating an atmosphere where anything is possible. The therapeutic role of imagination in Mesmer's animal magnetist movement, and in Breuer's work with Bertha Pappenheim, is compared with a clinical case in the author's own practice. Using dreaming as its model, the paper argues "imagining the impossible" is the basis of creative growth and therapeutic change.

Death, drawing and psychoanalysis

My childhood in Wisconsin was formed around my father's suicide. He'd landed at Omaha Beach and left the Second World War with a traumatic brain injury. As a boy, wearing his dog tags around my neck, I'd run my fingers around the edges of holes drilled into his skull to relieve the pressure on his swelling brain. I'd ask him to show me again the scars of bullet wounds in his shoulder and back. At night he'd tell me war stories, drinking whiskey from a water glass. Although alcoholism helped, my father's mind couldn't contain the violence of the war. When I was a teenager he threatened to kill us, his wife and two children. I kept a rifle hidden to protect us during his rages. Then, when I was 15, he shot himself with a pistol we didn't know he had. My father's suicide shattered our family and, four years later, propelled me a thousand miles to New York.

As a child I spent hours drawing. No one else in my family was artistic. By the age of 10 my mother began dropping me off at the

Art Institute when she visited relatives in Chicago, and I'd spend hours wandering the museum. My sister and I participated in summer programs at a local art museum, where in high school I took life drawing classes. The museum director told us stories of studying at the Art Students League in New York alongside Jackson Pollack. At university my first painting teacher was the pupil and assistant of Ad Reinhardt, an ascetic purist claiming to make "the last painting anyone could paint" (Lippard, 1981, p. 147). Dramatic declarations like this were a siren call.

At 19 I moved to New York to escape the remnants of my father's death and to be in the center of American art. Enrolling in Hunter College, I was taught sculpture by Tony Smith, maybe the most famous American artist of his generation. Tony was spell-binding. Often more drunk than my father, he'd recall painting *Blue Poles* with Pollack at midnight in an intoxicated Dionysian rite, and spontaneously recite *Finnegan's Wake* from memory. He'd weave together stories of Pythagoras' music of the spheres with descriptions of close-packing soap bubbles demonstrating why we have five fingers rather than four. He loved the idea of an invisible mathematical structure in the physical world affecting us emotionally. Beauty was in the numbers, proof this secret geometry was divine.

At Hunter I learned art as geometric abstraction. After graduate school my best ideas produced mediocre results and there was nothing captivating about the pictures I made. The light of divine geometry inspiring Tony dimmed in me. Though I worked hard, I'd lost my ability to make art. By the time I was 30 I wanted to kill myself. My father's suicide planted the certainty in me that I'd do the same thing. I entered psychoanalysis, which changed my life and the kind of pictures I made.

In the beginning my analysis was about staying alive session-to-session. My first hour ended with me asking the analyst, "Do you think I can keep from killing myself before our next appointment?" During the first year of my analysis I talked mostly on my father and his suicide. I struggled to paint but couldn't produce anything meaningful. Eventually I decided to do some drawings as I had as a child, just to fill the time before inspiration returned. I made portraits of my girlfriend, my mother, and my father's lips. Making pictures of people I loved felt important. I didn't realize it, but entering psychoanalysis reignited my childhood desire to draw. At first, I thought these drawings were inconsequential. Then I began exhibiting them, and eventually they became the basis of an emerging artistic identity. My artwork grew directly out of my psychoanalytic experience. Actually, I became an artist *as* I became a psychoanalytic patient. My analyst was the first audience for my creations. I was taught as an artist, and as a patient, to be personally expressive and truthful. I believed creativity was the heart of psychoanalysis.

Psychoanalysis changed my life. I couldn't get enough of it. After eight years of individual analytic work I entered the training program at the Center for Modern Psychoanalytic Studies in Manhattan. I'd had no previous education in mental health, but I was passionate about psychoanalysis, its history and theory of mind. It took me nine years to complete the Center's program. When I'd finished my clinical education, I traveled to Boston for a masters and doctorate in psychoanalysis, earning both degrees from the Boston Graduate School of Psychoanalysis. After 15 years of study I began to practice psychoanalysis.

By that time, I'd developed a regional reputation as an artist. I'd mounted a dozen one-person shows and participated nationally in 100 group exhibitions. Based on my drawings, I was elected to the National Academy of Design, America's oldest art institution. I was proud to be selected by my peers to join a group including Thomas Eakins and Willem de Kooning. My analysis and psychoanalytic education, and my modest artistic achievements, were milestones. It's easy to consider my experience in drawing and analysis as coincidental, but I saw them as related. They both took place in an altered state of consciousness. They were both open-ended mental processes, promoting freedom of thought. And, because my thoughts and feelings expressed in analysis were welcomed uncritically, they were both places where anything was possible.

Drawing happens in a meditative trance. Here's how it works. I alter consciousness to slip past its edges and enter an unconscious world. I hover at the boundary between my conscious and unconscious mind. With a foot in both worlds, drawing's a little like dreaming. From this vantage I engage in a rhythmic process of observation and recording. I study the shape of lips and ears, the texture of cheeks and chin, the tone of shadows under eyebrows and nose. Using pencil or pastel

I make marks on paper—little squiggles, dots, lines or soft gradations of color—trying to replicate patterns appearing before my eyes. The marks become echoes of the material presence in front of me arranged into forms on paper resonating with objects before my eyes.

Then a subtle emotional meaning begins to emerge from these collections of marks. They start telling a story. A nose becomes resolute. Lips appear to be on the verge of quivering. Eyes seem to swell with tears or hide in shadows surrounding them. Emotional life materializes from the marks rendering a complicated mind. A face becomes desiring but defeated. One eye seems optimistic and engaging while the other is guarded and world-weary.

How can graphite dust caught in the weave of paper generate feelings? Emotions seem to flow from the marks themselves. I'm not consciously aware of feelings associated with the marks I make. I discover these emotional meanings afterwards, like waking up from a dream. Where do they come from? Emotions emerge between mark and mind. By echoing a tiny bit of the world, a unique virtual reality is created, seeming to pulse with life. While the shapes and colors in a face originate in the material world I see, emotional meanings emanate from an immaterial unconscious I experience directly. I perceive the world with my eyes, but I live by my mind, unmediated by perceptual organ. How all this happens is a mystery. Art enters the world like automatic writing. And its unconscious origins are invisible.

The unconscious mind plays an even more mysterious role in my drawings. Thirty years ago, I was making a drawing of my future wife, Pat, that I entitled *Selene*, a name unknown to me at the time. It would be two years before Pat discovered she had a great-grandmother named Selene. This was the beginning of me feeling I wasn't alone in that meditative trance. When I finished *Selene*, I realized it was a better drawing than I was capable of making. How could that happen?

I was reminded of the 1980 Olympics when the American hockey team defeated the heavily favored Russians for the gold medal. The ragtag American amateurs were no match for Russian professionals. But the Americans played beyond their ability and won a match remembered as "the miracle on ice." For the next 30 years I had this experience repeatedly. I made pictures that were better than my ability, made seemingly by something more than me. It was humbling, hard to admit and hard to accept. I'd made every mark, but something seemed to be "drawing through me." Was this the basis of the Greek idea of muse, a personified source of creative inspiration? Over a period of decades, I discovered this was an aspect of the meditative trance: imagination is a dissociative process. The experience is depersonal or transpersonal. I wasn't making the picture. Something other than me was creating these little miracles. By drawing I came to realize imagination is the path to the miraculous living in the unconscious. Unexpectedly, over the years, drawing became a spiritual practice. Setting out as a young agnostic, after 40 years of drawing I'd accidently become a mystic.

Miracles and imagination in the birth of psychoanalysis

What does the history of psychoanalysis tell us about the role of miracles and imagination in mental and physical health? Psychoanalysis began in the laboratory of Jean-Martin Charcot. In 1885, 29-year old Sigmund Freud received a scholarship to travel from Vienna to Paris to study with Charcot, the most famous neurologist in the world. Freud was captivated by Charcot, who was a free-thinking charismatic teacher, and he savored precious hours spent in "the magic of a great personality" (Freud, 1892–94, p. 135). Employing a hypnotic trance, Charcot demonstrated hysterical paralyses weren't caused by lesions in the brain, but by ideas and emotions associated with trauma. Through Charcot's experiments, Freud became aware of an unconscious mind revealed by the trance, and the mysterious leap from idea to paralysis (Chertok, 1970; Ellenberger, 1965; Micale, 1995a, 1995b). Through experimentation with subjects hypnotically entranced, Charcot reconceived neurology as an interplay of mind and body.

Charcot began his career making anatomical discoveries about multiple sclerosis and ended it trying to explain miracle cures (Goetz, Bonduelle & Gelfand, 1995). There's a long history of serious people trying to understand miraculous events (Ellens, 2008; Grosso, 2016; James, 1985; Keener, 2011; Marshall, 2005; Winkelman & Baker, 2010; Woodward, 2000), and each of the world's religions incorporates these mystifying phenomena. Charcot didn't doubt miracle cures. He'd witnessed several in his own hospital, and he sent 50 patients a year to Lourdes (Hustvedt, 2011). Charcot just wanted to demystify the supernatural. Disagreeing with the Catholic Church, he claimed miracle cures were produced by the mind, not by God. Charcot's demonstrations of mind transforming body became a cornerstone in the foundation of psychoanalysis which emerged as a psychical treatment for physical ailments.

If miracles are violations of natural law, impossible events a rational person should dismiss, then Charcot concluded his career observing *the impossible*, and trying to understand how it happened. By contrast, at the end of his student's career, Sigmund Freud described miracles as wishful illusions disavowing painful reality. In 1933 Freud wrote, "miracles contradicted everything sober observation had taught, and betrayed all to clearly the influence of human imagination" (1933, p. 166). Freud concluded the impossible is impossible, and we're simply too weak to accept the hopelessness of this fact. If Freud observed miracle cures at Salpetiere—and it's likely he did—he ended up denying them. In his dismissal Freud links imagination with the miraculous. Did imagination play a role in the origin of psychoanalysis? Yes, although it's place is denied and misrepresented.

Psychoanalysis was born out of the magnetic tradition of Franz Mesmer (Chertok & de Saussure, 1979; Crabtree, 1993; Darnton, 1968; Ellenberger, 1970; Pattie, 1994). Living in a world captivated by scientific discoveries of gravity, magnetism and electricity, Mesmer proposed a superfine magnetic fluid bathed the universe penetrating all matter. Mesmer believed the distribution of this magnetic fluid within the human body affected thought, emotion and health. All forms of illness were caused by an obstruction of the natural flow of magnetic forces within the body.

What was important about Mesmer was his therapeutic technique, not his theory. Mesmer's treatment was interpersonal based on a state of mind created between himself and his patient that he called *rapport*. Believing he was magnetic, Mesmer passed his hands over the bodies of patients, inducing within them an altered state of consciousness. He "mesmerized" them. Today we'd say he hypnotized them. Once they'd achieved an interpersonal state of "magnetic resonance," where their bodies and minds "were one," Mesmer imagined his healthy organs restructuring the diseased organs of his patient. Employing hour-long treatments six days a week, Mesmer was successful at curing rheumatism and gout, epilepsy and chronic fever, digestive and respiratory ailments, paralysis and even blindness. He became a physician of last resort, sought out after traditional medicine had failed.

Mesmer was sensationally successful. An envious medical establishment, whose primitive methods were leeches, blood-letting and purgatives, demanded the government do something to protect their interests. A scientific commission chaired by Ben Franklin and led by Antoine-Laurent Lavoisier (the founder of modern chemistry) investigated Mesmer's work. The commission was noteworthy for its sophistication and rigor (Chertok & Stengers, 1992). They questioned Mesmer's theory, not his technique. The commission concluded sick people had been cured by Mesmer's method. But, they asked, had Mesmer discovered a magnetic fluid permeating the universe which affected human health? While they couldn't rule it out, they found no evidence for it. Instead, the investigators concluded Mesmer's cures could be explained by the patient and magnetizer's *use of imagination*, by the palliative effects of touch, and by patients' imitation of others (Bailly, 2002; Franklin, 1785).

The commission identified imagination as the therapeutic agent, and by rejecting its power the scientists inaugurated a new form of skepticism rooted in a fearful mistrust of the mind (Harrington, 2008). Imagination was both trivial and dangerous, and its significance denied. The commissioners claimed imagination was the enemy of rational thought, and a cure created through imagination was invalid because it defied explanation. Of course, the problem is imagination emerges spontaneously from an unconscious mind whose workings are invisible. Something that's both invisible and powerful is dangerous. As philosopher of science Isabelle Stengers (2003) remarks, the empirical evidence was dismissed: "the cure proves nothing" because patients had been "cured for the wrong reasons" (p. 16). Mesmer's technique was outlawed, he was disgraced, and medical leeches prevailed. Undeterred, the public continued to seek magnetic treatments simply because they worked (Shorter, 1992). And a review of medical records (Gauld, 1992) demonstrates Mesmer's method was the most effective medical treatment throughout nineteenth-century Europe.

Imagination similarly sits at the center of the origin case of psychoanalysis: Josef Breuer's treatment of Anna O. (Breuer, 1895; Borch-Jacobsen, 1996; Breger, 2009; Ellenberger 1965, 1970, 1972; Hirschmuller, 1978; Skues, 2006). For psychoanalysts this case represents the appearance of a new therapeutic paradigm. As analysts tell and retell this case the role of imagination is rendered invisible, so the cure appears rational rather than imaginal. Like Mesmer's commissioners, psychoanalysis sidesteps the role of imagination in Anna O.'s recovery.

Anna O. was Breuer's pseudonym for his young patient, Bertha Pappenheim. Bertha was born into a wealthy Orthodox Jewish family. She was bright, imaginative and well educated. By 16 she was fluent in five languages. Being female, a university education wasn't considered, and her life was constrained by her rigidly conservative parents. At 21 her father fell ill and for months Bertha devoted herself to his care as her own health deteriorated.

Bertha began experiencing a dizzying set of symptoms emerging during her evening *absences*, or dissociative autohypnotic trance states. Bertha called these *absences* "time-missing" because she was amnesiac of their contents. Bertha's illness began with a hallucination: She saw her fingers turning into snakes with death's heads replacing her fingernails. She stopped eating, experienced double vision, and was unable to recognize family members. Parts of both sides of her body became paralyzed, as did her neck muscles, preventing her from lifting her head off her chest. After four months of disabling physical symptoms, and no longer able to care for her father, she took to bed. Now her mental state worsened. Bertha developed two selves: one that was melancholy, and a second evil-self emerging during her *absences* which behaved destructively. Her speech disintegrated into a word salad drawn from four languages. She became mute for weeks, and then for months spoke only in English while believing she was conversing in German, causing her to feel misunderstood.

Breuer's reaction to Bertha's aphasia was the key to the first half of her cure. Breuer knew Bertha had been offended by her father, and to retaliate she'd decided not to talk about him. Breuer wondered if her vengefulness was related to her speech problems. So, in one of her autohypnotic trances Breuer insisted she talk about her father. She complied. Her aphasia subsided and the paralysis in her right arm disappeared. At that moment Breuer concluded many of her symptoms were based on unconscious emotionally charged memories. Thereafter, Breuer worked with Bertha each evening in her autohypnotic trance to help her talk about feelings and memories associated with the origin of each of her symptoms. One by one her symptoms disappeared. This became Bertha's famous "talking cure." Significantly, Bertha had no conscious awareness of either these memories or of this therapeutic process. As Breuer writes, "She never had any recollection whatsoever of her 'English' evening sessions" (Hirschmuller, 1978, p. 283). After three months Bertha was much better, but then her father died. She became suicidal and was temporarily hospitalized. This initiated a second phase of treatment where imagination clearly forms the basis of her recovery.

Bertha now spent much of her time in a withdrawn somnambulant state in which she recognized only Breuer who alone was able to feed her. Bertha became increasingly dependent on him. She was demanding and oppositional. Their relationship intensified and became stormy. Breuer doubled-down, increasing the frequency of sessions, coming twice daily and spending hours with her each morning and night. Overwhelmed by the demands of her treatment, after a year of therapy he privately contacted a sanitarium about the possibility of transferring Bertha's care. Then he abandoned the idea, and instead, took a different approach. To increase the pace of treatment, Breuer began hypnotizing Bertha in the mornings to determine the content of her evening autohypnotic trances. This strategy paid off. After listening to stories told during her evening *absences,* Breuer writes,

> she came out of her *absence,* was at ease, cheerful, set herself to work, spent all night drawing or writing, perfectly rational, went to bed at 4 o'clock … The contrast between the irresponsible invalid by day, beset with hallucinations, and the perfectly lucid person at night was most remarkable.
>
> (Hirschmuller, 1978, p. 285)

Now Bertha's therapy entered a final phase that mentally returned her to her most acute physical and psychological symptoms of the preceding year. Christmas was the one-year anniversary of her last contact with her father. In December 1881, during her evening dissociative *absences,* Bertha began to vividly re-experience the traumatic events of the same day from the previous year. During the morning hours she was consciously alive in 1881, but in the evening when she entered her autohypnotic trance, she lived the corresponding December day of 1880, losing all awareness of 1881.

These evening therapeutic sessions were conducted in a state of complete hallucination. Breuer (1895) writes, "She was carried back to the previous year with such intensity that in the new house she hallucinated her old room" (p. 33). In her trance Bertha saw the bedroom from the previous year even though she was now living in a different house, and she acted out her experiences of the previous year. This pattern of "temporal dissociation" continued for the next six months, and her hallucinatory reliving of her traumatic past brought her considerable relief. Once again, imagination—in this case a sustained pattern of hallucination—was the basis of her recovery.

Bertha announced her treatment would end on June 7th, the anniversary of being moved to a sanatorium after several suicide attempts following her father's death. Breuer considered this the most disabling point in her psychological illness. He describes their final session on June 7, 1881:

> On the last day—by the help of re-arranging the room so as to resemble her father's sickroom—she reproduced the terrifying [snake] hallucination which I have described above and which constituted the root of her whole illness. During the original scene she had only been able to think and pray in English; but immediately after its reproduction she was able to speak German. She was moreover free from the innumerable disturbances which she had previously exhibited.
>
> (Breuer, 1895, p. 40)

Creating perfect symmetry, Bertha ended her therapy by returning via hallucinatory trance to the beginning of her illness. Remarkably, Bertha chose to structure the final six months of her treatment as a daily sequential hallucinatory reliving in Breuer's presence of her life between the two most traumatic periods of her emotional crisis: her December convalescence when she was disabled physically, and her June hospitalization when she was her most disturbed psychologically. The final phase of recovery was accomplished through her creative regenerative use of this dissociative psychotic process.

Bertha's case has been consistently misrepresented within the psychoanalytic community beginning with Breuer himself (Gilhooley, 2002). Although she was largely cured of her hysterical symptoms, at the end of her treatment Breuer hospitalized Bertha for addiction to morphine and chloral hydrate he'd been routinely administering because he couldn't tolerate her emotional outbursts. It's unclear how these mind-altering chemicals had affected her trance-based therapy.

More importantly for the future of psychoanalysis, Freud's appropriation of Bertha's case as the beginning of psychoanalysis is misleading. Bertha's therapy and Breuer's technique are typical of Mesmer's magnetic treatments (Ellenberger, 1970; Hirschmuller, 1978), and bear little resemblance to the psychoanalysis Freud would develop. Psychiatric historian Henri Ellenberger (1970) says Bertha's treatment "is analogous to the great exemplary cases of magnetic illness in the first half of the nineteenth century" (p. 484). For example, the therapeutic technique of Puysegur, the most famous of Mesmer's followers, was to gently interrogate entranced patients about the origin of their symptoms (Conn, 1982). He was indulgent, invested countless hours in patient care, and allowed patients to design their own treatments, just as Breuer had with Bertha (Chertok & de Saussure, 1979; Crabtree, 1993; Ellenberger, 1970). In fact, Breuer's work with Bertha bears greater resemblance to Puysegur than to the psychoanalytic technique Freud developed. So, what Freud described as the origin of psychoanalysis was actually a "rebranding" of animal magnetism.

Compare Bertha's therapy with psychoanalysis. Bertha's treatment occurred in an *autohypnotic trance* of which she had no conscious recollection, while Freud's psychoanalysis would be conducted in a state of wakeful consciousness. Freud was frightened by the trance which promoted emotional entanglements with his female patients. Hoping to sidestep these challenges, Freud believed cure could be achieved by bringing unconscious thoughts and emotions under conscious control through reflective rational thinking. But in Bertha's therapy there was no conscious memory, no rational reflection, no understanding. Most importantly, in the last six months of treatment Bertha's recovery resulted from 160 sessions of hallucination. Dramatically, she cured herself through consecutive doses of insanity. That doesn't look like psychoanalysis to me.

In the rational world of psychoanalysis, the therapeutic role of dissociative psychosis in the case has never been discussed. This omission— the collective negative hallucination of psychoanalysis—is the most significant misrepresentation of Bertha's treatment. Like Mesmer's commissioners, through this omission psychoanalysts deny the therapeutic role played by irrational psychosis and convert Bertha's imaginal treatment into a rational one. This is the essential point. If mind transforms matter—and that's what Mesmer and Charcot and Bertha's case demonstrate—then what form of mentation accomplishes this feat? *Imagination.* Certainly, Bertha's hallucinations were dramatic imaginative actions—an immediate, active, emotional reliving—not an emotionally detached, rational reflection on past experience. Bertha's cathartic, action-oriented treatment, taking place in a dissociative autohypnotic trance, couldn't be further from the passive, conscious, rational, and insight-oriented thinking Freud employed. Today, young analysts aren't taught to orchestrate a "curative psychosis," but that's the actual lesson of the Anna O. case. That this fact has remained invisible for over a hundred years of psychoanalytic education says a lot about our fear of imagination. Using mind as the central therapeutic agent, Freud hoped he could substitute passive rational reflection for dissociative imaginative action. He was wrong, and Freud never achieved a clinical success equal to Breuer's work with Bertha.

Imagining the impossible in a psychoanalytic case

There are many ways imagination enters therapeutic practice. Here's one example which illustrates the therapeutic role of dissociative imaginative action occurring in psychoanalytic psychotherapy. It also shows how being an artist affects my psychoanalytic work.

Twelve years ago, I began seeing Frank. His son Anders had cancer. Frank wanted me to help Anders fight the disease. Anders didn't want my help, but Frank stayed to talk about his anger and despair. Anders suffered. He fought cancer for six years, enduring 10 surgeries and losing an eye before dying at the age of 23. Frank was devastated.

About a month after Anders' death, I had a dream in which I woke up dead. In fact, those words, "I woke up dead," echoed in my mind at the beginning of the dream. In the dream I hovered above my body lying motionless in bed. I floated down from the ceiling and circled my body, checking for signs of life. I laid there unresponsive. I really was dead. I figured it must have happened in my sleep. I was surprised by how effortless it was to move around. Being dead was easier than I expected.

Later that week, near the end of his session Frank said, "I had a strange dream earlier this week. I dreamt I woke up dead." Frank described this dream as a turning point, a sign from Anders. He believed his dead son was now guiding his mourning. I was surprised by the improbability of these mutual dreams. I mentioned to Frank that I'd also dreamt of waking up dead earlier in the week. He wasn't interested, so we didn't discuss it. But I was struck by the remarkable coincidence of these mutual dreams. Like Charcot, I silently thought I was observing the *impossible*, a little miracle appearing before my eyes.

During the next week Frank began writing a story about life after death that begins with the protagonist announcing, "I woke up dead." This short story evolved into a dreamy noir detective novel set in a timeless space between life and death. Frank had never done any creative writing. His education had been in science and mathematics, and he'd had a career in technology. Writing was brand new, and his preferred genre was science fiction. Frank attributed his newfound creativity to Anders whose artistic nature was now inspiring him. Frank worked on his novel continuously for the next three years, each week reading segments to me during sessions. This imaginative writing process became the focus of his mourning.

The month after Frank began writing, I began writing about Frank's writing. Frank had no conscious awareness of this, but as his novel progressed it made repeated references to twin authors writing the same paper. For example, in one chapter the main character and his psychoanalyst simultaneously declare they've written the same article, "The Myth of Mental Illness." In another chapter the protagonist and his double from a parallel universe have written identical scholarly papers. Like our mutual dreams of waking up dead, Frank describes twin authors creating the same text, each echoing the other. And as his novel progressed, the double became a dominant motif.

Although Frank had no knowledge of my personal life, there were several parallels between his novel and me. For example, Frank wrote a chapter in which a boy is raised by a shell-shocked war veteran whose unrelenting memory of combat disables him, renders him unemployable, and leads to his suicide. The boy is his father's sympathetic confidante. Frank's story mirrors my life growing up with my father. Consider the following detail. In Frank's story the boy's last image of his father occurs in a freezing morgue where his "breath formed jets each time he exhaled." Compare this to my description at my father's internment, written 20 years earlier, where the minister's "lips moved over stained teeth emitting clouds of frozen air," and where I say of myself: "I became the cold. My heartbeat rose and fell measured by breaths escaping, and then in seconds evaporating." Standing before the bodies of their dead fathers, the parallel images of the sons' frozen breaths is striking. Here's another example. In one of Frank's chapters the psychoanalyst places a pistol to his head and kills himself. I'd entered psychoanalysis believing it was inevitable I'd place a pistol to my head. That was my deepest trauma, a future I'd anticipated and struggled to avoid.

How could I explain these strange parallels between my life and Frank's imaginative writing? It looked like Frank was reading my mind. As Frank read his vignettes to me each week I came to believe the similarities between Frank's story and my life were the product of a symbiotic state of mind we'd created between us. Hyman Spotnitz (1985) described this merged mental state as narcissistic transference, and Harold Searles (1979) called it therapeutic symbiosis. Franz Mesmer's word for it was *rapport*.

Mesmer considered *rapport* to be the most intimate relationship between human beings. Magnetizers conceived of *rapport* as recreating the intrauterine relationship of fetus and mother. *Rapport* was a return to the womb, and "each cure achieved through animal magnetism goes through the same phases as the yet unborn child in its mother's womb" (Ellenberger, 1970, p. 153). *Rapport* and the hypnotic trance were inextricably entwined. Conceptually, the trance was a form of intrauterine thought which was inherently telepathic, as between mother and fetus. Medical researcher and Nobel laureate Charles Richet served as an intellectual bridge between the worlds of Mesmer and Charcot (Ellenberger, 1993; Wolf, 1993). Charcot consulted with Richet about hypnotism. Richet (1923) described the telepathic nature of *rapport* between patient and magnetizer "being such that the sensations of the former were perceived by the latter, who could also divine the thought of the magnetizer without the utterance of any word" (p. 104). It looked like Frank and I had established a telepathic *rapport* allowing thoughts to pass between us. My memories seemed to be appearing in Frank's stories. By the end of the nineteenth century, theorists concluded *rapport* was intersubjective: its therapeutic effect occurred because the magnetizer and patient were in a state of mutual entrancement (Hudson, 1893).

Here's a more elaborate example of *rapport* emerging in Frank's book. During those first months when Frank began writing his novel I had a strange premonitory experience. Each Friday morning I leave my home in Bellport and drive to Babylon to catch a 5:12 train to New York City. On this early December morning I stepped onto my porch and thought, "Flat tire." I checked the tires on my car, but I didn't have a flat. I drove to the train station. When I turned off the main thoroughfare to merge onto a two-lane highway, there was a problem. Coming up around a cloverleaf turn at about 50 mph there was a car immediately to my left traveling at the same speed. The driver didn't move over to allow me to merge. I thought of accelerating. But then I saw the flashing taillights of a vehicle parked at the edge of the cloverleaf about 50 feet ahead. I stepped hard on the brake and tucked in behind the other car. In an instant I passed a guy kneeling down changing his car's left rear tire. There's no shoulder on the cloverleaf, so his body was sticking out onto the highway. In the darkness I hadn't seen him, and I barely missed hitting him. I thought, "What a terrible place to change a tire." I was shaken by the realization that I'd come within five feet of killing him.

How it could be that 20 minutes earlier I'd thought "flat tire," and now I just missed hitting this guy changing a flat tire? "Another little miracle?" I wondered. I tried to make sense of this coincidence, this echo in nature. Could a part of my unconscious mind exist in the future? Maybe an unconscious part of me had already made this drive and was warning my conscious mind about danger ahead. Or maybe, in an unconscious form of awareness, when I stepped onto my porch I was actually in Bellport and Babylon simultaneously. In fact, if a part of my unconscious mind is untethered in time, where would I be spatially? Would I be "located" where my conscious mind is attending to reality? Is it possible that in my unconscious I could be in multiple times/locations, and location and time are only determined by conscious attention? What makes conscious attention the basis of reality? Maybe my unconscious mind is independent of space and time altogether, as some consciousness researchers propose (Baruss & Mossbridge, 2017; Kelly, Crabtree, & Marshall, 2015). I spent weeks pondering these questions leaving me with a deepening uncertainty about fundamental aspects of myself in the world.

That was an unusual life-altering experience, but here's the uncanny way it seems to appear in Frank's novel. After writing for about six months, Frank gave me copies of his first two chapters. At home I read his second chapter, a science fiction story in which a mathematician published a controversial essay demonstrating the existence of parallel universes. This paper upset a group of physicists who undermine the mathematician's career. Distracted by this professional conflict, while driving on a dimly lit road, the mathematician accidently side-swipes and kills a young man who was changing the left rear tire on his broken-down car. This event dramatically altered the mathematician's life and led to a mental breakdown followed by years of psychoanalytic treatment. In Frank's story the accident was attributed to "twilight, poor visibility, and too small a shoulder," all attributes of my near-miss. Although I remembered Frank reading this vignette to me months before, it was a detail lost in a sea of information.

During our next session I asked Frank when he wrote "Convergence." He began writing it in late August and finished it in October, a couple of months before my flat-tire experience. So, Frank wrote about a life-altering experience with a flat tire in a story involving a dramatic reconception of our place in space and time two months before I had my near-miss involving a flat tire—a near-miss that caused me to seriously reconsider my place in space and time. The parallels between these two events seemed too compelling to be coincidental. Was I again, like Charcot, observing the impossible?

I asked Frank about the date of writing "Convergence" to determine what came first, my flat-tire experience or his story, wondering if there was causal relationship between them. One thing must precede another to be considered its cause. Frank reading me this portion of this story months before my flat tire encounter may have predisposed me to interpret events in a particular way. But that couldn't explain my experience of thinking "flat tire" and 25 minutes later encountering someone changing a tire. In other words, this detail in Frank's story couldn't have meaningfully contributed to my experience. Looking at these two events in chronological sequence revealed no causal relationship between them.

But look at them the other way around. Frank appears to write about an experience two months before I have it. Could his story be a premonition of my premonitory experience? Talk about an echo! Was his story a memory from my future? Could my future experience be the cause of this portion of his story? That's *impossible!* A memory from my future can't cause Frank's present experience. Or can it? Anyway, I wondered, how could Frank even have knowledge about my future? On the other hand, if I presume that within this symbiotic state of *rapport* Frank has access to my unconscious, does his story "prove" my future exists within my unconscious?

I know, thinking like this makes everyone's head spin, including mine! Symbiosis threatens our sense of personal integrity. Of course, that's to be expected if *rapport* recreates an intrauterine experience of fused identities. Premonition alters our place in time, and time is the basis for our belief in a continuous self. To reverse our understanding of causality is simply too much. Anyone could respond, "Surely this is madness!"

Let's think about that. Bertha Pappenheim cured herself with 160 consecutive doses of hallucination. Is there a parallel between her hallucinations, her temporal dissociation, and Frank's writing? Actually, yes. Both are products of creative imagination spontaneously emerging from the unconscious. Both enter consciousness through an altered state called a dissociative trance. Both create animated virtual realities that momentarily take precedence over lived experience. Temporarily, Frank and Bertha can live—that is, *imaginatively act*—in these alternate realities. Both reverse the temporal sequence of conscious reality. Both relieve suffering. Both appear following the death of a loved one. The case of Bertha is presented so Breuer appears to independently observe her insanity: She's crazy and he's sane. In the case of Frank, madness—or maybe the miraculous—is the product of the *rapport*. The craziness emerged in the relationship. It was intersubjective, it wasn't either his or mine.

Anyway, I don't think this is actually madness. It's more miraculous than madness. Perhaps it's *imagining the impossible.* "What's the point in that?" you might ask. Like Freud, you could reductively conclude that miracles are impossible because they're impossible. Redouble your fortitude and find the courage to accept depressing reality. Makes sense, but the unconscious has a different idea. In the face of tragic loss, imagination erupts spontaneously in the minds of Frank and Bertha. Imagination is the only refuge for their despair. Seeing that makes me wonder if depression is an absence of imagination.

Imagination enters our lives most often through dreaming, the most common altered state of consciousness. Because dreaming doesn't subscribe to the constraints of reality, it's considered a psychotic process. In the words of sleep researcher Allan Hobson (1999), "Dreaming is not a *model* of psychosis, it is psychosis"; dreaming "is not *like* delirium, it is delirium" (p. 44). As Hobson declares, "There is no madness more delirious than dreaming" (p. 4). So, what's the value of slipping into an imaginative psychotic dream state several times each night? Hobson's associate, David Kahn, studies dreaming and creativity. Kahn says, "while dreaming we benefit by thinking the unthinkable and, importantly, believing it and experiencing it" (Kahn & Gover, 2010, p. 193). In our dreams we *live and believe the unthinkable.* That's the same as believing in miracles! Kahn's research shows that after dreaming people are more creative and inventive, and they are more capable of creating solutions to life's challenges. Human growth depends on this daily dream-dose of psychosis which serves as an antidote to the constraints of reductive rationalism. Ironically, regular dream-doses of madness—or the miraculous—may be necessary to cure the mental illness caused by rational thinking. From the perspective of the unconscious, rationalism is the problem, not the solution.

In our work together, Frank became an artist like me. Of course, he had no conscious idea of my background in visual art. And I never suggested he write, much less that he write a novel. Writing became therapeutic because Frank was free to be completely imaginative. Frank says if someone had asked him to write about the painful experience of his son's death it would have been paralyzing. He couldn't have written a word. Instead, Frank's writing was spontaneous and automatic. It was pure free association. He wrote about whatever came to mind and rarely edited.

Frank is amazed to have written a novel. "Where did it come from?" he asks. He never had an outline; words just arrived on the page. Like Bertha's therapy and my drawing, Frank's creative writing occurs in a dissociative trance—a dissociative trance akin to dreaming. In fact, Frank's novel reads as a long continuous dream. When he finishes a story he says, "Maybe I wrote it. I guess I did. I don't know where it came from." Frank's creativity converts anguish into a story that transports him, a story that brings him temporary comfort, a story that hopefully affects others. Frank says Anders is his inspiration. It's Anders' hand that guides him from the darkness of despair into the light. Frank knows his pain can't be stopped. But it's transformed by imagination.

References

Bailly, J.-S. (2002). Secret report on mesmerism, or animal magnetism. *International Journal of Clinical and Experimental Hypnosis*, 50:364–68. (Original work published 1784.)

Baruss, I. & Mossbridge, J. (2017). *Transcendent Mind: Rethinking the Science of Consciousness*. Washington, DC: American Psychological Association.

Borch-Jacobsen, M. (1996). *Remembering Anna O.: A Century of Mystification*. New York: Routledge.

Breger, L. (2009). *A Dream of Undying Fame: How Freud Betrayed his Mentor and Invented Psychoanalysis*. New York: Basic Books.

Breuer, J. (1895). Case 1: Fraulein Anna O. In J. Breuer & S. Freud, *Studies on Hysteria*, pp. 21–47. Standard edition. London: Hogarth Press.

Chertok, L. (1970). Freud in Paris: A crucial stage. *International Journal of Psychoanalysis*, 51:511–520.

Chertok, L. & de Saussure, R. (1979). *The Therapeutic Revolution: From Mesmer to Freud*. New York: Brunner/Mazel.

Chertok, L. & Stengers, I. (1992). *A Critique of Psychoanalytic Reason: Hypnosis as a Scientific Problem from Lavoisier to Lacan*. Stanford: Stanford University Press.

Conn, J. (1982). Nature of magnetic treatment. *Journal of the American Society of Psychosomatic Dentistry and Medicine*, 29:44–53.

Crabtree, A. (1993). *From Mesmer to Freud: Magnetic Sleep and the Roots of Psychological Healing*. New Haven, CT: Yale University Press.

Darnton, R. (1968). *Mesmerism and the End of the Enlightenment in France*. Cambridge, MA: Harvard University Press.

Ellenberger, H. (1965). Mesmer and Puysegur: From magnetism to hypnotism. *Psychoanalytic Review*, 52B:137–153.

Ellenberger, H. (1970). *The Discovery of the Unconscious: The History and Evolution of Dynamic Psychiatry*. New York: Basic Books.

Ellenberger, H. (1972). The story of Anna O.: A critical review with new data. *Journal of the History of the Behavioral Sciences*, 8:267–279.

Ellenberger, H. (1993). Charcot and the Salpetriere School. In M. Micale (ed.), *Beyond the Unconscious: Essays of Henri F. Ellenberger in the History of Psychiatry*, pp. 139–154. Princeton: Princeton University Press. (Original work published 1965.)

Ellens, J. (ed.) (2008). *Miracles: God, Science, and Psychology in the Paranormal.* Westport, CT: Praeger.

Franklin, B. (1785). *Report of Dr. Benjamin Franklin and Other Commissioners Charged by the King of France with the Examination of the Animal Magnetism as now Practiced at Paris.* London: J. Johnson.

Freud, S. (1892–94). *Preface and footnotes to the translation of Charcot's "Tuesday Lectures."* Standard edition. London: Hogarth Press, 1:131–143.

Freud, S. (1933). *New Introductory Lectures on Psychoanalysis.* Standard edition. London: Hogarth Press, 22:3–182.

Gauld, A. (1992). *A History of Hypnotism.* Cambridge: Cambridge University Press.

Gilhooley, D. (2002). Misrepresentation and misreading in the case of Anna O. *Modern Psychoanalysis,* 27:75–100.

Goetz, C., Bonduelle, M., & Gelfand, T. (1995). *Charcot: Constructing Neurology.* New York: Oxford University Press.

Grosso, M. (2016). *The Man who Could Fly: St. Joseph of Copertino and the Mystery of Levitation.* Lanham, MD: Rowman & Littlefield.

Harrington, A. (2008). *The Cure Within: A History of Mind–Body Medicine.* New York: W.W. Norton.

Hirschmuller, A. (1978). *The Life and Work of Josef Breuer: Physiology and Psychoanalysis.* New York: New York University Press.

Hobson, J. (1999). *Dreaming as Delirium: How the Brain Goes out of its Mind.* Cambridge, MA: MIT Press.

Hudson, T. (1893). *The Law of Psychic Phenomena: A Working Hypothesis for the Systematic Study of Hypnotism, Spiritism, Mental Therapeutics, etc.* Chicago: A.C. McClurg.

Hustvedt, A. (2011). *Medical Muses: Hysteria in Nineteenth-Century Paris.* New York: W.W. Norton and Company.

James, W. (1985). *Varieties of Religious Experience: A Study in Human Nature.* Harmondsworth: Penguin. (Original work published 1902.)

Kahn, D. & Gover, T. (2010). Consciousness in dreams. *International Review of Neurobiology,* 92:181–195.

Keener, C. (2011). *Miracles: The Credibility of New Testament Accounts,* 3 vols. Grand Rapids, MI: Baker Academic.

Kelly, E., Crabtree, A., & Marshall, P. (2015). *Beyond Physicalism: Toward Reconciliation of Science and Spirituality.* Lanham, MD: Rowman and Littlefield.

Lippard, L. (1981). *Ad Reinhardt.* New York: Harry Abrams.

Marshall, P. (2005). *Mystical Encounters with the Natural World: Experiences and Explanations.* Oxford: Oxford University Press.

Micale, M. (1995a). Charcot and *les nervroses traumatiques*: Scientific and historical reflections. *Journal of the History of Neuroscience*, 4:101–119.

Micale, M. (1995b). Charcot and the history of hysteria. In *Approaching Hysteria: Disease and its Interpretations*, pp.88–97. Princeton: Princeton University Press.

Pattie, F. (1994). *Mesmer and Animal Magnetism: A Chapter in Medical History*. Hamilton, NY: Edmonston Publishing.

Richet, C. (1923). *Thirty Years of Psychical Research: Being a Treatise on Metaphysics*. London: W. Collins Sons.

Searles, H. (1979). Concerning therapeutic symbiosis. In *Countertransference and Related Subjects: Selected Papers*. New York: International Universities Press.

Shorter, E. (1992). *From Paralysis to Fatigue: A History of Psychosomatic Illness in the Modern Era*. New York: Free Press.

Skues, R. (2006). *Sigmund Freud and the History of Anna O.: Reopening a Closed Case*. New York: Palgrave Macmillan.

Spotnitz, H. (1985). *Modern Psychoanalysis of the Schizophrenic Patient: Theory of the Technique*, second edition. New York: Human Sciences Press. (Original work published 1969.)

Stengers, I. (2003). The doctor and the charlatan. *Cultural Studies Review*, 9:11–36.

Winkelman, M. & Baker, J. (2010). *Supernatural as Natural: A Biocultural Approach to Religion*. Upper Saddle River, NJ: Prentice Hall.

Wolf, S. (1993). *Brain, Mind, and Medicine: Charles Richet and the Origins of Physiological Psychology*. New Brunswick, NJ: Transaction Publishers.

Woodward, K. (2000). *The Book of Miracles: The Meaning of the Miracle Stories in Christianity, Judaism, Buddhism, Hinduism, Islam*. New York: Simon & Schuster.

Chapter 5

My dual journey

An autobiographical account

Henry Kellerman

Psychologist/Psychoanalyst/Author

Why did I pursue a career as psychologist/psychoanalyst? That's the question many psychotherapists ask themselves. It also becomes a question that others are curious about whenever they discover what I do for a living. The general answer I've given myself was that I thought I'd be good at it. But although that answer is accurate insofar as it's what I really thought, it is, however, not specific. The specific answer would need, it seems, to have a genesis to it; to be part of a process that started very early on in my life and that then created a path through life onto which I navigated directly toward the profession of doing psychotherapy.

So, yes there was a genesis to my interest in psychotherapy, psychopathology (neurosis, psychosis), psychoanalysis, and all the rest of it. The unalloyed truth is that I'm in thrall to idiosyncrasy and always have been. It possibly could be said that I actually love pathology. Well, let me explain that. It's that I love to be near it, to see it, observe it with a clinical and, very importantly, with an empathetic eye. I feel strongly sympathetic with people who are severely and emotionally/psychologically ill (disturbed). I try to understand what it is they feel. But I must also admit that observing pathology (and its dynamics) is for me an aesthetic gratifying pleasure; it's like looking at something awesome, different, unusual, and deep—perhaps even, dare I say, beautiful.

I find it intriguing to be in contact with pathological phenomena because it offers me a chance to look at it, to observe it with a penetrating eye in order to see if I can intuit it, have insight about it, and basically have the privilege to see first-hand the essence at the core of such pathology—and ultimately perhaps to cure it; actually, to help people struggle better. Isn't that more accurate? The issue is never "cure." The issue is always working toward struggling better. You don't cure life!

So, again, how did it all start, or where did it all start, or when did it all start, or why did it all start? The answer, as one might expect, started, I'm reluctant to say, with a description that is usually assessed as a cliché; that is, with the relationship with my mother. And I believe I understand it. It was not that she didn't love me or that I didn't love her. It was not that I came from a broken family. It was not that I was neglected.

It was not that my father was cruel or an isolate or uninterested in me. I believe it all started because I felt sort of—betrayed! Yes, betrayed. And I felt this sort of betrayal when I was about two and a half years old. That's right, even two-and-a-half-year-olds can feel such things.

Up until I was two and a half, my mother didn't work at a standard nine-to-five job. She was with me all the time. There were no stranger nannies or mother's helpers or babysitters—that is, there were no people around who were not in the immediate family.

However, my grandmother (bubba in Yiddish) lived with us; mine was a Jewish immigrant family. The language spoken at home here in America was Yiddish. My bubba spoke no English except to say hello and goodbye and nod her head up and down for "yes" and side to side for "no."

Therefore, my first language as an American-born son was Yiddish. I learned English on the streets of the southeast Bronx in New York City. But at home, especially with my bubba, I spoke only Yiddish. My parents arrived in New York City in the very early 1920s not knowing a word of English. They learned "American" very quickly. So with my parents I spoke both Yiddish and English, but with bubba it was strictly Yiddish.

A pivotal situation occurred when I was two and a half years old. As I've said, my mother was my primary care-giver and was with me all the time. She was (and remained) a very loving parent. She was an extraordinarily talented person and could do almost anything, and further, do it with great élan. It would not be an exaggeration to say that she was on fire. She was beautiful, sang beautifully (had a smoky alto), was a great dancer, great cook, could sew anything, spoke several languages and was an actress (could do accents and all sorts of roles requiring what she had—rhythm and perfect pitch).

Although she had this perfect pitch, nevertheless, she was governed by traditions of her eastern European-ghettoed formative life which dictated screening out bad news.

That was the one area in which she, along with others of her generation (from the other side), were actually quite tone deaf. And what I mean is that when I was two and a half years of age, and completely accustomed to her attention, love, affection, companionship, and safe harbor, she, one day, suddenly announced that she needed to go to work with my father in a little luncheonette that they were going to open—a store that was located at street level of the four-story tenement-like apartment building where we lived.

My talented, beautiful mother apparently thought that telling me she would be only a stone's throw away from our first-floor apartment (one flight up) would mollify my apprehension and unhappiness about her departure—a departure that each day would bring her home in the evening. She reminded me that my bubba would always be there and then she introduced me to two young babysitters who arrived at our apartment at the precise time my mother was telling me all this. She must have timed it thinking it was the right thing to do. Each babysitter was to alternate their babysitting stints during the week.

I wasn't shaken by the news but I was definitely disappointed. "Betrayed" is really what I felt, but I couldn't put my finger on that particular word because, of course, I didn't know that word. I couldn't tag my feeling to that word until I was much older. And, of course, "betrayed" is a feeling, existing within the context of abandonment, and underpinned by disappointment plus anger. So the fact of the matter is that I was angry with my mother, but nevertheless, definitely also loved her.

Despite what I felt was her abandonment of me, I also with no doubt whatsoever knew that she was definitely doing it in order to save the family. That's right, two-and-a-half-year-olds can understand or feel a great many things—things most people do not believe two-year-old or two-and-a-half-year-olds can do. But they can.

So that's the way it was and this situation generated my first patient. No, it was not my mother. It was I who was my first patient. It was me.

At that time I also had a vague feeling that my father, handsome, intelligent, and the regular guy that he was, really couldn't make a living. Yes, even though I was that young, I still could sense that everything was alright in the family if my mother backed it all up. My father was as honest as they come; he was loyal, strong, and he had a lot of pride. He could not tolerate unfairness and had a sophisticated and democratic, even Marxist sense, that equitable distribution of wealth should be the norm. However, his practical sense was essentially perhaps naïve (perhaps he was in denial). He was also maximally risk-averse—the prototypical anti- or rather non-entrepreneur. He could not abide any thought that he might owe someone something and not be able to repay it. Therefore, his ability to make a living was challenged in contrast to the undeniable fact of his high intelligence. He was an avid reader who would inhale books. So my mother with her can-do attitude (who was incidentally always crazy about him) jumped into the fray, and they opened a little luncheonette where she was in the back cooking all kinds of Jewish foods and he was in the front serving and washing dishes.

And that's how I grew up—with my bubba in the house and my parents in the store. I also spent much time in the store with them, at least until I went to kindergarten at the age of four because my parents could no longer afford even the pittance babysitters were paid in those years, and they needed to get me off the streets.

Okay, the first day of kindergarten arrived and my mother ushered me into the classroom. I asked her to remain at the door and not to enter. All the other children had their mothers with them in the room, and these children, to the best of my recollection, were all crying. I was not crying, not scared, and not at all caring about anything but going to the other side of the room to the windows in order to look out at the street and to try to see where my block would be in relation to this window through which I was staring. Sure enough, there it was—the store and the building where I lived. Now I knew that if I needed to get the hell out of there, I could run out of the room, make an acute right turn, and head for the school door that would let me out into the street. Then I would make a dash for it and run diagonally across the street directly to the store. I figured it all out instantly, turned to signal my mother, and waved her away. She left.

I was perfectly fine. In retrospect, I believe that because I felt the abandonment when my mother went to work about a year and a half earlier, I also felt a sense of independence; that I would need to take care of myself and perhaps also all of those around me. So at age four

I was already getting set to do psychotherapy, especially with what I felt was my unusual sense of empathy with others.

At that point I felt, nay, I knew I could navigate my life and perhaps help in the navigation of the lives of others. I believe my kindergarten teacher, Miss Dubin (whom I loved and who, I sensed, loved me), also felt I had certain special mature qualities and, without asking, and on that very first day, appointed me president of the class. It was a class of five-years-olds, and I was four.

All in all, I grew up with a bubba in the house, while at that time I would usually hang out in the store after school. Those were three of my four venues (house, store, school). My fourth was playing ball in the street with my friends—especially Richie, my first and best friend (my life-long blood-brother). But there in the store was where I was essentially in training as a psychotherapist.

The customers were endlessly interesting to me and many of them had, to say the least, very idiosyncratic behaviors. And it was these idiosyncrasies that completely arrested my attention. It was there in that store where, in the sense of pathology, I was just beginning to understand the difference between idiosyncrasy and irrationality.

Mr. Jaskowitz

My next patient (as mentioned, I was my first patient) when I was in my early psychotherapy training (about six years old, leading to my first maturity as a budding psychotherapist a year later, at seven) was a 65-year-old man. I'll give him the name of Morris Jaskowitz. He was a Jewish immigrant to America, arriving here at about the age of 14, in the early 1900s. At the age of 24, he was a soldier in the First World War and was gassed during combat. Because of this trauma, he never recovered his normal mental functioning and was from that time on quite fearful and especially paranoid.

Mr. Jaskowitz's seemingly only respite from worrying about the FBI was when he displayed his artwork. To my young mind and sensibility, he seemed to be a very good artist. Along with this, his sketchbook, though artful, was nevertheless loaded with and contained features of what I could tell even then at that young age looked like, suspiciousness, guardedness, and vigilance. It was in the eyes of the figures he sketched. The eyes were highly and acutely articulated. They were wary eyes, and the line quality around the eyes was an anxious one—shaded and overprescribed (staccato-like) as if the figure he drew was in a pronounced state of ominous apprehension. It was interesting to me that even when I was that young, Mr. Jaskowitz spoke to me without feeling nervous; he didn't think that I was some kind of a spy or that I was out to get him. Of course, later on I understood more about Mr. Jaskowitz. I realized that he liked me and sensed that I was not malicious. He trusted me as a confidante and so would tell me stories about who he feared and why. It was my first close-up view of a paranoid delusional system. Mr. Jaskowitz was full of stories of how the FBI was tapping his phone and following him. Of course, I realized that the chief reason I had gained his trust was that even through his paranoid eyes, he nevertheless could see I was only a small child; for me to be an FBI agent, or even an FBI informant, was obviously preposterous.

Mr. Jaskowitz was a steady customer of the store, and, over the years, whenever we happened to be in the store at the same time and, while he ate his meal, he would talk to me. I began to understand him and it was my first lesson in psychology. What I saw was that one would never be able to argue logically with a delusion, no less a paranoid one. So I never tried to "logicalize" him out of his delusional thinking. I knew full well that if I tried it would be the end of his trust in me and the end of our friendship.

The point is that even with such a well-meaning and positive motive (of logicalizing him), I still would not be even one iota closer to helping him and certainly further away from that which fascinated me—being able to observe (close up) his feelings and his thinking—his mind.

Over the years there were many other customers who would demonstrate idiosyncratic or neurotic behaviors (not necessarily pathological or irrational) and, without fail, these people would interest me. Again, it occurred to me that, also without fail, I was never able to resist getting close to idiosyncrasy, or to the unusual—and not necessarily only to pathology.

Then it hit home. When I was about 14 years old, my bubba began displaying what in psychiatric lingo is called "an encapsulated delusion."

I only understood its basic meaning (and reason for being) when I was in my thirties and already a practicing psychologist/psychoanalyst.

Bubba

My bubba, Pessie Pellis, born in Ukraine in 1864 (Civil War time in America), only really communicated with my mother (who was her daughter), me, but only infrequently with my father. My father and she never really liked one another, and they never addressed one another by name. They simply started talking to one another whenever necessary. That sort of interpersonal behavior also fascinated me. It told me something about how people are stubborn with regard to expressing pleasant behavior which they feel is equivalent to yielding—when angry with the other person. At the time I sort of knew what it meant but not as a crystallized thought. I later considered this little non-interaction that my father and my bubba created as another important building block of my training as a budding psychotherapist.

Thus my bubba was my third patient, starting when I was a small child but gaining its full measure when I was about 14. My bubba was really alone most of the time. She had very little interface with neighbors. She would talk aloud to herself even when coming from the market where she shopped for her special foods in stores run by Jewish owners who also spoke Yiddish. I would frequently see her speaking audibly to herself while she was walking. At home she would also talk to herself out loud.

Bubba was also a very stubborn person who could never admit to being wrong. Her feelings were more important to her than "truth." I later realized that many people consider ideological positions more important than truth. And no matter how often their ideological positions may have empirically actually proved to be wrong, they still never take the position that they possibly could be wrong about anything. And that was my bubba. I quickly developed a sense that truth trumps ideology every time. The trouble, I noticed, is that with delusion truth means nothing. Although in a descriptive sense a delusion seems to be the furthest extrapolation of the ideology—its apotheosis, the deification of something, or the most extended point of the ideology. However, a bona fide delusion is really quite something else. From a psychoanalytic point of view, rather than its seeming relation to a belief, the delusion relates to the subject's *wish*. As a belief, it would be expected that the delusion could be confronted by logic. But this is where the alleged connection between delusion and belief disintegrates. The delusion can only be reached (touched) by understanding the person's *wish*. My bubba's encapsulated delusion illustrates this point. And here it is.

As mentioned, when I was about 14, my bubba developed an encapsulated delusional system. This meant that she was reasonably normal in her thinking about everything except one thing. This delusional immovable and encapsulated thought of hers contained two parts. The first claim was that I would sneak into her room when she wasn't there, open her trunk (which literally had not been opened for more than 30 years), and, with a razor blade, slice the threads from the hems of her dresses, which again hadn't even been looked at or touched by anyone for all those years. These articles of clothing actually traveled with her from the old country. They had been in her closet or in her trunk for those decades. They were also articles of clothing she never wore, and, in fact, she had them for many years even before she arrived in America. Second, she also claimed the same for the dresses (and shoes) that she always wore—the ones she had hanging and stored in her closet—those that were purchased for her here in America. In these cases the hems of her dresses and flaps of her shoes were in perfect condition. But that didn't matter to her. It was a discrepancy she simply disregarded.

Despite my sense that it was not possible to argue with a delusion, nevertheless this got the best of me and I pleaded with her to believe me that I didn't do any of that. Of course she wouldn't listen. I reminded her that all I was interested in was playing ball with Richie and my other friends and that I had no interest whatsoever in her articles of clothing—and I said it all in Yiddish, of course, because that's the only way we could converse. I think I also felt (and most likely continue to feel) that if one speaks Yiddish, then how bad could it be? Finally, one day, after bubba was out of the apartment shopping, I persuaded my parents to check bubba's trunk and check all the hems of her dresses both in the trunk and in her closet. They did so. No hems were torn or severed and none of her shoes had any damage. I was vindicated of any wrongdoing and was relieved that my parents could see I was entirely innocent.

In any event, and in short order, I no longer lived at home. At 17 I left for college and that was it for living at home. My bubba died at the age of 94. At the time I was 20.

From a psychoanalytic perspective, and many years later, the meaning of her delusion became obvious to me. She was very definitely a lonely person. She had no friends (despite the fact that there were two other elderly Jewish neighbors on our first-floor apartment house where each of the four flights of our building had three apartments). What was always interesting to me was that none of the three elderly neighbors ever had much interface with one another and never even stepped foot in each other's apartment. To this day their sense of implicit partition puzzles me. The greetings they offered one another (in Yiddish, of course) were addressed with surnames.

I would occasionally ask my bubba whether she ever had girlfriends in the old country. She would then regale me with stories about her best friend Rokhl. We would also occasionally sit at the window and she would ask me about various people that were walking along on the street. I would tell her anything I knew about them. It was that my bubba wanted a friend. She was really *wishing* for someone to visit with her in her room, in her domain. It was that precise *wish* that she translated into a delusion. Freud said it: In reality wishes are frequently denied, but in the psyche no wish will ever be denied. That's why Freud also said that we love our symptoms. We love our symptoms because they are our wishes realized, albeit in neurotic form. Therefore, by definition, by bubba must have loved her delusion despite the fact that it gave her a problem. She loved her delusion because as a symptom it represented a gratification of the *wish* to have someone be in her room—a familiar person with whom to break bread, with whom to talk and tell stories—a peer, a friend, a companion, or in a way even some other relationship. But, as a delusion, she translated the wish so that her own psyche (a psyche that did the translation) would not permit her to know and focus on just how lonely she really was. She just didn't want to know. It also dawned on me that bubba was angry at the unfairness at not having such a peer-friend. This later brought me to the realization that in order to pop a symptom, one must have anger repressed. I began to see that as an axiom.

Thus, I was early on gestating an education in the psychology of the person's psyche (self to self) as well as in the psychology of interpersonal relationships (self to others).

Simon

When I was about 15, I had my fourth patient. It was Simon. He also would come to eat in the store, and that's where he revealed to me what he considered his most precious thought. It was this: Simon felt that he was the only person in the world who understood how both animate objects (people, animals) as well as inanimate objects (chairs, tables, napkins, etc.) also felt. Then when I was already eight and a half, one day while sitting opposite me at a table Simon pulled a napkin out of the napkin-holder resting on the table and said to me: "See, kid, I can't even tear this napkin apart because I can feel the pain it would cause the molecules being pulled apart." Again, I understood many years later that Simon was very angry about the world (especially people in it), but it was all underneath, beneath his consciousness; his anger was repressed. As a repressed emotion, the anger he felt was disguised as its positive opposite, a concern for all living things. And, to Simon, living things meant everything—animate and inanimate. Years later when I left for college I no longer saw Simon. But I definitely remembered him and probably permanently retained a healthy respect for molecules.

But there was more. At the age of 27, I began my private practice as psychologist/psychoanalyst at a Gramercy Park address in New York City. And, lo and behold, there was Simon. He was the daytime doorman of the building. We hadn't seen one another for a decade. The last time I saw Simon I was 17, and here I was now 20. The moment he spotted me he said: "Kid, it's you!"

He was the same Simon with the same concern for molecules. Of course by this time my psychoanalytic doubt index was at an all-time high—about how people can say one thing but really feel the opposite (frequently without really knowing they were feeling the opposite). In this respect, I knew without a shadow of a doubt that Simon was angry about almost everything and that he felt the world had dealt him a very poor hand. Therefore, his concern about not even hurting a molecule had another more menacing and insidious meaning to it. To exaggerate in order to underscore this point, I would illustrate just how angry Simon really was with the world by saying that yes, he actually would not want to separate a napkin because the separation would indeed hurt the molecules. Rather, he would really, underneath it all, want to explode an atomic bomb; that's how angry he was and didn't know it.

I then discovered that Simon lived in the underground garage of the building in a derelict car at the far wall abutting the building's boiler room. Obviously, he would be warm in winter. He sponge-bathed in the staff locker-room/bathroom in the basement. Simon was alone.

Yiddish theater

My early sense that I felt I could almost understand how people felt by how they looked and by any numbers of their physical postures and manners of speech also corresponded to probably the seminal experience of my life. This seminal experience was my participation in the Yiddish cultural world as the person who personified what the immigrant Yiddish-speaking population wanted: a sense of continuity with values they considered to be an imperative. This meant they needed someone, a young person, to reflect and actually represent the achievement of their objective in the New World—that Yiddish would flourish in this new miraculous country—the good ole U.S.A. And so, as my Yiddish was indistinguishable from that of someone who was born and raised in the old country, then some people from the leftist Yiddish high-brow cultural life in America came my way, and after speaking to me in Yiddish, brought me into the inner sanctum of the Yiddish secular cultural life. As such, I became, in short order, the tip-of-the-spear of such immigrant hopes of what they could accomplish with respect to how Yiddish could be successfully anchored in America. It all started when I was seven years old, precisely the time when I also became this budding seven-year-old psychotherapist having my psychotherapy office located in a hole-in-the-wall little luncheonette in the southeast Bronx. It was then that I began performing in a wide variety of Yiddish cultural events including performing prose and poetry of Yiddish writers and performing them in front of a microphone in virtually each and every major performance venue in New York City, including narrating major cantatas with a 100-voice Yiddish chorus along with solos by Metropolitan Opera notables while I narrated the entire shootn' match. These venues included Madison Square Garden (at a Holocaust Memorial event), Metropolitan Opera House, Carnegie Hall, Town Hall, Manhattan Center, Waldorf Astoria Ballroom, and in cities such as Philadelphia, Boston, Miami, and Los Angeles. In addition, I performed in Yiddish theater with the Ensemble

Theater and with the great Maurice Schwartz on Second Avenue. My oeuvre consisting of all my work in this very special part of my life is contained in my performance archive of 10 volumes, housed at the Dorot Division of the New York Public Library (the Yiddish art division), at YIVO (the Institute for Jewish Research, Archive Division, New York City), and at the Yiddish Book Center (Archive Division) in Amherst, MA. I am also represented in the multi-volume *Lexicon of Yiddish Theatre*, Volume VI, 1969, pp. 5885–5886; 5871–5872, edited by Zalmen Zylbercweig, and in the 2016 edition of *New York's Yiddish Theater: From Bowery to Broadway*, published by Columbia University Press, compiled and edited by Edna Nahshon, with a reminiscence of my work on page 193. The sense of the contribution I made in this seminal experience of my life began as stated at seven with a heavy concentration of performances each week for 10 years. Then at age 17 to 27, I limited my engagement in this arena to only a few performances a year. In those 20 years, I had memorized tons of material and was part of scores and scores of theater plays in which again, I needed to do lots of memorizing. In addition, although some actors are great at rehearsals as well as at legitimate actual performances while the opposite is true for others who may be terrible at both rehearsals and performances, and then again while others are either great at rehearsals and terrible at performances, or, terrible at rehearsals and damn good at performances, I personally fell in this latter group. I could not abide rehearsals and therefore at rehearsals I could not rise to the occasion. But when it came to the real thing is when I became in Yiddish: The Vunderkind. The following is what one of the reviews said about me and this quite frankly represents just about what others had also said:

In Yiddish:

Dee program bashtayt fun Henry Kellerman, bagapter yunger kinstler, oistaytcher funem Yiddish leed un vunderlekher illustrator funem Yiddish vort.

In English:

The program will feature Henry Kellerman, incredible young artist, interpreter of Yiddish literature, and the wonderful illustrator of the Yiddish word.

So, the possibly daunting question becomes, why psychotherapy and not the theater? The simple answer is that I could no longer imagine memorizing volumes of material as well as the thought of needing to continue to do so on a regular basis. This prospect was so toxic to me that I then, with certainty, rejected a number of offers to participate in legitimate theater as presented in major venues such as on Broadway and in film. I never looked back. I proceeded to gain a Master of Arts in experimental psychology, a Master of Science and a PhD in clinical psychology, and then completed a five-year postdoctoral training in psychoanalysis. I've now been in private practice for many decades and in addition I became an author/editor of more than 30 books with the 35th at the moment in preparation, entitled: *The Unconscious Domain*. Both of my careers have been a privilege to experience. I'm comfortable in my office and do not need to feel what I always felt as the tyranny of rehearsals. My need to just do it on the real stage in an extemporaneous environment anchored in training and education is what has continued to illuminate my spirit—especially understanding moments of truth. These moments of truth then also depend on a specific gift of virtuosity (the *science* of doing the *art*) in this process we call psychotherapy—that is, enabling one to struggle better. It's how I feel now as a psychologist/psychoanalyst/author, and how I felt as an interpreter of Yiddish literature where in another way I was also able to contribute to the greater good—being in a position to offer people cultural nourishment in an important cultural milieu. Interestingly, my tenure in the Yiddish cultural world was also where I sharpened my understanding of character structure that writers spend arduous hours crafting—such as intuiting: personality generally, and character formation specifically; conflict expressed in peak pivotal moments and the corresponding emergence of mutative interpretation; the performer's need to know how to deliver subject matter to the audience in a pre-digestive form; and, the very important interaction with the audience that must be honest. The audience must be respected so that authenticity becomes the issue. In addition, it was important to learn that patience is required in both venues, relating to an audience and relating to a person. These, then, have been the components of my dual journey of wonderful diverse, intricate, and uninterrupted highs—especially as I've said, because I was enabled to contribute to a greater good—akin to a pilgrimage. Yes. It has all been a privilege.

Chapter 6

Improvisational play for a psychoanalyst-musician

Robert J. Marshall

I'd like to convey to the reader the parallels in my functioning as an author, psychoanalyst, and jazz pianist. The similar styles, while in different realms, namely writing, conducting psychoanalysis, and improvising jazz, seem to stem from a common source and follow a similar common pathway.

My musical and educational roots

Taking piano lessons at age seven in 1935 was no fun, although I enjoyed the attention of my attractive piano teacher, Miss Hyatt. Despite the efforts of this lovely and talented teacher, I seldom practiced. But my next piano teacher, Victor, who was a gifted professional swing (1930s jazz) pianist, caught my attention because he improvised. How wonderful, I thought, that this man plays such exciting and enchanting music without looking at music. It was magical. Entranced, I practiced the fundamentals of technique and reading music. Victor also introduced chord structures needed to improvise. He wrote out his improvisations of several standards for me to practice. I was even willing to practice technique in order to improvise.

At about the same time, my father took me on a large party fishing boat that accommodated a small upright piano. As the boat headed home with the jolly fishermen with their full pails of fish and, I suspect, their fill of beer, they enjoined me to play piano. The appreciative audience showered me with praise and with many dollar bills. More magic – I could play, be applauded, and paid for playing!

During World War II when I was 14 years old and when civilian musicians were scarce, Victor introduced me to a big band. The members, much older than I, were very warm and supportive, but told me to go home and practice playing the charts (arrangements). I complied because I yearned to play in a band that produced such wonderful music and offered such comradery. At the same time, a young enthusiastic music teacher arrived at Passaic High School and established a dance band around a couple of talented schoolmates. My parents were so taken by my interest in music that they bought me a record player with their hard-earned money on which I began to listen to vinyl 78s of jazz orchestras and musicians where improvisation was in the forefront. I lay awake at night turning the dials on my radio trying to find jazz stations. I began to imitate artists such as Teddy Wilson, Benny Goodman, Dizzy Gillespie, and Charlie Parker and ventured into improvising.

It was only much later in life that I realized that I was the recipient of a musical gift bestowed upon me by my father, who, without taking any lessons, could play virtually any tune on the piano. He could play a complex harmonica, and later in life began to play an accordion. Genetics are at play because my children became proficient at the oboe and bassoon (very difficult instruments) while my sister and her children were also talented musically. My mother and wife, always appreciative audiences, were part of a supportive milieu.

While I was doing well enough in my high school studies, I was being drawn into the music field. I began playing with big bands and small groups for which I was paid fair amounts of money. Music became increasingly central. I was cajoled into playing double bass for the high school and city orchestra. I even arranged three charts for a big band for which I was paid virtually nothing. I was in the company of men somewhat older than I who were entertaining. They smoked, drank, experimented with drugs, and consorted with women among other libidinous activities that fascinated me and alarmed my parents. As no one seemed to support my interests in studying music, and because I did well in high school sciences, I enrolled into a nearby engineering school where, because of little talent and interest in calculus, electricity, and spatial geometry, I was asked to leave. There was no room for improvisation at that college, just vaguely interesting drudgery. I often wonder, "What if I had gone to Juilliard?"

It took me about a year or so to realize that given the level of my musical talent, no support from my parents, and my wanting a stable family life, music was not a viable career. I entered Rutgers University in 1947 where I found pleasure in studying the liberal arts and found time to help establish the University Jazz Club, organize jazz concerts, and play music on weekends. My commitment to college life ended my association with a big band because I could not be relied upon to play the gigs, nor could I attend the rehearsals. I recall my last gig with the big band. With my replacement at the piano, I walked onto the floor where dozens of couples were dreamily dancing to a wonderful arrangement of "Moonlight in Vermont." I was flooded with feelings. I was thrilled to hear the talented tenor man soloing, the five-part harmony of the sax section, the mellow backup of the five-man brass section, and the steady soft beat of the full rhythm section. As happy as I was hearing the harmonies, and proud that I had helped assemble that orchestra, tears rolled down my face knowing that I would never again be a part of this fun-loving, dedicated, cooperative group. To this day, nostalgia ripples through me and even a few tears of happiness yet sadness dribble down my cheeks as I hear a big band perform. I have the same reaction when I hear about a successful cooperative event like our moon shots.

On Rutgers campus, many of my friends were psychology or pre-med majors who talked of psychoanalysis and aspired to be psychoanalysts. Excited by this new world, I aimed to be a psychoanalyst. Some of my friends had discovered the presence of a campus psychiatrist and at their urging I began psychotherapy with Jay Fidler, who at the time was a candidate at W.A. White Institute. In his warm and accepting manner I was able to freely discuss what was on my mind. He asked me to talk *ad lib* and I complied. In the musical metaphor, he welcomed my improvisations and all the notes I could play.

Another influence was the anthropologist, Ashley Montagu, who was a brilliant lecturer and elegant Englishman who opened his office to biweekly four o'clock teas for his students where we could talk about anything. Occasionally, a small group would repair to a local tavern for a beer and hamburger where we continued our discussions. His degree of academic informality and penchant for integrating psychoanalysis with anthropology and other fields provided an exciting model for me.

After my graduation from Rutgers, I was accepted at The City College of New York in the school psychology program that was loaded with talented psychoanalytically oriented educators such as

Kurt Goldstein, Ruth Munroe, David Beres, and Katherine Wolf, who was Rene Spitz's assistant. These teachers turned me on. I worked hard and enjoyably for them, reading and writing papers and reports that seemed to come easy for me. In retrospect, writing reports was improvisational play for me. I was creating something out of virtually nothing. I continued my analysis with Joseph Steinert from the W.A. White Institute. In using the couch, talking was easier. In the musical metaphor, I did not have to practice, I just improvised for a quiet and, I assumed, appreciative audience.

In the meantime, I was not neglecting my music. I had an easy, steady weekend gig with some fine musicians who taught me how to sing in their harmonious quartet. Summertime found me playing piano at resorts. I was p(l)aying my way through college. I use the word "playing" and not "working" because playing music was never work.

Upon attaining my master's degree at CCNY, I was accepted at Teachers College, Columbia where I took clinical psychology courses. In following the then current roadmap toward a psychoanalytic career I met Simone, who was a vibrant, beautiful Fulbright Scholar from France and who also aspired to be a psychoanalyst. Attracted to my playful attitude and perhaps my musical world, she accepted my hand in marriage. Throughout our 65-year relationship, I felt she was an unstinting admirer and support to virtually everything I did, although she might have rendered a different opinion. We were successful in raising two wonderful, psychologically and musically minded children.

After a year at Columbia and without adequate funds, I reluctantly left Teachers College and Simone for the graduate program at the University of Buffalo, where I was offered free tuition, an internship, and an assistantship to a professor, Marvin Feldman, who had a psychoanalytic orientation. Highly motivated, I contributed to my professor's research and wrote clinical reports and papers that were not only a joy to compose but were judged to be superior. As opposed to the larger universities, the relatively small department functioned in a friendly, informal collegial manner which was appealing to me. I was pleasantly surprised that as part of the curriculum for my class, the department provided group therapy conducted by a psychoanalyst, Hyman Levin.

While an intern at the Psychological Clinic at the university, I was also playing jazz and cocktail piano at a bar/restaurant on weekday evenings where my name and photo were prominently displayed in the window. An uptight professor who visited the lounge wanted me dismissed from the program, citing something akin to conflict of interest. After a departmental inquiry, I was asked to tell the lounge owner to take down the sign and put up a more general ad about live music. I certainly was not about to tell my professors about my playing Sunday afternoon jazz concerts in a scuzzy bar in the steel town of Lackawanna.

I was fortunate in being able to write easily because of mine and Simone's "dissertation disasters." After having my dissertation proposal on psychoanalytic symbolism approved, I searched the literature, and collected data. Suddenly, my two major committee members left the department. Unable to find qualified professors to continue the work, I had to find a topic that was synchronous with the interests of a new committee. Ironically, I chose the topic of "conformity," which was of current interest. At the same time, Simone discovered that her committee chairperson had left the university and had lost her work including data that she was about to analyze. Not finding professors who were willing and able to help her continue her topic, she, too, had to find a topic that was consonant with the interests of a new committee. Highly distressed by the perfidy of her first chairperson and the surprising academic politics and her preoccupation with our baby, she was about to abandon the dissertation process. Because I had the time, motivation, and the penchant for researching and writing, I assisted her in evolving a study that not only qualified her for her degree but was good enough for publication in *The Journal of Clinical and Consulting Psychology.*

I discovered my true love for writing during a summer vacation in France. I had been asked to write a chapter for the forthcoming *Handbook of Child and Adolescent Psychiatry* (Marshall, 1979). Ensconced in a comfortable home on the Cote d'Azur with a view of the Mediterranean Sea, my wife, her mother and friends would provide me with breakfast and set up my desk overlooking the sea. Everyone either vacated the house or were quiet while the *Professeur/monsignor* wrote from 9 AM to 1 PM. A wonderful lunch ensued, followed by a siesta, a visit to the beach, cocktails, a light dinner, conversation, and bed. Within four weeks I had written a long chapter that was accepted with virtually no editing. The writing flowed not only without much effort, but with pleasure. Could I become another Hemingway who followed a similar schedule but with more drinking and fishing? I began to compare my writing tempo and creativity to my piano playing.

Playing jazz and writing

I always had a good sense of rhythm and timing. For example, I never needed a metronome and was always relied upon to establish and keep the beat even with complex Afro-Cuban–Latin rhythms. I played drums intuitively and when I saw that many pianists were better than I, I turned to the double bass to earn money. In a writing session, I feel that I can pace myself and maintain a steady, rhythmic flow of words until I get physically tired.

There is a certain order in the sequence of playing a jazz tune. There is the intro, the statement of the melody using an established progression of chords, the improvisations around those chords, and a return to the theme. In writing I see a similar pattern. I state the theme, elaborate on it, and provide a summary of the theme. However, the main part is the improvisations on the theme and the chord patterns. The rules about the structure of a chord as well as customs about their sequence are analogous to the grammatical tenets and conventions in ordering words, paragraphs, etc. As free as improvisation may seem to be, there is an underlying discipline in writing, and playing, jazz and, as will be discussed, in conducting psychotherapy. As I write, I am not aware of any customs or canons and do not know what I am going to play or write next. I may have a general idea where I want to go and somehow usually get there.

Even in writing my books, as I sat down to write, I seldom had an idea about what I would write for the day until I began writing. I used no conscious outlines. Sometimes I had no idea what the next sentence would be – as in improvising jazz. I might think of a word or idea just as I am writing it just as I may hear what I am about to play. Most famous jazz musicians have a solid education in theory that they unconsciously tap at the existential moment of improvising.

A significant difference between writing and playing jazz is that in jazz one does not have the liberty of changing what had been played, however imperfect. In a performance or even in practice, as with many musicians, I continue despite mistakes. A certain amount of sloppiness is tolerated in practice or in a performance especially if the musician is trying to express something brand new or complex. Sometimes the "mistake," as in psychotherapy, can lead to a productive outcome (Gilhooley, 2011). The concept of "good enough" applies here and is reminiscent of my mother reassuringly saying, "It's OK. You can't see it from the railroad station" when I had not done something well. In writing on the computer, I will ignore spelling and grammatical errors for I have the luxury of editing what I have written and even subject it to a spell/grammar check. In recording a musical session, if mistakes and dissatisfaction abound, a retake is made. It is said that the consummate jazz singer Billy Holiday and her highly professional accompanists rarely had a retake. On the other hand, Stan Getz, it is said, was seldom satisfied. In a live performance, the lay person seldom discerns how the professional player is experiencing his/her solo except to watch the other musicians. Their attention, movements, and smiles usually reflect the goodness of a performance. While I look forward to recognition and approval of my writing and my jazz improvisations, at this point in my life I am pleased just to be able to play in both arenas.

The confluence of psychoanalysts and jazz musicians

My playing with musicians who were psychotherapists spiked my interests in the relation between psychoanalysis and jazz. However, except for one psychologist who later authored an article about the topic, we seldom talked of the psychological significance of jazz. I think we were pleased to be playing with each other and happy to leave our psychoanalytic personae in the office.

I began playing with a few musicians lead by Mort Schillinger at the New York State Psychological conventions. Later, I was invited to play with a group called "Three Shrinks and a Fink" lead by Everett Dulit who found gigs at psychoanalytic parties and conventions. Eventually, I founded my own group, "The Oedipus Wrecks," which played *gratis* to enliven innumerable professional functions. To my consternation, in some circles I seem to be recognized more for my music than for my professional activities.

I have found musicians/psychotherapists to be a cut above the average professional in that they evidenced superior organizational skills, were more social, creative, and "off-beat."

Conducting psychoanalysis

As a student and neophyte therapist, I assumed that there was a "correct procedure" that could be learned. I was raised to believe that there were immutable facts of science, math, and physics – a belief that extended to the behavioral sciences. As a matter of fact, even in the third year of college, one of my psychology professors earnestly intoned, "College students are not supposed to have creative ideas." In my graduate days, dominated by the scientist–clinician model where Bridgman's (1927) operationalism abounded, I presumed that one could discern the "truth." Those professors who propounded a phenomenological, humanistic point of view were marginalized and derided.

Even in my first year in psychoanalytic institute, much to the chagrin of one of my experienced Viennese supervisors, Elizabeth Zetzel, I was looking for a map, a procedure, a formula for conducting an analysis. The classroom instructors warned of the dangers of "wild analysis" and countertransference while suggesting that we stay within the confines of traditional theory and technique. Most of my educators seemed to downgrade improvisation, just as Freud was askance of countertransference. My fears and rigid attitudes slowly were eroded by some of my supervisors in two ways: I found that some of my supervisors' advice was meaningless or lost me a patient; some of my supervisors did encourage a more existential position. One of my analysts taught me that there were rules of thumb, but no absolutes and that I should listen to my inner promptings. As I left my linear way of thinking and discovered the world of nonlinear dynamics systems, I felt more comfortable with ambiguity and not knowing as advocated by Pine (1985). Theory and textbook techniques receded as I learned that my feelings were an important source of data that could be used to advance progress. Imperceptibly, I began to improvise in conducting therapy, especially when I was conducting therapy with adolescents and children where rules and boundaries were more elastic.

My first three analysts, Jay Fidler, Joseph Steinert, and Harold Guerney, encouraged me to talk freely – to play. But in retrospect I was playing by myself. They were not very interactive and may not have known how to use my transference. My next analyst while I was training at The Postgraduate Center was Abram Kardiner, who had been analyzed by Freud. He loosened me up as he told me of Freud's more human side and some of his limited views. My last analyst, the contro-versial Hyman Spotnitz, eventually taught me how to play with him. Some individual and group sessions were spent laughing, sometimes hilariously, that induced me to write about humor (Marshall, 2004). Yes, there were serious, silent, angry, tearful times, but relative to my previous analytic experiences, there was an interactive movement and lightness that I described, Marshall (2018). Moreover, Spotnitz experi-mented with many controversial techniques which gave me license to innovate (Spotnitz, 1985). Over the course of my analysis I journeyed from a child playing by himself, quietly and perhaps enjoyably, to a child engaging in parallel play with another child or group in a more animated way. I became looser, more feelingfull, confident, and willing to take risks.

One of my supervisors with whom I worked many years was Lia Knoepfmacher, a highly intuitive, even mystical, Viennese analyst who had been trained in modern psychoanalysis by Spotnitz. She and I worked in a synchrony that led to developing my intuition (improvi-sation) and, in turn, led to remarkable progress of my patients that I recorded (Marshall, 1972, 1976, 1979, 1983). I found that the use of modern psychoanalytic theory and techniques freed me and vastly improved my clinical functioning. The success that I experienced gave me grounds to write about my work spurred by my identifica-tion with Kardiner's and Spotnitz's extensive authorship. Incidentally, Kardiner was a fair violin player, Knoepfmacher was a gifted cellist who played with Albert Einstein, while Spotnitz had little musical tal-ent as did Freud.

When I conduct analytic sessions, I believe that one should begin a session with no memory or agenda. The patient calls the tune, states the theme, I listen, and when invited, join in largely as an accompanist. I may begin to remember fragments of other sessions or experience emotions so that the therapy becomes an interactive, intersubjective process where the patient and I are in an unending fractal reiteration and development.

I have become an ardent advocate of the importance of induced feelings, that is, unconscious feelings that the patient wants to commu-nicate to me – feelings that they are not yet willing to experience (pro-jective identifications) or feelings that had been present in the parents.

And so it is when playing with another musician. For example, when playing with just a bassist, drummer, or saxophonist, we had to listen to and intuit each other to play well. In a way, we tried to establish an unconscious mutual language based on musical, affective and behavioral cues. Good musicians are always listening to the others and building upon that communication. Playing music with others is communication. On the other hand, playing by oneself is communing with oneself and perhaps the audience. For me, playing with other musicians is by far a more satisfying experience.

In listening to patients and to music, I have a very good ear in hearing auditory non-verbal communications such as subtle changes in tone, timbre, tempo, inflections, pace, and decibel level. In the music world, I am usually called upon to help tune the instruments. That is, I would play my "A" and the instrumentalist would play an equivalent note and adjust the instrument such that that my piano and his instrument would literally be on the same wavelength. I attend to discrepancies between a patient's words and affect as when a patient laughs about a horrible event or lifelessly speaks of being enraged. I also hear the harmony between the words and the emotional music. Famous jazz musicians usually learn the words to a tune before they can improvise well on that tune. Words *and* music count. As the song goes, "You can't have one without the other." Occasionally, I might refer to a line or title of a well-known song to reflect a patient's feeling. For example, I am fond of referring to "I've got you under my skin," when a projective identification is in the air, or "Across the crowded room," when referring to an unexpected emotional attraction to another.

There is a common emotional reaction that I have in improvising in jazz, writing, and psychotherapy which is akin to Maslow's (1998) "peak experience" and where I seem to be transported to another world. In the music realm these moments are characterized by the expressions "in a groove" or "swinging." It is an emotional high where everything seems to come together in the music and in rhythmic body movements as evidenced by Stevie Wonder as he plays and sings. In writing, the descriptions have to do with inspiration, excitement, and emotional satisfaction. In conducting psychotherapy, the patient and therapist seem to merge into a common feeling state or synchrony Marshall (2018) and may represent part of Ernst Kris' (1956) "good hour." I have always come away from a musical session feeling liberated, excited, and pleased, as after a productive therapy session.

There are similarities in playing for a singer and in conducting psychotherapy. The first rule is that the accompanist must lag a split second behind the professional vocalist. I try to follow the patient's lead. Sometimes, amateur singers need to hear the note before s/he can sing it and so it is with new patients who sometimes need some direction. Another rule is that the accompanist does not distract the singer with flourishes and musical displays. I try to supply just enough to support the singer. This principle is in line with the "contact function" wherein the therapist provides the right amount of stimulation to keep the patient talking. Another analogy is that the singer needs the accompanist to play in the right key, which means that the musician must accommodate to the singer's range.

The concepts of harmony and dissonance are relevant. In playing my favorite music, Dixieland, swing, and bebop, I try to render my accompaniment in harmony with the soloist or the band. That is, we improvise in the same key, tempo, and use the same chords. Dizzy Gillespie introduced some dissonances, for example, the flatted fifth (the Devil's note) in a provocative or fun-producing manner. He and others began to use complex chords that to me are intriguing. However, the chords and chord sequences of subsequent musicians like John Coltrane make little sense to me. The analogous therapeutic principle is: stay within the harmonic structure of the patient. It's likely that some patients may need a Stravinsky kind of complexity that I cannot supply. On the other hand, I may be able to provide supply the simplicity and repetition of a "doo-wop" (50s style) song which would match the pace and level of the needs of some patients, such as depressives or children. Flexibility and range of repertoire are key.

All of us have been faced with occasions where we felt completely lost and did not know what to do. I had that sense when I was assigned my first child patient. When I shared that feeling with my supervisor, she replied reassuringly, "Just remember that you were once a child." She was saying what a jazz musician says to another who claims he does not know a tune, "Fake it, man." The expression does not imply deceit but "do the best you can."

There is another element that is present in playing jazz, writing, and conducting psychotherapy: the employment of humor. For example,

Charlie Parker, famous and accomplished "bebopper," would inject humor into his solos at a nightclub. For example, if Judy Garland walked into the club, Parker would incorporate strains of "Over the Rainbow" into his solo. Similarly, I may insert humor into my narrative as an enlivening change of pace, or judiciously employ humor to underscore an intervention during therapy.

Group therapy and music

The analogies between conducting group therapy and playing music in an ensemble are many but somewhat beyond the scope of this article except for a few remarks about my experience in large orchestras and bands and my training in and conducting group therapy (Marshall, 1999, 2003) and supervision (Marshall 1998, 1999).

In a classical orchestra where the musicians are dependent on the conductor who is frequently revered, it is difficult to conceive of a 50–100-person orchestra that is run democratically or therapeutically. However, in the several 6–12-piece dance orchestras that I've played in, the leaders were variable in their style and musicianship. Sometimes, the leader was a respected instrumentalist such as a Benny Goodman who was a consummate musician but, according to lore, was a taskmaster who demanded precision from his musicians. The players listened to his commands and suggestions out of respect and fear of being fired. In another dance band, the leader was a mediocre musician who, by his wealth and ownership of a 1950 Cadillac convertible and a pistol, was tolerated and feared. I have known of group leaders who were excellent individual therapists but did not have the training or disposition to run a group.

In well-run orchestras in which I played, the leaders were usually respected instrumentalists who operated democratically. They allowed for a great deal of discussion among the musicians and between sections about how a piece should be played. There seemed to be a willingness to play as well as possible and cooperate. Paramount was the musicians' abilities to listen to other players in the section and orchestra. Harmony and synchrony were the operative terms. As in group therapy, cliques would form outside the band which created some dissonance in the band's functioning.

In a small jazz group there is usually an informal leader. He may call the tunes, set the beat, and specify turns in playing. Considering that the leader is primarily a member of the group, it is incumbent upon that the leader to hear not only the individual voices, but the voice of the group as a whole.

In another analogy we may consider the issue of conducting an analysis of the group relative to conducting an analysis of individuals in a group. Given the training in individual psychotherapy, and without training in group psychotherapy, most analysts tend to focus on analyzing individuals in the group setting. Although the group therapist is the titled leader, s/he can be considered as another group member and be subject to the vicissitudes of being in that position. If things go awry, in an otherwise well-run group, the group may call the leader's attention to the problem and the leader will resolve the problem. Moreover, in a well-run group, frequently the leader does very little and seems to function as another group member, except that s/he collects the fees. In general, I have found that a leader of a well-functioning jazz or therapy group is egalitarian, demonstrates no favoritism, cares for the group as a whole and respects the individual members. As a leader or member of a jazz or therapy group, I usually have left the session feeling satisfied, energized, and therapized. In addition, songs frequently lingered on after a jazz session and themes and conversations lingered on after a group therapy session.

I have found that in playing jazz and conducting groups, the theme is immediately stated. In a group, I attend to the first few moments because I have found that the rest of the group session may be a reiteration of the initial theme. For example, a supervisee presented a case where there was no consensus about any interventions – the theme. The group shifted to a new problem where the group hit upon a solution. It so happened that that solution was the answer to the mystery of the initial presented case.

At Montrose V.A. Hospital where I was the psychologist assigned to the "suicide and assaultive" building, and where I was engaged in milieu therapy. (Marshall, 1965, 1968), I noted that there were a couple of patients who had been musicians which gave me the idea of starting a music therapy group. I had not the slightest idea of how to run the group. It was improvisation but with anxiety because of the vulnerability and unpredictability of the patients. With two saxes, drums, mandolin and my playing piano, we began. We played a few charts and managed to "jam" on a few standards. Frequently a patient would stop playing when, for example, he would hear a voice commanding him to stop. We processed the interruption and went on playing. The popularity of the group grew to the point that the head of the music department complained that some of her patients/musicians were talking about threatening suicide or assaulting someone to enter my group.

I discovered a patient on the assaultive ward who had no history in his chart except that he had been hospitalized because of a psychotic episode in the streets on New York City where he had been pounding on his conga drum. On the ward he was mute, stood at attention and unpredictably struck out at passersby. I obtained a conga drum and arranged for his attendance at my music group. Despite dire warnings of the staff, he appeared at our group with two burly, skeptical nursing assistants. Carlos focused on the drum, and gingerly touched it. Over the course of several sessions, Carlos slowly began to drum and infused new rhythmic life to the group. His behavior on the ward improved and he even said a few words. My experience with the group combined my love of music with conducting therapy plus giving me something to write about.

Improvisation in other fields

While I have described my subjective experience in the realms of writing, playing jazz, and conducting psychotherapy, I have explored only one small corner of the universe where improvisation holds sway especially where concepts such as "inspiration" and "creativity" are relevant. I believe that any of the visual and written arts, sports, comedy, cooking or perhaps any human endeavor may be dealing with the same parameters. The medical field also is subject to improvisation as indicated by Dr. Charles Wilson (2018), a brilliant brain surgeon and researcher who, when asked how he was able to perform the most delicate and painstaking surgeries, replied that he did not understand the process except to say, "It's sort of an invisible hand – it begins almost to seem mystical."

References

Bridgman, P. W. (1927). *The Logic of Modern Physics.* New York: Macmillan.
Gilhooley, D. (2011). Mistakes. *Psychoanalytic Psychology.* 28(2):311–333.
Kris, E. (1956). On some vicissitudes of insight in psychoanalysis. In: *Selected Papers of Ernst Kris.* New Haven, CT: Yale University Press.

Marshall, R. J. (1965). A guide toward establishing a patient government. *Mental Hygiene.* 49:230–237.

Marshall, R. J. (1968). Stages in the development of a patient government: A case study. *Psychiatric Quarterly Supplement.* Part 2:1–13.

Marshall, R. J. (1972). The treatment of resistances in the psychotherapy of children and adolescents. *Psychotherapy: Theory, Research and Practice.* 9:143–148.

Marshall, R. J. (1974). Meeting the resistances of delinquents. *Psychoanalytic Review.* 61:295–304.

Marshall, R. J. (1976). "Joining techniques" in the handling of resistance and negative countertransference in the treatment of children and adolescents. *American Journal of Psychotherapy.* 30:73–84.

Marshall, R. J. (1979). Countertransference with children and adolescents. In L. Epstein and A. Feiner (eds.). *Countertransference: The Therapist's Contribution to the Therapeutic Situation.* New York: Jason Aronson.

Marshall, R. J. (1979) Antisocial youth. In J. D. Noshpitz (ed.). *Basic Handbook of Child Psychiatry.* New York: Basic Books.

Marshall, R. J. (1982). *Resistant Interactions: Child, Family, and Therapist.* New York: Human Sciences Press. Reprinted in paperback, Jason Aronson. Translated into Japanese.

Marshall, R. J. (1983). A psychoanalytic perspective on the diagnosis and development of juvenile delinquency. In W. S. Laufer and J. M. Day (eds.). *Personality Theory, Moral Development, and Criminal Behavior.* Lexington, MA: Lexington Books.

Marshall, R. J. (1991). Meeting the resistances of delinquents. *Psychoanalytic Review.* 61(2):295–304.

Marshall, R. J. (1993). Perspectives on supervision: Tea or supervision? *Modern Psychoanalysis.* 18(1):45–58.

Marshall, R. J. (1993). Mother and child as therapists to each other: A psychoanalytic version of filial therapy. *Modern Psychoanalysis.* 18(2):143–155.

Marshall, R. J. (1995). Pinel: The first modern psychoanalyst? *Modern Psychoanalysis.* 20(1):25–34.

Marshall, R. J. (1998). The interactional triad in supervision. In M. H. Rock (ed.). *Psychodynamic Supervision: Perspectives of the Supervisor and the Supervisee.* Northvale, NJ: Jason Aronson.

Marshall, R. J. (1999). Facilitating cooperation and creativity in group supervision. *Modern Psychoanalysis.* 25(1):181–186.

Marshall, R. J. (2003). Hyman Spotnitz: Recollections. *Modern Psychoanalysis.* 33(2):23–39.

Marshall, R. J. (2004). Getting even on the psychoanalytic couch. Humor and play in psychoanalysis. *Modern Psychoanalysis.* 29(1):63–76.

Marshall, R. J. (2018). Synchrony: A unifying concept. *Modern Psychoanalysis.* In print.

Marshall, R. J. and Marshall, S. V. (1988). *The Transference–Countertransference Matrix: The Cognitive–Emotional Dialogue in Psychotherapy, Psychoanalysis, and Supervision.* New York: Columbia Universities Press.

Maslow, A. (1998). *Toward a Psychology of Being.* New York: Simon and Schuster.

Pine, F. (1985). *Developmental Theory and Clinical Process.* New Haven: Yale University Press.

Spotnitz, H. (1985). *Modern Psychoanalysis of the Schizophrenic Patient.* 2nd ed. New York: Human Sciences Press.

Wilson, C. (2018). Obituary. *The New York Times.* March 8, p. A19.

Chapter 7

A Parisienne's passage through an American psychoanalytic world

Robert J. Marshall for Simone V. Marshall

As Simone's husband of 64 years, I began to write this piece for family when Simone's health began to fail. When Dr. Rachman asked to me to write about Simone, I shifted from the third to the first person, which enlivened the narrative. Robert J. Marshall, PhD.

Post-war Paris

After World War II, mired in the dank archives of Parisian libraries, translating US Army Jeep manuals into French, I dreamed of being a psychotherapist. When I graduated to translating American psychological journals, I fantasized being a psychoanalyst. I didn't know until years later in my personal psychoanalysis that my ambition was spirited by my need to help my father, who suffered from bouts of severe depression because of manning a French 75 cannon for four years at the horrendous battle of Verdun and being the only survivor of a five-man gun crew.

In viewing the American psychological literature, I often envisaged myself studying in the US, because the Americans were so far ahead of the French. Because training in psychotherapy was open only to the medical profession, I reluctantly consigned myself to my work for the French education system and gravitated to hanging out with analytically oriented psychiatrists in St. Anne's Hospital.

Walking through the corridors of the Sorbonne, I spotted a bulletin describing Fulbright scholarships to study for a doctorate in Clinical Psychology in the United States. Halfheartedly applying, I was astounded and thrilled upon being accepted into the program and looked forward to an eventful and fulfilling education at Teachers

College Columbia University, which was my first choice because I loved the excitement of the big city.

In the fall of 1951, with little money and after a storm-tossed trans-Atlantic trip on the *Ile de France* with another Columbia-bound Fulbright student, we faced a longshoreman strike in New York harbor that lasted a couple of days. Despite our eagerness to disembark, we enjoyed the partying with the skyscrapers of NYC in the background.

Columbia Teachers College

At Columbia, I did well in my course work despite my unfamiliarity with the English language. My encounters and interviews with some of my mentors and professors somewhat dismayed me in that they spent half of the interview looking at my body. One famous professor could not take his eyes off my *décolleté*. The department head spent most of his time obsessively telling me about how many times a week he vacuumed his Turkish rug while furtively glancing at my legs. I became very conflicted about American men's attention to me. I knew that I was attractive and enjoyed men's notices. On the other hand, I felt irritated with men who responded to me stereotypically as a "sexy French babe," who, given a Hershey bar, was ready to dance the cancan, and jump in bed with them. This dynamic clouded many relationships and eventually emerged in the transferences and countertransferences with my patients in analysis and was addressed in my personal analysis.

Not inspired by the professors, or the class work, save that of an anthropology course with Otto Klineberg, I complained to my advisor about not being involved in clinical work. My advisor, responding to my need for psychotherapeutic exposure, took me to the Jewish Board of Guardians, whose fabled psychoanalytically oriented outpatient service was headed by Sam Slavson. Slavson took an immediate interest in this bright, pert, French lass. Knowing that I had only $100 when I arrived in America, and hard-pressed to pay my rent, he found work for me in teaching French to some of his psychiatric colleagues and friends. Thus began a relationship wherein he served as an advisor, mentor and godfather throughout his life. I could not fathom, but accepted his benevolent, fatherly attraction to me.

My advisor acquainted me with the venerable Bellevue Hospital where I met and was squired by psychiatrists associated with the

William Allanson White Institute. Besides teaching French, I sup-
plemented my income by appearing on several radio programs that
treasured my student status, accent and verve. I was so well liked by
the program "Name That Tune" I was eventually selected to be a par-
ticipant in its first television program, where I earned over $500 – an
enormous sum.

During my first year at Columbia, I met Bob, who also was a student and who attended some of my classes. Bob virtually gave up on
trying to meet me because to him, I was always surrounded by a crowd
of French-speaking students and ardent suitors, as he put it, "Like a
queen bee swarmed by workers." Although I held him in the corner
of my eye, he managed to get my full attention by a ruse. Knowing
that I was systematically late to a large evening lecture class, he posi-
tioned himself near the door and reserved a chair/desk for me. We
traded notes and whispers, and after class we walked down to a West
125th Street Chinese restaurant where we shared an order of egg rolls,
shrimp in lobster sauce, fortune cookies, and much tea. We were always
the last to leave to the chagrin of the waiters. Thus began a romance
that blossomed into marriage two years later. When Bob first proposed
marriage to me, I could not bear to think of the legal, social and personal ramifications of such a prospect. I had gained a sense of security
and did not want it disturbed.

To satisfy my need to know about America and to gain some distance from Bob, I traveled across the country with four other students
in a DeSoto convertible during the summer. This trip helped me gain
an important perspective on American culture and people and reinforced my wish to remain in this grand country of opportunity. The
streets were not paved in gold, but I sensed the openness, freedom, and
grandeur that I craved. The trip also provided me with many adven-
tures about which I could spin entertaining tales.

In the fall, I continued my studies at Columbia while Bob, not able to
afford the tuition at Columbia, pursued his fortunes at the University
of Buffalo. We exchanged love letters, arranged to meet during vacations, and after some turbulence, including the chagrin of my parents,
particularly my possessive father, we married in the fall of 1953. My
bereft father consoled himself with the idea that American men were
ruthless cowboys who quickly divorced their wives. In part, I still
believed this image after being exposed to the crude GIs in Paris. I also

believed that French men make poor husbands, but was hopeful that Bob would not turn into the faithless men I knew about. Also, I was afraid that my marriage would mirror that of my parents. It took me a long time to give up this fear.

Marriage and dissertations

Papa refused to attend the wedding, sent no present, and forbade my mother to attend. This was a heart-wrenching turn of events that hurt and angered me. I realized that no matter how much I loved Papa, I had to free myself of my limiting attachment to him. As a good father surrogate, I experienced Slavson as steadying me emotionally and supporting my professional striving. He attended the wedding, walked me down the aisle, and brought an appropriate household item as, was the custom in the early 50s.

Completing all my course requirements, I began work on a dissertation proposal that was accepted. I laboriously searched the literature and began to collect data when, much to my distress, my committee chairperson suddenly and mysteriously left the university. After many inquiries, he admitted that he had lost my papers. Forced to change chairs, I chose to work with an easy-going professor despite his insistence that I change my study to coincide with his interests. So much for academic integrity and freedom.

I gathered all my papers, including my new marriage certificate, and shuffled off to Buffalo with Bob. During the year in Buffalo, NY, I worked as a child therapist at an outpatient clinic while transitioning into my new dissertation project – events that increased my appreciation of the professional opportunities in the United States and fueled my determination to become a psychoanalyst.

Suddenly, an event blocked the way to my professional aspirations – Bob's draft board caught up with him. Rather than being drafted for two years of uncertainty, including the prospect of fighting in Korea, I helped Bob choose entrance into a five-year stint in an Army Officer training program that provided us reassurance that we would be together in professional settings with financial benefits. We had been poor but didn't know it. Suddenly, we were going to be rich on his $222 monthly salary plus benefits.

Seemingly free for the summer, we used our meager finances to travel to France on the *Ile de France*. Within two weeks, Bob was summarily called back to the US by the Army, which assigned him to Letterman Army Hospital in San Francisco, a large training center. My family thought he was a complete lunatic because he had to pack and be on a plane within a day. Of course, Papa's mood brightened.

I had to remain in France to obtain a visa which had been denied me because, according to the US Embassy, I had tuberculosis. This was a subterfuge, for it was the McCarthy era, and I was suspect because of association with Communist friends. No doubt I was considered an imminent threat to the security of the US because I was married to an officer in the US Army from whom I could glean all sorts of military secrets. Such was the paranoia of the time. Through Bob's father's political connections and Bob's irate medical buddies at Letterman Hospital, I returned to the states in November 1954.

Motherhood

Nine months after I arrived in San Francisco, I gave birth to Gabrielle. I enjoyed my pregnancy (except for being badgered into eating liver) and our several months in San Francisco where I was free to read, paint, make baby clothes, sew on my new sewing machine, visit the Bay area, and attend parties with the lively group of Letterman psychiatrists and psychologists. Unfortunately, I was plagued again by a couple of crass RA (Regular Army) doctors, who saw me only as a French broad rather than an intelligent, cultured doctoral student. One leering Colonel plied me with a sweet-tasting alcoholic drink that made me sick for days. *Couchon!* (Pig!) Despite that encounter, I thoroughly adored San Francisco and its environs, but I could not settle there because I missed the change of seasons and the cultural heritage and beauty of my Paris.

After a year's internship, Bob was assigned to the University of Buffalo where he was to write his dissertation for a year before being reassigned for three-year payback duty. Contentedly pregnant, I painted, taught a French conversation class at the university, worked on my dissertation, and, as in Paris, enjoyed the company of the bright, lively graduate students and professors in the small Psychology department. I began to develop a sense of security and maturity that I had never experienced. This momentary pause allowed me to think and talk about the fear that had pervaded my life caught in the tumultuous conflicts of my parents. Moreover, I began to realize the terror that I had experienced during the war in Paris: the sound of the jackboots of marching German squads; the threat of being whisked off the street for minor infractions of seemingly arbitrary law; the early morning long food lines to garner a couple of rutabagas, a few grains of chicory, or foul black bread.

After many inquiries about the arrival of our belongings from San Francisco, we were told that the truck carrying all our possessions caught fire and completely burned. I felt demolished because my treasured French books, souvenirs, our love letters, and especially a crib that I had lovingly painted were gone. To be compensated, we had to draw up a list of our belongings, dates of purchase, and refer to a government list of depreciation. The task became interesting, because I had a photographic memory of all our belongings plus a fantasy of things that a couple would normally possess. After a literal act of Congress, we received a compensatory check. Somehow, I was more sanguine about these events than Bob.

Getting close to little Gaby's birth, I began to have signs of an imminent birth. With prepared bags, we began a two-hour car trip to a hospital at Sampson Air Force base in Romulus, NY. Within a couple of miles of the base, we freaked out when I broke my waters and believed that I would deliver by the side of the country road. We proceeded to the hospital where I was warmly received, but was told that the OBGYN docs were busy and that I would be delivered by a doctor on call – a psychiatrist. Fortunately, I had an uncomplicated delivery of a beautiful healthy baby. In a couple days, we filled our car with goodies from the PX and returned to campus where we spent our time taking care of Gaby and writing our respective dissertations. Did Gaby's delivery doctor help Gaby choose her own psychiatric career?

Shortly after Gaby's birth, we heard a loud knocking on our apartment door. Upon opening the door, we were faced with two burly men who identified themselves as Immigration officials and gruffly asked for me. When I came to the door with my baby in my arms, they had handcuffs ready to arrest me for allegedly being an illegal immigrant. Remember that we were in the McCarthy era. Fortunately, I had my papers in order, but my newfound sense of security vanished. I was thrown back into the terrors of my adolescence: my parents had sent me to school to the relative safety of Cahors, a city in the southwest of France where some of my family were farmers. One evening, I stretched the curfew time and was arrested on the street by a squad of Mongolian dragooned Soviet soldiers lead by a German officer. I was especially afraid of the Mongolians who were unpredictable and threatening. I'll never forget the innumerable watches that they had stolen and strapped onto their arms. Ironically, I was glad to see the German officer who controlled the Mongolians. Dispatched to German headquarters, I was interrogated. But thanks to a friend of mine who worked in the office and who vouched for me, I was released.

In my personal psychoanalysis, I found that these terrifying experiences shaped many of my expectations and relationships. It took me a long time and much work to allay my sense of insecurity and sort out my allegiances to France and America.

We're in the army now

With the academic year ending, Bob and I were alarmed to find that we were to be stationed at a small Army outpost in South Carolina for three years. What would happen to my data collection and consultation with my committee? Where would I go for a psychoanalysis? To our relief, we found that the Army was political. Through the influence of a psychiatrist who befriended us at Letterman and who was to be Chief Psychiatrist at the Mental Hygiene/Hospital complex at Fort Dix, NJ Infantry Training Center, Bob was assigned to that desirable station.

In a comfortable apartment and with Bob's 9–5 position, we could spend lots of time together and with our little Gaby. Visiting Bob's family was comforting and joyous. The proximity to New York allowed me to finish my dissertation with the "help" of our four-year old daughter who delighted in pounding the keys of an old Marchand calculator that she termed "peuter." I also achieved a dream by beginning a personal analysis with a French-speaking psychoanalyst from the New York Psychoanalytic Institute who was recommended by Slavson. With a devoted nanny and a playschool for Gaby, I found time to teach at a local school. The class was interesting to me because some of the kids were bright, energetic "Army brats" and some kids were "pineys" whose benighted parents lived in the pine barrens in hovels and old school buses. Because some of these kids came to school with no breakfast, I had to plan for them to be fed. I had to leave the job because I was not certified as a teacher. Through Henry David, Chief Psychologist of New Jersey who was a consultant at Fort Dix, I got a job at The New Lisbon Institution for Retarded Males. I performed intellectual and personality evaluations and conducted psychotherapy with inmates who would now be diagnosed on the autism spectrum. As grim as the position was, I somehow felt some affinity to the children and institute because of its long and important history in the evaluation of mentally challenged children and because it reminded me of some of my work in the education department in Paris. Again, I was amazed at the ease with which I could be employed in the field of psychology.

After two years at New Lisbon, I upscaled to working a couple of days a week at The Rutgers University Psychological Clinic where I tested children, conducted child and family therapy, and supervised graduate students.

I was beginning to appreciate some of the advantages of "being in the Army," because our psychiatrist friend had been very helpful in cutting through the ponderous bureaucratic structure to provide me with subjects for my dissertation. The cut rate values at the PX and Commissary and Officers' Club were attractive. The medical services were solid, and we had access to free flights to Paris. On the other hand, I hated all things military and especially disliked the white-gloved formality of army wives who seemed to live for their afternoon teas. I was delighted to hear from those women that I would never become a "good Army wife."

Thanks to the Military Air Transport System (MATS) and the fact that a senior Air Force Officer at adjoining McGuire Air Force Base was being seen by one of Bob's colleagues, our little family flew round trip to Paris for about $25. We made peace with Mama and Papa during our four weeks of a stay in France. It seemed that bringing little Gabrielle, named after my mother, completely changed my father's attitude toward my marrying Bob. Papa seemed to fasten himself onto little Gaby and was relieved that I was not married to some gun-slinging, cigar-smoking, ugly American GI. Our summer visits served to perk up my father and brought a softness to his grim face when he looked at little Gaby. He had me again, and me as a little girl.

He revealed his ground plan to me which validated my plan to escape to America. While we were staying with my folks in a small rural community in the southwest of France, Papa asked me to take a job as a teacher in the local school. I inquired, "But Papa, what would Bob do?" Papa readily replied, "Il fera le menage" – "He'll keep house."

When Bob was nearing the end of his (our) military service, we were offered many benefits to "reup" and perhaps extend to 20-year service to become a bird colonel and Chief of Army Psychology. Among the promises were stations in Hawaii, and even in France. We halfheartedly agreed to visit posts in France and Germany (Stuttgart and Heidelberg). Despite the prospect of being near my folks in their declining years, my unabating dislike of the military, my distaste of anything German, our unrelenting desires to become psychoanalysts, and a desire for family stability brought an end to our military ambitions. I guess I could not stand the built-in predictability and security. With the publication of my dissertation (Marshall, 1960) in *The Journal of Clinical and Counseling Psychology* in 1959 and my MA in Developmental Psychology and PhD from Teachers College Columbia, I was ready to storm the portals of psychoanalysis.

Beginning to realize my dreams

Completing his military service, Bob was offered a position as Ward Psychologist at the Montrose VA Hospital. Although I preferred that we live in NYC, I reluctantly agreed to settle down in the suburbs, raise children, and then return to NYC. Slavson, who summered in Croton-on-Hudson, found us a reliable real estate broker who located a pleasant house for us to purchase with the help of a GI loan. With a newly minted PhD I easily found a job as a part-time school psychologist in Ossining, NY. I tolerated my work but was displeased with my office which was "in the tower," which required considerable marching up and down stairs. After failing to obtain a more suitable office, I had the idea of inviting the school superintendent to my office. After winding his way up the staircase, he readily commiserated with me about the relative inaccessibility of the office, especially for parents, and found me a new office. Wanting to do more treatment rather than testing and consulting with parents and teachers, I found a job in Monsey, NY at an outpatient clinic that was manned by competent therapists and headed up by Dr. Woody English, a respected member of the W.A. White Institute. I began to feel that I was on the ground that I wanted to tread.

With the birth of our second child, Annette, five years after Gaby, I spent considerable time with her and Gaby. Bob's 9–5 VA job with a short commute made for lots of family time and an extensive social life. Despite my enjoyment, I was eager to return to the psychological field and improve our finances. I became tired of pinching pennies like Papa, who constantly worried about money, living on his meager pension and fearful of monetary devaluations. Although Bob was oriented to attending a psychoanalytic institute, he seemed too comfortable in his day job and seeing a few patients in our home office. I was ambitious for him and nudged him to advance his career and make more money.

Each summer we spent considerable time with Slavson who loved our daughters, especially Gaby who sidled up to him like a content grandchild. I aired my ambitions with Slavson who thought that I should wait until Annette was two years old to venture into the professional world. He also advocated for my going back into personal psychoanalysis, begin a private practice, and obtain private supervision. He disliked psychoanalytic institutes, I suppose because he had no formal training in psychotherapy. Although he was "the father of group psychotherapy," he held only a degree in engineering from Cooper Union and learned about groups on his own. He tended to favor the New York Psychoanalytic Institute, perhaps because of its adherence to Freudian therapy. He especially disliked the W.A. White Institute, believing that they were "too social and superficial."

In the meantime, Bob, to my jealous satisfaction, had taught part-time at Hunter College, had obtained his Diplomate status in ABBP, had begun his psychoanalysis with Hyman Spotnitz (recommended by Slavson) and had applied to the Postgraduate Center for Mental Health. I was terribly conflicted and especially weighed down by the prospect of spending less time with my daughters who were thoroughly delightful and lovable. We considered that they were very healthy, bright, sensible girls who enjoyed school and their friends. We decided to hire live-in nannies and *au pair* young women to care for the kids.

We were always uncertain about the consequences of our being away from the girls during the week. However, we all looked forward to the weekends and vacations.

Gaby was asked by one of our inquisitive neighbors, "Why is your mother going back to school?" to which Gaby promptly replied, "So that her patients can lie on her couch."

I had applied to and was accepted at the White Institute. The White Institute seemed to fit with my interpersonal orientation, and because of my contacts with White faculty, I was almost guaranteed acceptance. I was ecstatic at the prospect of beginning training as a PSYCHOANALYST. I was also thrilled in my finding a house under construction overlooking the Hudson River on four acres. We were active in designing the floorplan of the house to accommodate a private practice, parties, and guests. Financially, the purchase was a gamble for us, but it seemed too good to pass up. I was on the move.

Upon entering the White Institute, I had mixed feelings about the classes. On one hand, they were stimulating, but on the other I found them to be dominated by very bright men who debated competitively at a highly intellectual level. Frequently, I was unsure of what was going on, except that I wanted the instructors to bring the discussion to a more feeling level. I felt intimidated, frightened, and angry. Moreover, I was astounded when several students rebelled against an instructor and drove him out of the class. I could not appreciate the level of anger and revolt, thus could not participate. Certainly not like the atmosphere of respect for authority and tradition I had known in the Sorbonne.

I gravitated toward the foreign students who were from South Africa, Japan and Brazil and with whom I forged lifelong friendships. I could identify with their struggles and discomfort. Because I could not and would not readily engage in the tumultuous class discussions, several instructors felt that they did not know me. They were right to a degree. I could not easily make the shift from the large lecture classes at the Sorbonne and Columbia to the small class discussions and arguments. But I was a diligent student in that I took copious notes in class and from the readings, and did my best to participate in class.

Another shift that distressed me was the move from my previous analyst and the one assigned to me at White. She was an acolyte of Fromm and rather than listen and analyze me, she frequently lectured me and advised me – and not always to my best advantage, for she frequently sided with me against my husband and wanted me to take action. Maritally, I had been in a dangerous environment because I realized that by the end of my training I was the only person in my class who had not divorced, separated, or who otherwise was not alienated from her spouse. This was the age of individuation, realization and independence the hippy era. These were values I thought I sought.

It took a great deal of subsequent work, time, and money to remain married and maintain my beloved family. Bob and I went into marital therapy with a leading therapist. We left him because he was rather passive and tended to doze off in our morning sessions. I consulted with Bob's analyst who I grew to hate because he seemed to side with Bob. I also attended group therapy sessions with Bob's analyst, which only heightened my negativity. After I had finished my training analysis, I found a fiery Hungarian analyst who wanted me to sue Bob's analyst for alienation of affection. I experienced Bob as controlling and siding in with our daughters against me. Part of the problem was that Bob's parenting style was more *laissez-faire* than my more stringent expectations and I frequently felt his daughters loved him more than me.

With continued analysis, we began to resolve our conflicts and got along better as we saw our kids maturing. At the same time, our practices were thriving and we were taking longer, more interesting vacations. We became adept at designing our travels so that they were tax-deductible. On one of our six-week vacations, we participated in a convention in Tokyo, lectured to student psychoanalysts in Kyoto, and attended conventions in Sydney, Hong Kong, and Hawaii. In retrospect, I believed we were on the cusp of feeling secure and actualizing ourselves. I think that rather than striving for our own individual independence, we were becoming a couple.

In the meantime, against my better judgment, I joined a group practice in Yorktown Heights that Bob helped develop. Although the group provided me with patients, I had grave difficulties getting along with some of the members and could not tolerate the politics and pettiness of the 12-member group. I found that I was not a good team player because I had to abrogate too much of my need to be independent and exercise control. I resigned and incorporated the group practice patients into my home practice in Croton-on Hudson.

Feminist assertiveness

I became active in a cooperative nursery school that our children attended where I was asked to discuss issues of discipline, creativity, and child rearing. At first, anxious about presenting, I became more comfortable when I saw that parents enjoyed my conferences and workshops. In accepting invitations to speak at surrounding school districts, it did not escape my attention that my private practice was increasing. But something was emerging from my presentations and practice – the status of women in our society. I was meeting many bright, talented, anxious/depressed women who were suffering from stay-at-home-itis. I seemed to fire up several women to want to leave their kitchens and full-time child care and do more with their lives – go back to school, start/continue a professional career and in general, become more politically and socially active. I started a *pro bono* group because by that time, I had had some experience and training in group dynamics and therapy. I felt alive and meaningful as I worked with these women to become more assertive and I had the fantasy that I was freeing my mother from her socio-cultural peasant slavery and from the harsh bonds of her husband. Bob did not know what the hell was going on in these meetings held in our living room every week. I'm not sure that I did, but I was carried along by the current of feminism sweeping the country with Gloria Steinem, Betty Friedan, and my favorite, Simone de Beauvoir.

Because Croton-on-Hudson had a strong socialist background, there was support from the community. I had a strong ally in the local newspaper that was willing to publish the activities and news of *The Croton-Cortlandt Women's Center*. As we gained in numbers and influence we extended our influence into the school system and challenged the sexist bias in education and advocated for more math and science for the girls. We influenced the physical education department to open all the sports to girls and provide for equal locker-room facilities. As we became politically active, we probably scared the daylights out of many men who were used to having a passive woman catering to their needs. I think I frightened my family by expressing a phrase I came to like – "I'll fix their wagon" – which later became the source of our household's amusement and verbal armamentarium. My assertiveness emerged again when Bob asked what plans we should make if he should predecease me. I replied in a matter of fact manner, "You aren't allowed to die before me." That was that. I think Bob came to accept and appreciate my assertiveness. I trust that my girls have learned to speak up for themselves.

When it came time for us to move to NYC, the Woman's Center planned an extensive lunch for my farewell that was attended by about 200 women. I felt very honored, but disappointed because I had not been able to recruit the next leader who had the energy, organization, and vision for the continued work. The organization limped along for a couple of years and eventually collapsed. But I had made my mark, had helped many women, and made my life more meaningful though hectic.

Coinciding with my feminist activities, I allowed myself to expand my interest in art. Always a dabbler, I began to take lessons in Japanese art and calligraphy. The latter endeavor was a compromise between my penchant for order, yet spontaneity. Later, as I unwound emotionally, I took lessons in realistic and abstract art. Perhaps my involvement in art represented a microcosm of my way of life and my way of conducting psychotherapy – instilling some sense of order out of ambiguities.

In retrospect, my feminist interlude gave me a chance to work through my sense of powerlessness in the French and American professional culture and allowed me to feel that I should never have to be in the subservient position that had been my mother's and her sisters' fates. I realize that my insistence on buying my own automobile, a Mercury *Marquis* (NB), substantiates my hypothesis.

On the move

My feminist orientation and needs for independence provided little leeway for our daughters to choose a lifestyle – they were to go to college and pursue a secure career. Their identifying with their bright, ambitious, college-bound friends made our parental roles easier. Although there was some dabbling with anti-authoritarian groups and some false starts, our children were on their professional way. While it was difficult to acknowledging their rebellion, which I secretly admired, I was determined that they be given every opportunity to achieve a secure life.

When our children were in college, it was about time that I asked Bob to keep his promise to move to NYC. We were both reluctant to give up our comfortable home overlooking the Hudson River, but Bob more than I because he had a thriving practice in Westchester County and loved to maintain our house and gardens.

While we were planning our move to NYC, we made an extensive trip to Egypt which put us in touch with the limits of our mortality. Suddenly we wanted a second home. We unconsciously wanted to build our own pyramid. After searching for 15 years for a vacation home, we decided on East Hampton, because it was 100 miles from NYC. One of our daughters was living there with her family, and it was a lovely area dominated by nature and sea life. It was an area that would guarantee visits from friends and our progeny. We were pleased to find that several W.A. White psychoanalysts had second homes in the area. We could not find anything that suited us, so we bought some land and built a house overlooking Gardiner's Bay.

Upon completion of the new house, we moved to NYC where I had already established an extensive practice. While Bob was beginning his NYC practice after completing his analytic training at the Postgraduate Center for Mental Health, I found a comfortable office that I shared with Bob and some W.A. White colleagues.

One of the most meaningful experiences of my life occurred when I was about to show my Mom my new offices. I had designed a bronze plaque with my shingle to appear at the entrance to the office building at East 86th & Park Avenue along with about 10 other professional plaques. When I showed the plaque to Mom she approached in awe and gently caressed the metal. She then turned to me and gave me one of the few spontaneous hugs I ever received from her. Gone were the envy and jealousy, and in their place emerged maternal pride. We shared a good cry right on the sidewalk. Her referral to the plaque always gave me the glow I had yearned for. I believe that she was especially touched by the fact that I had included my maiden name – S. Verniere Marshall, PhD.

My mother was also impressed with another accomplishment – I had purchased a house with five rental apartments with my earnings and some money she had given me. I always liked the idea that my parents owned their own apartment in Paris and that they also owned their retirement cottage in the country. I particularly enjoyed renting apartments to young couples who liked Croton and had put down their first stake in the community. My expenses were minimal because

Bob enjoyed maintaining the house and yard. I was a *landlady*, a position that gave me much satisfaction, a tax deduction, and finally, a tidy profit in my own bank account when I sold it.

My apartment house and office with its elegant plaque were very meaningful to me. They represented my independence and freedom from France, from my parents, and even, if I wished, from my current family. This realization came clearer to me after I left these quarters and leased a three-office suite. I virtually owned my terrain – a necessary feeling after suffering from my family's financial insecurity and the terrors of the Nazi occupation. I felt lucky and grateful.

Another step served to sooth me – being registered in *The Who's Who of American Women.*

Psychoanalysis and life in New York City and East Hampton

Bob and I finally decided to buy an apartment in NYC. We shopped very carefully, because we were looking for a large apartment with a view in which we could eventually practice. Life was good. Our kids were flourishing, our practices were full, our vacations were rewarding, our social life was active, and we were seen as "a formidable couple." Eventually, I moved my practice to my home office where I felt very comfortable.

My experience at the White Institute helped shape my innate therapeutic style. In general, I was a somewhat active, truly interpersonal analyst who worked in the "here and now" as well as the "there and then." I believed in studying my induced feelings, countertransferences, and bringing them into play. If I interpreted, it was in the broad context of the patient's relations and the transference. I had come to trust the meaningfulness of my feelings and somehow had learned to use them to advance the patient's progress. I believe I was more interested in the patient's behavior than in his "understanding." I loved the "inquiry" but was not averse to directing certain patients. Sometimes I felt like a therapist rather than a psychoanalyst for I experienced considerable gratification in watching my patient's grow. I had come a long way from my trepidatious "treatment" of my father.

I began holding group therapy sessions that I loved. With my experience with colleagues in running groups, some Tavistock workshops, frequent attendance at AGPA in institutes and conventions,

I cobbled together enough credentials, and with the recommendation from Slavson, I received a certificate from the American Group Psychotherapy Association (AGPA).

An important part of my life was devoted to helping Bob in his career. Although bright and energetic he seemed to hold back in promoting himself and advancing his career. I, on the other hand, was more outspoken and ambitious. We made a good mutual assistance team and helped each other in diverse ways. In fact, one psychoanalyst characterized us as an "intimidating couple." I was more socially active than Bob. Being out there was not only part of my nature, but I found that cultivating professional friends would enhance our practice. We became famous for our parties, especially as Bob was a musician and invited his friends to play jazz. At our Croton house, we entertained for all the holidays – especially New Year's Eve, the fourteenth of July, birthdays and anniversaries. I think some would say that our parties were lavish, especially at our pool overlooking the Hudson River. We often entertained up to 40 people. People would readily travel from NYC for our festivities. We held hilarious themed costume parties and an uproarious event where people were requested to tell one eighth-grade joke or two fourth-grade jokes. I was realizing an adolescent dream of being a vivacious actress. I fact, I had studied with the actress Simone Simone in my youth.

Occasionally, we would host a party at my new office. One party was memorable. When Bob had his book published, we invited virtually all the professionals we knew. Because the party was held on a Sunday afternoon in March, we thought that about half of the invitees would show up. We were mistaken. Virtually everybody showed up! I learned the definition of a crunch party. We were honored to have many distinguished guests including the heads of five or six psychoanalytic institutes. At one point, we freaked out because someone said that we had run out of scotch and then food. Somehow, we managed to get more liquor especially for the W.A. White people. The party ended in a farcical manner. As people began to retrieve their winter coats from our rented coat racks in the hallway, one of the racks collapsed, at which point a hysterical, drunk woman was screaming that someone had stolen her mink coat.

Another way that I helped Bob and our practice was to support him in his writing. I admired his talent and noted that he would write only when asked for a paper. A publisher asked us to write a book on transference and countertransference. Because my writing skills were limited, we agreed that I would write one clinical chapter and Bob would write the rest (Marshall & Marshall, 1988). As deadlines approached, I had to find ways to keep him writing to meet deadlines. I recall a Sunday in NYC which Bob reserved to write a chapter. As a break, we attended a nearby street fair where Bob dawdled. He knew it and I knew that he was reluctant to return to his task. I felt that I had to literally herd him back to the apartment. On occasion, Bob suffered a disappointment as when an editor returned his manuscript. I was always there to support him and restore his morale. I was his cheer-leader, not only because I wanted Bob to actualize all his gifts, but his success made me more secure professionally and financially.

Oddly enough, we never shared cases or worked together. We might talk about a patient now and again or I might ask Bob to supervise me in a difficult situation. We seldom discussed theory or technique in any deep way. I think we had learned not to take our patients home. We had come to value our time together and with our children. Moreover, our theoretical and technical orientations were different. Bob leaned toward a Freudian and modern psychoanalytic model while I took a more cultural, pragmatic approach, based on my feelings. Perhaps Sullivan's concept of a security system appealed to me.

Although I cherished being a graduate of the White Institute, I seldom participated in the political and professional activities. I had fashioned satisfying and lasting relations with some of my colleagues and senior analysts. Coming from the French college system of a hierarchical separation of student and faculty, I reveled in seeing some of my professors in a relaxed social setting as in the White yearly retreats where I drank wine with them as peers and observed them singing and playing poker. I surmised that they were functioning in the easy-going tradition of Harry Stack Sullivan and Clara Thompson. We often visited the homes of a couple of my beloved teachers, and reciprocally, they visited our home. These relationships were enhanced after we built a residence in East Hampton, NY where many W.A. White people had second homes. These social and collegial relations were an unanticipated but welcome bonus of attending the White Institute. I felt a sense of pride and fulfillment in my associations with these very human, bright, accomplished people.

Ease

As my professional life unfolded, I thoroughly enjoyed my work, especially as I found out more about using my feelings. As we spent more time traveling throughout the world, enjoying life in East Hampton, and being with our children and their families, I let my practice dwindle. I felt secure socially, professionally, financially, and with Bob and myself. I found myself organizing my possessions, taking diligent care of myself, putting photos in albums, and planning our next vacation. Our kids and grandkids provided me with especial pleasure.

As my life transitioned from an ambitious pursuit of a professional life and emotional and financial security, I began to realize that I was forgetting patient data and felt that I was slipping. My best guess was that I had been subject to a series of mini-strokes from which I was quick to recover. Despite Bob's kidding me about "Who listens?" and "Who remembers?" and assurances from my doctors that I did not have Alzheimer's disease, I felt something was changing – something was wrong. I slowly and sadly terminated my individual patients, but found grave difficulty ending a long-term therapy group that felt familial. As we had worked for many years as a cohesive, helpful unit, we had to work emotionally for several months before we could part.

And so, my reader, we must part. Although I ended my professional life, I frequently had the feeling that I would live forever with my family and friends.

I shed a few tears and in the words of Edith Piaf, *"Je ne regrette rien."* I have an enhanced sense of ease, curiosity, puzzlement, but with an odd mixture of my old emotional companions – insecurity and accomplishment.

And this is where I must say, "Au revoir."

References

Marshall, S. V. (1960). Personality correlates of peptic ulcer patients. *Journal of Consulting Psychology.* 24(3):218–233.

Marshall, R. J. & Marshall, S. V. (1988). *The Transference–Countertransference Matrix: The Emotional-Cognitive Dialogue in Psychotherapy, Psychoanalysis, and Supervision.* New York: Columbia Universities Press.

Chapter 8

How I became a psychoanalyst

From Shakespeare to psychoanalysis, from Freud and Lacan to Ferenczi and beyond

Clara Mucci

English as a way-out and a place of belonging

When I was born, my family lived in a rural area of central Italy and at home everybody spoke only the dialect of that region. When I was 19 months old we moved to the industrial north of Italy where my father had got a job with the railroad. This was an enormous leap forward for my father, whose family had for generations made their living as farmers. Because I was so young I had the privilege of going along with my mother and father when they first moved north. My sister, who was 6 years my senior, had to finish the school year, and so she remained with my paternal grandmother in the countryside for a few more months. My sister has always kept a bond with the countryside that I never really had; she was able to speak the dialect of the family, while I was never taught that dialect and my parents were proud of teaching only "real Italian" to me.

It was the sixties, Italy was still experiencing the post-war boom of economic expansion and there was already a growing desire for more equality and a greater recognition of basic civil rights. And yet, because we came from the south and there were two children in the family, nobody wanted to rent an apartment to "immigrants" (as they felt we were), so instead of living in the major city of the north-west where my father worked, Turin, we lived in a small provincial town, Asti, where somebody had "generously" rented their flat to us.

So, change and a move and also an enthusiastic though problematic start became my family environment, while the "language divide" (and the expectations that this probably meant on their part for me), the fact that I spoke Italian and my sister and my parents still spoke mostly the dialect, created, I suspect, a symbolic fracture that was there to remain. Even if I did not realize at the time, this sense of being different, of being somehow in-between our family's rural past and the industrial present, in-between dialect and Italian, probably made liminality a part of my identity. I think I was in-between cultures and lifestyles and mentalities and, I guess, as such I had all the privileges and the exclusions of in-between creatures like Turner's "liminal personae" (Turner, 1982) discriminated against and yet considered somehow powerful because of their inhabiting a special symbolic position (at the "threshold"). So then it is not surprising that my first book on Shakespearean tragedy *Liminal Personae*, explored figures of marginality and subversion rooted in the language of Shakespeare's plays (Mucci, 1995).

In truth, this inclusion/exclusion ambivalence in my life goes a little deeper than the move north and the question of language. I was the second daughter born into the family and, as one female child was already enough in that poor rural landscape, the birth of a second child could only be justified if the child were a male. The toast made at weddings "best wishes and may you have male children!" is indicative of the southern peasant mentality. When well-wishers would come to visit my parents for the newborn baby girl, they would say "Oh well, best wishes, anyway."

The second divide I experienced within my family was rooted in food. The northern region (Piedmont) where we had moved was close to France and the traditional cooking of the area had been greatly influenced by French cooking over the centuries, making it much richer and more elaborate than the simple vegetable and home-made pasta dishes of the south. My mother continued to cook the traditional meals for my father and sister but for some reason I seemed to refuse that food and she had to buy for me certain "industrial foods," that were quite the opposite of home-cooked food. There is also a funny episode about the only attempt that my family made to enroll me in a nursery school run by Catholic nuns when I turned three; they basically asked my parents to take me out of the school because not only would I not eat the food but I would inspire and convince all the other kids to refuse to eat that food! So my first introduction to an Italian official institution of some kind was ... one of subversion and rebellion! Language and food, what we might term the maternal side, (don't we say "mother-tongue"?) were therefore a bit problematic for me at the beginning of my life, but also the introduction to the first social and institutional places were not easy: I was restless, a bit defiant and extremely vivacious and extroverted, always singing and leading the other children around me.

I think my birth or the first years of my life also meant for my parents a challenge and the opening of a new socially ambitious phase that I somehow came to represent for them. They particularly wanted me to be well-behaved and well-introduced in the "outside world" and in the northern, more developed environment. In those years I literally spent most of my time playing outside, and spent very little time inside. They also say I started reading at 4, not because somebody taught me how to read, but simply because I kept asking everybody, especially my sister, what the letters on the street signs or in the papers meant, and I eventually linked the images of the letters to the sounds in words, another way I presume to appropriate and control and read my environment and possess it.

But reading was also linked to another strange pattern of mine; one of my first memories (beside the fact that I fell down a balcony a couple of meters high at the age of two and everybody thought I had knocked my head off forever and that at a wedding party at the age of three I started drinking all kinds of alcoholic beverages without supervision with some funny results: do you detect some neglect?) is of having a book open in front of me, and pretending I was reading a language that I called "English." I invented words and kept speaking that foreign language. Where I got the idea of "English" I cannot tell; the only thing I know is that my father spoke a few words of that mysterious and evidently fascinating language, a few words that he had learnt during the brief weeks that some English soldiers spent in their farm during the Second World War. So I suppose that was a way for me to "own" my private, exclusive language, a language of my imagination, to counterpose to their dialect, and it was a sort of "paternal" language (a father tongue?). So my invented English was my father-tongue, an invented place where I was still by myself but having a lot of fun, a space that was truly my own, a place of imagination and liberty, that I did not share with anybody.

Of the entire family, my father was the only one to actually have a curiosity and openness towards foreign languages and the world "outside" and that must have been very significant for me. He was the more social, extroverted, expansive, intelligent, courageous and curious man who had been the first and only member of his entire family to have the courage to move to the north and to turn his back to the family land. In contrast, my mother had never worked outside of the home, had even fewer years of education than my father, and although she had been raised under the rule of silent submission that all women and young people had to respect in a land of fathers, she harbored within herself that fierce and indomitable resistance that is typical of all dominated beings (women especially). So, while I think she did not seem to me when I was young that she had much to offer that I wanted to imitate, I do think I inherited her resiliency, independence and quiet defiant resistance of the patriarchal world.

Although Italy is a modern European country it is still plagued by vestiges of a regressive cultural heritage expressed in its deep-rooted attitude about domestic violence and women's role in the family and in society. Data from the National Institute of Statistics (ISTAT) show that a woman is killed in Italy every three days by a male family member either because he does not want her to leave him or feels betrayed by some behavior of hers or by her excessive freedom in her lifestyle or attitude; or he feels offended in his "honor" by what she does. Up until 1981 the so-called *delitto d'onore* (crime of honour) defense was still valid in Italy. Under this defense a male member of a family would receive only a minor penalty for killing a female member of the family who had "dishonoured" the family through marital infidelity, adultery or other sexually improper behavior. It was thought that the male's behavior in such circumstances was justified and understandable as a vindication of the family's honour. So, from an anthropological point of view, we are really a Mediterranean country where the domination of women is a fact that nobody contests or even notices compared to the more independent women of the western world.

So when I say I liked to speak the (invented) language of my father I probably meant a language of more freedom and less restraint, if not of true liberation, a language of expansion, of enterprise, of choices and possibilities that are of one's own making, not of another's (the husband's, the father's, the brother's, another male who has decided a female's destiny). And although this regressive mentality is present throughout the country it is certainly stronger in the south of Italy than in the north.

Discovery of Freud

My childhood had been active and eventful; my adolescent years were the darkest and gloomiest of my life. We moved from the north back to the south and I lost not only my friends and a less narrow-minded environment, but the possibility of staying outdoors most of the day. My sunny, extroverted and fiery temper became gloomy, very introverted and nostalgic of my past on the Ligurian Riviera, in Savona, where we had moved after a few years in Asti.

I did not like my new school mates, or the new teacher for the last year of elementary school or many of the professors. I was always very good at school, but I felt totally out of place, estranged and left out.

It was in my adolescent years that I discovered Freud. I am not sure how, and it must have been before my sister gave me a book by Freud when I was 15, because recently a friend from middle school sent me a note I had written her when I was 13 in which I mentioned Freud and psychoanalysis. At high school, when classes got boring, my school mate and I would play "free associations": we gave each other a word to free associate from; I am not sure how it was decided on who was the winner, but that is the game we played almost daily in class.

After Liceo Classico where I graduated with honours and after I had been invited to try the exams to enter a famous school in Italy, La Normale di Pisa, for honor students (but I would have had to pursue Classical Studies, which at that point I hated), I was unsure what to do next and my parents could not help me in the decision. I decided to enrol in a program of English Literature at the university of my local town, Pescara, so that I would not be a financial burden for my parents if they had to support me elsewhere. I was not sure what to do, but I knew I was going to use "English" to go abroad. English would be both my passport and my place of happy exile, as it was in a sense when I was a child.

Finding Shakespeare and a familiar (canny and uncanny) place of imagination and studying English Literature, I got to the land of Shakespeare's drama. Could I have found a richer and more fertile soil, a more inviting shore, a deeper and more complex humane and fascinating landscape? The language of the plays and (his?) imagination absorbed me totally: it was the most articulated poetic language I could imagine. Similarly to what Freud says about interpreting dreams, Shakespeare proved that the work of imagination, discovery, decodification and interpretation is potentially endless, and I felt that intriguing and powerful suspension of layers of meaning and references lurking there and was intrigued with finding ways of extracting it through my literary and theoretical training. There I found an uncanny familiarity, again a belonging and a magical abode: inclusion and exclusion, domination and submission, love and hate, creation and destructiveness, extreme joy and luck and extreme unhappiness and misfortune, sometimes sudden reversals of fortune and ways out that became ways of re-encoding destiny in life's trends. The language of punning, of seduction, of reversals, of kings who became humane when they encountered folly (King Lear); buffoons more in touch with truth than anybody else (the Fool); women who possessed a capacity to direct events through their subversive social and linguistic positions (the witches in *Macbeth*); deformed creatures who seemed to be pure bodily drives and could barely talk the language of the island but were endowed with a language and a capacity to reflect on their own conditions that was deeper than the master's himself and in their profundity reached pure spirituality and compassion (Caliban/Ariel). I was attracted to an entirely new world, open to endless possibilities, in language and body. And it seemed to hold within it all of the threatening and enchanting potentialities of the human mind and desires, the passions and the struggles of identity and destiny, not differently from what psychoanalysis was also trying to express about human mystery. The more I was to read theories of criticism and thought, in the university years in Italy but mostly in my future doctoral program at Emory, in the ILA (Institute of Liberal Arts) in Atlanta where I was going to be between 1988 and 1993, with psychoanalysis, feminism, deconstruction or postcolonial studies, the more Shakespeare seemed ready to illustrate those theories to me, and seemed also to have anticipated all those theories.

"The lunatic the lover and the poet are of imagination all compact," the Bard said in *Midsummer Night's Dream*, and it seemed a treatise on literature and psychoanalysis, still somehow to be explored and mapped out. It hinted at primary and secondary processes, before Freud had been born; it made concrete and powerfully evident the "revolutionary force" of poetic language of which Julia Kristeva wrote (Kristeva, 1984), explaining how extremes are in touch somehow and capable of being reversed (again, a lesson Freud were to teach). On top of everything, it also unpacked a liminal world of imagination and power that intrigued me and gave confirmation of how power (even when disguised by gender division, as in the *Taming of the Shrew*) rules the world, how it can spoil the good in human beings and how what is marginal was probably symbolically central but got repressed (like the Fool and the Witches demonstrated with their lingustic practice and their subversive bodies, and similarly to the status of "truth" in a Lacanian view of the unconscious; see Lacan, 1966; Mucci, 1995, 2001).

With the so-called "Last Plays," the most renowned being *The Tempest*, Shakespeare gave me, among other things (Mucci, 1998) that sense of "unfinished business" that probably identifies for me what life is mostly about, especially after the time of youth is over, and at the same time highlights the possibility of "Fernweh," as the German language calls it, a nostalgia for a place that you have never reached but still is there almost to guarantee a trace of desire and possibility still open, stirring a tension inside and a movement forwards, a tension that as far as I am concerned becomes unfortunately most intense as life becomes shorter.

To keep a chronological order to illustrate my route before I reached the shores of Emory in 1988, I should add that after graduating in English Literature in 1984 in Pescara, my original family region, where I had come back after my childhood in the north, I had gone to Rome to teach for a year, and then I was offered a few hours of teaching in London, at one of the polytechnics. It was the mid-1980s. London was interesting, rather overwhelming, fascinating, full of exciting new things, but the experience of being abroad was tough emotionally. I taught Italian conversation, and it was a very pleasurable and rewarding experience.

One of my colleagues at the Polytechnic of Central London (now Westminster College) was Riccardo Steiner, the Italian Kleinian psychoanalyst who had also become a historiographer of psychoanalysis. We spoke about my passion for psychoanalysis, and about my Italian thesis on the Fool in *King Lear* and punning. He encouraged me to attend the Freud Memorial Lectures held at the University College, London (1985–1986). There I attended the lectures of Joseph Sanders, Hannah Segal and other eminent psychoanalysts of the British

Psychoanalytic Association of those years. I was terrified at being in that environment of renowned thinkers, but I kept going.

I had no idea what I would do after that inspiring year in London; but I knew I missed my readings, my classes, I craved for more courses to take, more things to read and I was a bit nostalgic for the student life with its research and writing, so when my Italian dissertation advisor told me about a program in the United States looking for some talented international students where I could pursue a PhD in an interdisciplinary field within the Humanities including psychoanalysis (and offering money towards tuition), I applied for a grant there, and I got it, for four years.

At this point, together with the excitement, I was scared, but deep down I knew I was going in the direction of nurturing life and sustaining my identity, my understanding, to enlarge and deepen my conscience, not only my learning and my intellectual knowledge. I alternated between being very open and enthusiastic and extroverted about experiencing the world, and being very shy and introverted. In this last regard, Emory was challenging. Having to introduce myself for the first time to new people, speaking in class was very difficult; in addition, I was speaking a foreign language, even if it was the language of my expansion and discovery. When in 1988 I received the scholarship from Emory, I was teaching English at high school as a permanent teacher within the Italian system, and I was living in Tuscany (where I had chosen to enter the national competition).

Teaching at high school in Tuscany turned out to be one of the most inspiring human circumstances I have ever found myself in. I adored the students and the students adored me. It was endearing. The vocational school they were attending was preparing them to be chefs, waiters and hotel managers. Although they were not particularly keen on English they were extremely sensitive and very kind and generous people. They were in their youth and by themselves, so a bit fragile and vulnerable, and I sensed this very strongly and this created a powerful bond of love and affect and respect among us. I felt very close to them, and they were close to me. I had become for them the last member of a new family, emotionally supportive, professional and gentle. When after a year I finally left for Emory, their cards and letters followed me for months and sometimes years to come.

Atlanta "epic" years: Emory, first personal psychoanalysis and surroundings

Finally, in August 1988 I went to Emory, and it was the most significant change in my life up to then, definitely a turning point, not only for my professional life.

I felt immediately at ease there, or at least things went easier than I had expected. Atlanta was a warm, easy-going ("Southern," I understood later) environment, and at the end of the 1980s was a very open, still not too busy and not too polluted a city; it looked like a garden to me, so different from the crowded, noisy and polluted Italian cities I knew. I enjoyed my circumstances, having a room in the upstairs of a real house (not an apartment), with a yard, a garden, a cat, and I began being very sociable again. People were very friendly, very encouraging and very interested in my background, in what I was doing, even in my ideas, which seemed to me at that point totally incredible. It was the first time I was asked to discuss my ideas, in class, in the papers I wrote, in conversation. In Italy the education system is not interested in what you think when you are in training, and what you have to say, except when you become a professor, or a researcher, but when you are a student, even a graduate student, you need to show that you have retained a lot of information very well, but no professor would even think of asking you what you actually thought about anything (I am different now as a professor). So it was for me an incredible world, an enchanted island, full of imagination, discoveries, theories, lots of readings and lots of writing; writing was also a novelty for me as writing papers is not part of the Italian university method (we only write a dissertation at the end of a degree course, but all the exams before then are oral). So the English language and the writing became another great form of expression for me in that new system. The courses were extremely interesting, and I could also put together a few directed studies on my own, with a reading list of my choice, mostly in psychoanalysis and anthropology, in addition to Shakespeare's plays; those were the subjects I had chosen to work on in the interdisciplinary program at the ILA (Institute of Liberal Arts). Unfortunately the program was closed a couple of years ago.

Emory had a huge and very beautiful campus. The swimming pool there was my retreat when I was too tired or too hot to read any longer, and it was such a pleasure to be on campus with my friends that I literally spent all my time there. There I had also a "carrel" (a place to study) first and a closed room in the library afterwards, when I was writing the dissertation, and there I literally spent all my days including weekends, all year round. This was also a novelty for me as no such provisions exist in Italian university libraries. The library was my second home, or perhaps I should say my first home; it was the most extraordinary and fascinating place, 10 floors of books on shelves. I could read everything, everything was at hand, I could take all the books I wanted, I could not believe it. The first time I asked an Emory librarian how many books I could borrow at once, I could literally not believe it, he kept saying "all the books you want" and because it made no sense to me (a library in Italy allows you to take up to two books at once, after one hour or so of searching and most of the books you search for are missing or not there), I literally could make no sense of that answer; afterwards I realized that I could take (and return on call) all the books I wanted, AT ONCE. The first year in Atlanta I lived in the upstairs of a beautiful old house in Little Five Points, the alternative part of town, with a nice big porch. My room had a mattress (no bed), a table and chair and an armchair; a few days after my arrival, the entire upstairs was all crowded with my borrowed books, on the floor, on the table, on the chair, on the armchair, books were everywhere. They were not only my course books, but also all the reference books, the texts I needed to write my papers, and other books, books filled the place and my excited mind, I was the happiest woman in the world, and I was astonished that anybody would actually pay me (the fellowship included both tuition and living expenses) to study and then express what I thought! And so I took my "reading job" very seriously: when my housemates left in the morning to go to work, I would be sitting at a little table downstairs with my reading, when they came back after work (if I had no classes to go to) I was still sitting there, and it felt as if time had not passed at all. That was really my enchanted world, the isle in the tempest where there was no need to be afeard ("Be not afeard the isle is full of noise," says Caliban, the supposed monster, to the shipwreck sailors stranded in Prospero's or Shakespeare's island).

Again, I could not believe that and it was the most inspiring and powerful experience in my life, combined with the wonderful friends, scholars and professors I met and had lunch with (also, the idea of having lunch with a professor in Italy was unheard of, as most universities are state universities with thousands of students). Not only did they have lunch with me but they were actually interested in what I had to say! It was unbelievable. My first reading list had Jung in it at first, then Freud and other psychoanalysts, but I eliminated Jung almost immediately because after reading the first two books I felt his ideas about animus/anima and all the mythology around it were very biased, dated and also antifeminist. It was not intellectually engaging or liberating for me, while the more I read Freud the more I understood how radical his thought was, especially at his time, and then the reading that Lacan did of Freud, his "return to Freud" through structuralist parameters or antistructuralist parameters seemed to me so powerful and convincing and once again radical and revolutionary, especially when working with poetic texts.

Literature and psychoanalysis (and myself)

While I was at Emory I wrote a paper for one of my courses on literature and psychoanalysis. It was my first paper to be accepted for publication ("The blank page as a Lacanian object a," for a Journal called *Literature and Psychology*; Mucci, 1994). It was inspired by a reading of "The blank page," a short story by Karen Blixen, where the blank page is the sheets of the first night of a famous princess in Portugal, which does not show any traces of blood, leaving all the witnesses in doubt of what the first night had been like. I had written basically that the page that remains unwritten, like the blank page, is a sort of "object a" in the Lacanian definition of our connection with a desire that relentlessly and by definition escapes us, and which is rooted in an impossibility; because desire marks the subject's position towards their desired object and towards existence, it is the place of a lack, a void, that remains forever open to cause desire, the place of a forever lasting tension. Once again, I think it explains a tension I have always felt in my life, a nostalgia for a place I have never been, as impossible and irrational as it sounds. I think it is the place of the radicalization of our desires, and some places or some people evoke that very strongly, a place of "love" or "sacredness." In my experience, this place of desire, tension to love and sacredness is also linked to what makes the state of writing possible, the alone-ness that becomes a connectedness, far more reaching than the real connections. I guess writing puts the self in connection with a third, a symbolic self of alterity, which helps us connect to the sphere of meaning (which is a place unreachable for us by definition). I also think it says something about the special realm that unites two people in therapy, not always pleasurable but often filled with awe and somewhat extraordinary.

I think Virginia Woolf has somehow shed some light about this strange connection, when she writes about writing as receiving a "blow" (in consciousness? Within consciousness? A moment of revelation and therefore/nonetheless traumatic?) that she receives when she writes, which makes things more real, unbearable, and yet more present:

> And so I go on to suppose that the shock-receiving capacity is what makes me a writer …: I feel that I have had a blow; but it is not, as I thought as a child, simply a blow from an enemy hidden behind the cotton wool of daily life; it is or will become a revelation of some order; it is a token of some real thing behind appearance; and I make it real by putting it into words. It is only by putting it into words that I make it whole; this wholeness means that it has lost its power to hurt me; it gives me, perhaps because by doing so I take away the pain, a great delight to put the severed parts together. Perhaps this is the strongest pleasure known to me.
> (Woolf, 1941, *Moments of Being*)

In my graduate years, given my background in which women still suffer marginalization and even my mother's generation has been discriminated so that if there is some money in a family to educate just one out of five children in the family, the money goes towards the education of the only male in the family, I developed strong feminist ideas, and I guess my background (or intergenerational stories) played an important role in that. I became passionate about Julia Kristeva, Nancy Chodorow (1999), Shoshana Felman (1983), Jonathan Culler (1988), Barbara Johnson (1997), Kaja Silverman (1983), Peter Stallybrass and Allon White (1986), and the more I read the more my feminist thought was strengthened. I suppose in some ways I was taking revenge not only for my mother's unfinished years of education, but the fact that my two grandmothers were both illiterate (I say this in retrospect, I was not aware at the time of why I was doing what I was doing). I did not know exactly at the time but I am sure now that a part of my craving for learning and studying and writing and acquiring "knowledge" came out of the eagerness to read and count and speak that women of only one generation before me had had. I remember my mother always saying to me: "If only I could speak like you!" Meaning, "If only I had the power of language and the command of Italian language that you have thanks to your education ...!" I guess my epilogue to my mother's words would be *Acheronta movebo*, "If I cannot move the heavens then I will move hell." My mother's underworld was unexplored terrain for me, but I nonetheless understood the frightening memories with which it was populated. Again, I think psychoanalysis and the work done on myself were also a way to be in touch with the hell of her own experience, the elaboration of her "phantasm," namely, the unelaborated residue of an impossible (for her) mourning, which had become intergenerational. I did not know, when I was in therapy, why my mother seemed to come from a place of mourning and tragedy; after the end of my many analyses or psychotherapies (three, in fact) I knew that there had been loss in the family right before she was born and other deep traumatic events.

I became more and more aware of my own "phantasms" only through my own analysis, and I owe all these discoveries to my first analyst, an MD who was doing a residency in Psychiatry during my Emory years. This experience was also part of my epic years and also part of those pivotal years in Atlanta. I still had emotional problems connecting when it came to being social and in groups and I also could not write the papers on time; I felt it was too much for me, even if overall I was doing very well. So I decided to go to the university doctor to ask to see a psychotherapist. I was given a psychiatrist at first who seemed to me superficial and arrogant. The second one I saw, James A. McCoy, MD, would become my therapist for the rest of the time I was at the university (three and a half more years) and I have resumed contact with him recently, so he is still in my life. He was doing his internship at Emory as a psychiatrist while still practicing as a thoracic surgeon; African American, he was in his early fifties when he was training at Emory and also taking classes at the Institute of Psychoanalysis.

I will never forget how powerful our sessions were; all the emotions that I was capable of covering up in a lot of words in Italian would come out straight away in my still reduced or limited, but for this reason even more powerful or evocative, English. Most of the time he would simply repeat to me the words I was saying to him, so that I could take notice of what I was saying, and that simply overwhelmed me, because he had a way of giving me back the words I was giving him in a way that created a huge impression on me; I was forced to take knowledge of my story, of my feelings, of all the displaced parts or the fragmented parts I had inside, and he would both contain and give back to me my awareness. The language, I think, had a special renewing effect on my identity, as if I was inscribing new meanings and new versions of my story in wholly different vocabulary, and I felt a lot of hope and understanding even though there was also utter pain in those new/foreign words. (Now if I were to translate this process into neuroscientific terms, I would say the words and the emotions have created a new web of connections in my brain that emotionally and relationally were not there before.) Sometimes (most of the time) the sessions were so powerful and intense that the next day I had to stay in bed, with the comfort of the bedlinens and the blankets all around my body. I felt as if my skin would come off if I were to get out of bed, that it would be ripped off in pieces. I felt as if I needed to be held like a newborn and that I could only be relieved by the comfort of the bed-linen and the warmth of the blankets. There are no words to describe what I went through, and I certainly will not try to find them here, but that was the deepest, most intense and somehow most highly symbolic and transformative experience of my life, only comparable to a strong and somehow desperate love relationship.

The years at Emory gave me that experience too, and separation after the feeling of finally belonging with mind, body and spirit was also excruciating. I guess literature and lots of writing and working helped me in overcoming that loss; by then they had become a bit of a habit for me.

But from my original disorganized attachment, I think I was going towards "earned secure." I had learned that I could survive, and I am indeed a survivor. My early years had in some ways put me in touch with feelings of psychical death, extreme deprivation, abuse and loss.

One little episode from my years at Emory that I want to recall here is when I needed to leave to go back to Italy for a couple of weeks and I gave my therapist a little wooden box. Is was nicely carved with decorations, and the wood had a nice rose smell which I liked. He took it, acknowledging the gift, and said nothing. When I came back from my trip home, he returned the little box to me saying that I did not owe him anything special apart from what I was already giving him through our work together and through the payment of the therapy. I was both puzzled and disappointed, but then I realized that I had spent all my life until then feeling that my inadequacy (my basic fault somebody would say) had to be mended by giving the other something more or something that was mine in order to be accepted, while in reality I did not need to do or be anything else except myself. It was a highly symbolic and utterly reparatory act that, like many of the things he said which became real actions even if purely on the symbolic level, a real form of reparation. He was treating me differently from the way anybody else in my life had treated me, with the recognition of and total respect for who I was, and not simply for my intelligence or for other qualities of mine. This recognition and acceptance was all the more poignant coming from a man whose understanding of marginalization and discrimination, repression and injustice was deeply intergenerational and deeply felt "under the skin." He knew the sense of exclusion that I had suffered. He was capable of giving me a sense of the sacredness of life not just in others but even inside of myself that I had never experienced in my life. This sense of the sacredness of life was constructed and preserved in the bond of therapy, and I was then capable of carrying it around with me in my relationships with others. I feel very fortunate and very grateful that he is still present in my life. Meeting him signaled a moment of rebirth for me and certainly a determining moment in my final decision to become an analyst myself (even though at that point I was still very far away from having a clear idea about it).

My advisor at Emory was Robert Paul, a renowned anthropologist and psychoanalyst and until recently Director of the Emory Institute of Psychoanalysis in Atlanta (one of the few Institutes actually connected to a university in the US and in the world I presume). In his presence too, with his deep knowledge and warm humane understanding and attention for me, I felt moved and very motivated to do my best, in a safe and sacred place. In those years (1988–1993) I discovered that the French department was in the vanguard in using psychoanalysis and psychoanalytical theory to interpret literature. Those were the years when Lacan and Lacanian theory were at the height of their prestige and were being widely used to re-read canonic literature. I was still studying Shakespeare plays, but Lacanian theory was my real passion. Castoriadis and Lyotard were among the visiting scholars who came to the French department at Emory. And in the last years of my stay Cathy Caruth and Shoshana Felman also came, but I had already finished my course work by then.

But the encounter with Shoshana Felman's writings left the deepest mark in me, in my readings of English Literature text and I guess in my life. It was first of all a paper, "Beyond Oedipus: The Specimen Story of Psychoanalysis" (1983). I don't know how many times I have read through the paper, and each time it has the power of performing almost a magical effect. It seemed to do what the paper was about, namely the performative power of texts, the infolding of the writing which had such a powerful spell, and also its content, basically how the Oedipal story recounts the story of each subject, each of us, according to Lacan, because we are doomed to repeat in our life our story precisely because we don't know it. So we are played out by our loss, or our repressed chapters, the blank page in our life so to speak. Oedipus is doomed to kill his father and marry his mother, precisely because he does not know his story, the story of his origin: because we repress or, I now would say, dissociate our real story, our innermost truth is hidden, especially to us. This is in fact the mystery of our life story, for us to solve during the length of our life, and our parents mysteriously and unwillingly take part in that unfolding, creating its origin and contributing in presentia and even in absentia, after death. The mystery of our life is in our life itself, in the story of our life, but we can learn this only through the figure composed in our path, in our life treading: again, literature and Karen Blixen's image of the stork in *Out of Africa* (Dinesen, 1994) come to mind: through broken pieces of drawing, one piece after the other, as we go along life, we, hopefully, create or build up a full image, an image subsuming our own life destiny (for Blixen, the image of the stork).

I finally met Shoshana Felman years after going back to Italy for good (I went back in 1993 because my father had a stroke) when I was in New York in 2004 for my semester as visiting scholar at Columbia and before my training with Kernberg at the Personality Disorders Institute in 2005. I had written to her since I was in the States, and she invited me unexpectedly to her retirement party at Yale, in a private house. I cried most of the time, for the emotion of having finally met my inspiration. She was in front of me, nervously holding a Fiji plastic bottle of water in her hands. I thought it was one of the most important moments in my life and career. It certainly marked an emotional peak in my career as psychoanalytic literary critic. But my life had more detours in store for me.

Back to the real world: going back to Italy

The five years (1988–1993) I had as a leave from my Italian teaching job expired, and I had to decide if I would go back to Italy or if I would be looking for a job in the States. I had passed my PhD exams, I was ABD, as American students would say, and had (in 1993) won a competition to participate in the Summer session at the renowned Dartmouth School of Theory and Criticism, where Juliet Mitchell, Homi Bhabha, Gayatry Spivak and Robert Scholes, among others, were teaching that year. I was writing my dissertation which was to be the first book I would publish (*Liminal personae*, 1995). But at the end of that summer my father had a stroke. I had to decide in a few days what I was going to do. He was alive, but severely impaired, paralyzed on the right side of his body, and speech-impaired. I had left Italy in serious conflict with him, also about going abroad. Looking back, however, I thought I may have expected too much of him – even my sister had said that going abroad to study was something that only rich young males could do. It was the whole culture that disapproved, not just my father. I decided in two days to pack my stuff and go back to Italy. I had had three and a half years of therapy at that point, and I felt that I had to resume touch with him/them and from there work out my radical family difficulties.

In the meantime, to postpone going back to my teaching job in Tuscany, I entered a doctoral program in English Studies in Milan, where I also started a Lacanian analysis.

This second encounter with an analyst (Dr. Antonello Sciacchitano, Milan) was also very serious and very painful but, as people say, "rewarding." I just think (having become a Ferenczian afterwards) it could have been less painful, shorter, less authoritarian and a bit more sympathetic, but certainly it was once again powerful and extremely helpful. Wherever I was (either with my parents in Abruzzi or in Tuscany later on when I went back to my job) I would go to Milan for the weekend to see my analyst, for three sessions a week, and he would allow me to see him on weekends too. There were tough and strained moments, but thanks to the therapy and the work with him I overcame fundamental destructive tendencies that never came back. I am very grateful to him too.

For Lacanians, the moment a subject completes analysis he/she is authorized to become an analyst himself/herself, but this certainly did not feel right for me. At that point, I was an associate professor of English Literature at the University of Chieti-Pescara. It was 1999. That very year, our university had opened the department of Psychology. To become a psychologist and psychotherapist, I knew I would have to do five years of coursework, then a year of internship, then pass the board exams, and finally start a four-year psychoanalytic psychotherapy training in a licensed institution. I just embarked on this path and did one thing after the other, keeping up the necessary pace, keeping to my very busy schedule (which luckily was pretty flexible), adapting and adjusting my life to all my various commitments and duties. In the meantime, I was still teaching my courses on Shakespeare and Literary theory, and writing my books, so in the mornings and afternoons I was a professor of English, and in the evenings and nights I was a student of Psychology. In 1998, my second book came out (*Tempeste. Narrazioni di esilio in Shakespeare and Karen Blixen*; Mucci, 1998) on the Tempest and Karen Blixen's rewriting of Shakespeare's romance. I probably felt that after Emory "the revels were now ended," and whatever strength I had was my own, and the magic circle of my previous American years was gone, but it sounded more real to be in Italy, to build my own identity, back to earth (and starting a cycle of reconciliation with my family I understood later, or even of forgiveness I would now say). The book on the *Tempest* is the most Lacanian of my books, and there is a lot in it on exile. In 2001 I wrote on Macbeth and the witches in *Il teatro delle streghe* (*The Theatre of Witches*; Mucci, 2001); it is a book on the construction of femininity in Elizabethan times and the fact that the language of the witches, full of riddles, puns, metaphors and metonymies, was a perfect language to describe the work of the primary process of poetic language, similar to the rhetoric of dreams: it was in fact a sort of unconscious speech defining the course of action in the play, revealing the truth by disguising it through language precisely as it happens in the unconscious and its linguistic disguise according to Freud's theory of Der Witz (Freud, 1905), applicable to the pun and poetic language, and to Lacan.

In 2003–4, right before finishing the Psychology degree, I spent a semester in New York researching and giving lectures on Shakespeare and on Italian Literature. While there, I started following the debate on recovered memories of abuse that was then going on. I had very strong ideas about that theme. I knew from my own experience (my own analysis) that one could in fact remember episodes that had been dissociated or repressed (at the time I could not have told the difference). Fascinated by dissociated or repressed memory I kept reading and reading and eventually came upon writings on the related theme of survivorship, specifically Holocaust survivorship. The experience of those who had "encountered death" and "had remained alive," as Robert Jay Lifton powerfully writes in that amazing book that is *Listening to Trauma*, edited by Cathy Caruth (see Lifton, 2014), was extremely close to what I myself had felt, so these accounts seemed incredibly familiar to me, although I felt almost guilty because in a sense I had no right to declare my familiarity with those who had really lived through the Holocaust in first person. But this was what spoke to me in the most powerful and compelling way (the "intermediate region" in psychoanalytic-Freudian terms) and that powerful experience created the basis for my first book on trauma and the Holocaust which begins with the debate between Freud and Ferenczi on their respective theories of trauma and then moves through the recovered memory debate and finally goes on to the experience of massive events. That book was originally my dissertation for my psychology degree (I graduated in 2004). For months as I was writing the dissertation my companion was my cat Sweetie, who lay down on the table next to my computer during the long nights while I worked on that project. (I have dedicated my last book, *Borderline Bodies* (2018), to him, among other people.)

Writing on Shakespeare and literary theory had been a powerful emotional experience, but nothing in comparison with the emotions that I had to elaborate and face and deposit on those pages. The book that came out of that, *Il dolore estremo. Il trauma da Freud alla Shoah* (*Extreme Pain. Trauma from Freud to the Shoah*; Mucci, 2008), was the product of the most totally engaging experience of writing in which I had ever been involved. It was almost a physical experience. While it had been mostly my mind that became all absorbed when I was in the Shakespearean terrain, now my body and emotions were involved too.

One of the gifts that come with writing is that you may attract people with ideas similar to your own to your life, and that was the case for that first little "solely psychoanalytic" book (with no literature in it); that book attracted new friends to my life with new occasions for discussion with new people interested in the same topics, and this is, I think, the precious benefit of writing for which I am very grateful. Unfortunately the book was in Italian, so I could not really share this experience of mine with my American friends and none of my books until then had been translated or written in English, until *Beyond Individual and Collective Trauma* (Karnac; 2013) came out.

New York, 2005–2006

Another extremely meaningful and extraordinary moment for the direction my life was to take was when, after graduation in Psychology in 2004 in Italy, I asked for a period of fellowship that would count as my Italian internship at the Institute of Personality Disorders, directed by Otto Kernberg. Another amazing time in my life started then. Otto was for me (as I used to say) what Freud was for the Vienna of the early nineteenth century. I still can't believe how extraordinary my experience was and it is extraordinary even the way I got in touch with him: literally a friend of mine in the States who knew how passionate I was about his work on personality disorders made an appointment with him on my behalf (without me knowing it). And so I went. I was in his office, with a copy of my most recent book in my hands for him (*A memoria di donna, In a Woman's Memory*, 2004; the title is in a sense a pun, a play on words that created a feeling of estrangement, because the Italian language has "In a man's memory" to allude at what everybody can remember, but no such saying exists with a female subject and if the sentence is reverted into the female form it creates a feeling of estrangement and alienation in the listener, which was exactly what I wanted to provoke. I wrote a dedication to him, in front of him, at the moment of leaving. One of the first things he said to me in our brief encounter in his office was that I needed to add "Doctor" to my signature. It was his first acknowledgement of how I needed to reinforce my self-esteem and to start seeing myself differently, given all the things I had done. I still felt I had done nothing and I was still at the beginning. When the possibility came, I spent a semester at that renowned Institute between 2005 and 2006. It was unfortunately the year that his wife Paulina fell sick, and then passed away, in April, when I had just gone back, and so I never had the chance to meet her.

Kernberg is not only a passionate researcher and a first-class clinician, with an incredible expertise and extraordinary professionality and psychoanalytic knowledge, but everything he did and said I felt arrived after a long process of internal searching, continuous study and sensitive and keen reflection and comparison with other theories and a practical application in the therapeutic process. That is why no matter what one asks him, his answer is a distillation and a synthesis not only of his own theories but also of the theories that contrast with his own. Clearly for him what works best for the patient's disorder has priority and the theory is secondary: "I would never sacrifice the patient for the theory," he used to say, and I could not agree more. I guess that was an inspiration for me, his way of looking for what really worked for the patient and their suffering and his total devotion and integrity to the practice.

As a fellow there, not only could I attend his amazing interviews on Friday mornings at the Presbyterian Hospital in White Plains, plus all the supervisions of doctoral students in training in Psychology and in Psychiatry, and their organizational and general supervision meetings, but he even found time to devote an hour a week to me for discussion, debate, observation regarding any argument I chose. And he would always start the meeting with the incredibly humble and generous offer "What can I do for you?", explaining that I could use the hour to clarify something that I had seen in the hours of supervision, or psychoanalytic theory, or to posit personal questions.

Kernberg is also a most intense and enthusiastic teacher and researcher. He is also a master of integration and I think usually not enough recognition has been given to him for his capacity to extend the psychoanalytic theory in ways that are not as traditional as they might sound. The dyadic process at work in the TFP (Transference-Focused Psychotherapy, the psychotherapy Kernberg devised specifically for the treatment of borderline personality disorders; Clarkin, Yeomans, & Kernberg, 1999) was for me a revelation and I have been able to combine it with the victim–persecutor dyad I derive from Ferenczi theory (see my last book on personality disorders and affect regulation theory, *Borderline Bodies*). Of course, we give to trauma theory and to the question of aggressiveness (innate or derived from trauma and abuse) a very different value, as is also the case with regard to attachment theory, but what I learned in that semester planted the seeds for many ideas that I would develop in the future. Over the years, I have gone back to observe his study and clinical research group at least twice a year, also establishing an important friendship with Frank Yeomans, whose fascinating story is also related in this book. In our routine, we could in the same day visit a hospital for the criminally insane in Montebello and hear about the interview of a patient who had decapitated his mother and planted her head at the foot of a tree his mother visited, and then we would drive in his sturdy BMW at full speed to his office in Manhattan, sharing his reflections on friends being "the trees of life," as Borges would say, or on the last movie he had seen that weekend at home (he would get very special rare movies while also spending the weekend dictating his papers) or the latest Italian novel he had read (for instance, by Oriana Fallaci), and in the middle of all this he would suddenly look perplexed and puzzled because before reaching the office he needed to meet a patient with whom he needed to arrive at an important decision, like adding an extra session or revising the contract, and he would communicate that to me …

Together with the experience of my training school in Italy (SIPP, Società Italiana Psicoterapia Psicoanalitica) in the Milan branch, what I know in my clinical practice (besides what was taught to me by my patients in the struggles we had) started with Kernberg's teachings. It is to Kernberg's supervisions and his own vignettes or his tapes and sentences that sometimes I mentally return to solve a riddle or to decide what to do with a patient (even if, as I said, I became a Ferenczian-relational analyst!).

With him I learned what is possibly the most relevant lesson about my omnipotence and about "letting go" (it was about a suicidal patient I have described in my last book). And New York with Riverside Park (along the Hudson River) in particular and a few more places became for me the place of all possible nostalgia and hope.

Back to Italy in 2006, I took the board exams the following year. I passed them, and started seeing my first patients. In the meantime, I had published my psychology dissertation. Ferenczi trauma theory and his difference with Freud's theory was the first chapter. In my job, I had moved from the department of English to that of Humanities, where I really liked my colleagues, and started the psychoanalytic psychotherapy school in Milan. It was open enough to give me the direction on psychotherapy I felt I needed and a very solid background, but still I felt it was not open enough. No attachment or neuroscience and certainly nobody was speaking about Ferenczi at the time (things are different now, and the teaching of Ferenczi is part of the second-year theory class that I am presently teaching and I have asked now to teach him in other curricula in relational training schools in Italy, such as the ISIPSe). I also received excellent supervision in those years and enjoyed the classes and the readings. I finished the school in 2012 and became a member.

In the meantime, personality disorders had become more and more my interest thanks to my borderline patients, whom I really liked (one of my supervisors, who has become a friend over the years, Dr Antonello Correale (Correale, 2006), used to say that I had "adopted" them). To work with borderline patients was and is a challenge, but I feel they are the patients I feel closest to, and I thank them for having allowed me to enter the threshold of trauma and survivorship and for the resilience their life teaches us.

The trauma study years: 2008–2018

While in the process of writing my dissertation for my Psychology degree which became my first book on trauma (Mucci, 2008), the articles that struck me the most were written by a survivor who had really been in a work camp during the war years in Europe and was now a psychiatrist and psychoanalyst in practice at New Haven, CT. This survivor and trauma theoretician and clinician was Dori Laub (1992, 2005), who unfortunately died recently, unexpectedly.

I decided to meet him over the summer of 2008. I took an appointment, went to see him in his unpretentious office in New Haven. I remember sitting in his office waiting for him to open his door at the given time, and thinking what I was going to say. Why I was there.

It was easier than I expected. There were not so many things I needed to say. He had the most powerful understanding of the few scattered words I said, and his intensity was extreme. The silence with him was the warmest and a sort of companionate vicinity I had felt only in therapy. We were very happy for our brief discussion, I mostly spoke about what had struck me about his articles, and I left. Even if words were scant or imprecise, we had a channel for connection that I can't describe properly but was there. One year afterwards, I wrote to him saying that I wanted to spend a few days at the Fortunoff Archives at Yale to listen to the tapes of Holocaust survivors. He offered to give me hospitality and so I stayed four days with him, with his wife Johanna Bodenstab, who also became a friend (she had also spent years in Italy, I discovered, and was to my surprise completely fluent in Italian) and their dog Buster. The fortune plant I had given Dori the year before had become almost a tree in their home. Johanna died three years ago and the loss was utter for Dori and for the huge community of their friends. Now Dori also has left us, on June 23, 2018. And a few months before also Giovanni Liotti, to whom I owe the inspiration on disorganized attachment and dissociation (Liotti 1999), who also had become a sort of companion soul, with whom I exchanged literature books and poems, has passed on. The world is emptier or more opaque without these lights and I certainly feel a bit more lonely year after year for the friends and soul companions I have lost.

As always, I owe to my readings and my writings having found the best companions of my life path.

In the meantime, I had published my last books on Shakespeare (Mucci, 2009), a book on Elizabeth I's cultural background and the powerful symbolic net she had created and that was created around her and in the same year I published an edited work with some of my best young colleagues and previous students of mine, on "Shakespeare' s last plays," the romances (Mucci et al., 2009). I knew it was a farewell for me, as in the Epilogue of *The Tempest*, which I cannot repeat without crying even nowadays, and I would not have written more on Shakespeare's plays. My research, my writings and my conferences now revolved all around psychoanalysis, issues of trauma and forgiveness, and borderline personality disorders.

In 2009 I took a class in London on personality disorders at the Anna Freud Center, taught by Peter Fonagy and Antony Bateman (Bateman and Fonagy, 2006). I was curious to compare what I had learned from Kernberg in NY on TFP and I wanted to know what Fonagy and his group had to offer. I was disappointed by the fact that there was no psychoanalysis or psychodynamic processes really involved in the mentalizing treatment and although overall useful and interesting I felt they had given up what I felt should have remained the foundation.

That January I found in the Karnac Bookstore on Finchley Rd, a few blocks from both Freud's house and the Anna Freud Center, a book on relational trauma with an article by Allan Schore (1994, 2012).

Allan Schore was new to me. It was a total revelation.

Finally, a lot of things clicked in my mind. The mother–child relationship; the traumatic development; the pathologies depending on the amygdala connection or lack of connection, the importance of the gaze, of the body, the right brain! I could not believe that everything had already been done, and by one man! The most intense intellectual and emotional experience I had had in years, and the intricacy of deep and illuminating interdisciplinary work: the excitement was extreme. Implicit memory explained why the body could remember and the subject could not know; dissociation was the main response to traumatization, and created the basis of severe mental pathology, not repression, as Freud had thought.

I felt that contemporary psychoanalysis should have been doing precisely what Allan Schore was doing, rewriting the psychoanalytic path through the new understanding we now had, thanks to affective neuroscience, infant research, developmental psychobiology and psychopathology, neuroimmunopsychobiology and so on.

Of course, the theory on trauma had to be rewritten on the basis of what on one side Ferenczi was doing (the reading of his *Clinical Diary*, 1932, was unbelievable as was his "Confusion of Tongues" paper, 1933) and Schore was doing and putting into words and clarifying with tons of scientific articles and a huge volume of research exactly that path. The victim–persecutor dyad that seemed to be essential to me in the roots of the traumatic and violent developments even intergenerationally (something Dori Laub had clarified) was clearly hinted at by Ferenczi and thoroughly and brilliantly connected by Allan Schore's neurobiological thought. So another intellectual and humane path was open to me.

The rest is present history; the connection between Kernberg's work on personality disorders (Kernberg, 1984), Ferenczi's theory on trauma (1932) and all the work the Ferenczi Association was doing in Italy (Bonomi and Borgogno, 2001) and internationally (Aron and Harris, 2005; Rachman, 1997), Schore's developmental intersubjective work came all together in the book I wrote (Mucci, 2013) actually to convince the Italian Ministry of Education that I could move from teaching English Literature to Clinical Psychology and now have given rise to my last project on personality disorders and affect regulation therapy (*Borderline bodies*; Mucci, 2018). Most of my present Ferenczi friends or companion psychoanalytic voyagers or explorers were drawn to me by my first book on trauma written in English first and only afterwards in Italian, *Beyond Individual and Collective Trauma* (Karnac; 2013, which became *Trauma e perdono* in 2014) and we are still moving together to explore new territories, and I am very grateful to each one of them for that.

References

Aron, L. and Harris, A. (2005). *Relational Psychoanalysis*. Innovation and Expansion. Vol. 2. Hillsdale, NJ: Analytic Press.

Bateman, A. and Fonagy, P. (2006). *Mentalization Based Treatment for Personality Disorders: A Clinical Guide*. New York and Oxford: Oxford University Press.

Bonomi, C. and Borgogno, F. (Eds.) (2001). *La catastrofe e i suoi simboli (The Catastrophe and its Symbols)*. Turin: U.T.E.T.

Chodorow, N. (1999). *The Reproduction of Mothering: Psychoanalysis and the Sociology of Gender*. Berkeley, Los Angeles, London: University of California Press.

Clarkin, J., Yeomans, F., & Kernberg, O. (1999). *Psychotherapy for Borderline Personality*. New York and Toronto: Wiley and Sons.

Correale, A. (2006). *Area traumatica e campo istituzionale (Traumatic area and institutional field)*. Rome: Borla.

Culler, J. (Ed.) (1988). *On Puns. The Foundation of Letters*. Oxford: Basil Blackwell.

Dinesen, I. (K. Blixen.) (1994). *Out of Africa*. New York: Vintage.

Felman, S. (1983). Beyond Oedipus: The Specimen Story of Psychoanalysis, in Davis, C. R. (Ed.), *Lacan and Narration. The Psychoanalytic Difference in Narrative Theory*. Baltimore: Johns Hopkins University Press.

Ferenczi, S. (1932 [1988]). *The Clinical Diary of Sandor Ferenczi*. Ed J. Dupont. Cambridge and London: Harvard University Press.

Ferenczi, S. (1933). Confusion of the Tongues between the Adults and the Child (The Language of Tenderness and of Passion). *International Journal of Psychoanalysis*, 30: 225–230.

Freud, S. (1905). *Jokes and Their Relationships with the Unconscious*. New York and London: W.W. Norton, 1960.

Johnson, B. (1997). *A World of Difference*. Baltimore: The Johns Hopkins University Press.

Kernberg, O. (1984). *Severe Personality Disorders. Psychotherapeutic Strategies*. New Haven: Yale University Press.

Kristeva, J. (1984). *Revolution in Poetic Language*. New York: Columbia University Press.

Lacan, J. (1966). *Ecrits*. Paris: Ed. du Seuil.

Laub, D. (1992). Bearing Witness or the Vicissitudes of Listening, In S. Felman and D. Laub (Eds.), *Testimony: Crises of witnessing in literature, psychoanalysis, and history* (pp. 57–74). New York and London: Routledge.

Laub, D. (2005). From speechlessness to narrative: The cases of Holocaust historians and of psychiatrically hospitalized survivors. *Literature and Medicine*, 24(Fall): 253–265.

Lifton, R. J. (2014) Giving death its due: An interview with Robert Jay Lifton. In C. Caruth (Ed.), *Conversations with Leaders in the Theory & Treatment of Catastrophic Experience* (pp. 3–22). Baltimore: Johns Hopkins University Press.

Liotti, G. (1999). Disorganization of Attachment as a Model for Understanding Dissociative Psychopathology, in J. Solomon and C. George (Eds.), *Attachment Disorganization* (pp. 291–317). New York, NY: Guilford Press.

Mucci, C. (1994). The Blank Page as a Lacanian Object a. *Literature and Psychology*, XXXVIII: 23–35.

Mucci, C. (1995). *Liminal Personae. Marginalità e Soversione nel teatro elisabettinao e giacomiano* (*Marginality and Subversion in Elizabethan and Jacobean Drama*). Naples: ESI.

Mucci, C. (1998). *Tempeste. Narrazioni di esilio in Shakespeare e Karen Blixen*. Pescara: Edizioin Campus.

Mucci, C. (2001). *Il teatro delle streghe: il femminile come costruzione culturale al tempo di Shakespeare* (*The Theatre of Witches: Femininity as Cultural Construction un the times of Shakespeare*). Naples: Liguori.

Mucci, C. (2004). *A memoria di donna: Psicoanalisi e narrazione dalle isteriche di Freud a Karen Blixen. (As long as Women Remember: Psychoanalysis and Narration from Freud's Hysterics to Karen Blixen)*. Rome: Carocci.

Mucci, C. (2008). *Il dolore estremo: Il trauma da Freud alla Shoah. (Extreme Pain: Trauma from Freud to the Shoah)*. Rome: Borla.

Mucci, C. (2009). *I corpi di Elisabetta: Sessualità, potere e poetica della cultura al tempo di Shakespeare (Elizabeth's Bodies. Sexuality, power and the poetics of culture in Shakespeare's time)*. Pisa: Pacini Editore.

Mucci, C., et al. (2009). *Le ultime opere di Shakespeare. (Shakespeare's Last Plays)*. Naples: Liguori.

Mucci, C. (2013). *Beyond Individual and Collective Trauma: Intergenerational Transmission, Psychoanalytic Treatment, and the Dynamics of Forgiveness*. London: Karnac Books.

Mucci, C. (2014) *Trauma e perdono. Un approccio psicoanalitico intergenerazionale. (Trauma and forgiveness. An intergenerational psychoanalytic approach)*. Milan: Raffaello Cortina Editore.

Mucci, C. (2018). *Borderline Bodies, Affect Regulation Therapy for Personality Disorders*. New York: W.W. Norton.

Rachman, A. (1997). *Sandor Ferenczi: The Psychoanalyst of Tenderness and Passion*. Lanham, MD: Jason Aronson.

Schore, A. N. (1994). *Affect Regulation and the Origin of the Self. The Neurobiology of Emotional Development*. New York and London: Psychology Press.

Schore, A. N. (2012). *The Science of the Art of Psychotherapy*. New York: W.W. Norton.

Shakespeare, W. *The Norton Shakespeare*. Ed. S. Greenblatt et al. New York: W.W. Norton.

Silverman, K. (1983). *The Subject of Semiotics*. Oxford and New York: Oxford University Press.

Stallybrass, P. and White, A. (1986). *The Politics and Poetics of Transgression*. Ithaca, NY: Cornell University Press.

Turner, V. (1982). *From Ritual to Theatre. The Human Seriousness of Play*. New York: PAJ Publications.

Woolf, V. (1941). *Moments of Being. A Collection of Autobiographical Writing*. Ed. J. Schulkind. New York: Houghton Mifflin Harcourt, 1985.

urney to peace and love

from priest to psychoanalyst

Benito Perri

I am the eighth of 10 children born to Vincenzo and Assunta Perri, both of whom were born in Calabria, Italy. Clearly my early years were influenced by the culture of southern Italy. My father first migrated to this country at the age of 12. He arrived here with his father and a younger brother, clearly in the hope of securing employment with financial remuneration. Such opportunities were not available in southern Italy. All three worked soon after they arrived, and my father never stopped working until he passed away at age 74. He made three return trips to his home town. On one of these trips he married my mother, who was chosen for him by his parents. There were subsequent return trips resulting in the birth of my two older sisters. Eventually my father brought my mother and two sisters to this country and they settled in Brooklyn, New York. It is hard for me to imagine what it was like to traverse the Atlantic Ocean on a steamship. After returning those three times to Italy with his father and brother, he alone opted to remain in the United States.

What was my experience to be the eighth child in a family of 10 children, the youngest eight of whom were born over a period of 13 years – an indication of how little maternal attention was provided by my mother, who opted to manage the family grocery store at the same time. Legend has it that my mother "popped" us out of her womb and returned to work the same day.

What is the effect on a child whose mother chooses to work in the family grocery store rather than devote her loving attention to the developmental emotional needs of her children? Normal maternal attention to her children was delegated to a woman who came every day to care for us as well as serving as a "wet nurse" to provide us with breast milk. As I examine my sense of self and relationship to women, I have to hypothesize about what my relationship to my mother was and hers to me. Did I expect every other woman I dated to provide me what I needed but did not receive from my mother? We know that to grow up in a healthy fashion, the infant and young child requires loving intimacy from his/her mother in a relationship in which both find satisfaction and enjoyment.

I ask myself, "Did I love my mother?" I examine my relationship to women to answer this question. As I have found it difficult to love a woman for who she is, I would have to answer that my mother's lack of satisfying my most basic needs made it difficult to love her or even see her for who she was. Again, as an infant in need of love, specific attention to my unique nature and character was absent, as best as I can surmise. Consequently, in no way could I have reciprocated a love which I never experienced. A humorous aside: When my mother attempted to address one of her sons, she would call out all our names until she got the right one. To detail the significant determining factors in my development I list the presumed absence of any strong love from my mother resulting in a failure to have my developmental needs met. My father expressed his anger in fits of rage and physical beatings, especially when he was drunk from homemade wines. I believe my reaction to this included (a) suppression of my own rage resulting in prolonged attacks of asthma, requiring many visits to the emergency room of the local hospital; (b) no identity of a healthy self; and (c) a need to find a career in my life in which I would excel (in competition with siblings) and receive the attention I failed to receive from my mother. I would like to emphasize that the example of my parents' initiative to travel to a foreign country has left a permanent impression in my psyche. I have taken the initiative to develop my personality and career choices in many different ways as will become clear in this chapter.

Today, as I reflect with amazement at how my mother consistently gave of herself to each of her 10 children in the most loving way she knew, I feel great love for her. She maintained her self-respect despite constant outbursts of rage from my father. The fact that all 10 children grew up relatively healthy and happy and went on to have successful careers and form their own families is a testament to the good-enough parenting of both my parents. At the present time, I have come to appreciate the love and bonding with my siblings (only two of whom are alive today). Try to imagine the extended family which may result from 10 siblings marrying and bearing children – in-laws and their families, nieces, nephews, grandchildren and great-grandchildren. Words cannot express the loving affection which I continue to experience with all these family members.

I will first cover my years from my entry into adolescence until my ordination as a Catholic priest at age 25. I summarize this period into my spiritual development and the obstacles to my sexual development. Over the course of 12 years of seminary life, I had incorporated into my sexual development that the life of a Christian should be motivated by love and service of others, particularly the poor and needy. Accordingly, I opted to spend the summer of 1959 when I was 23 in the city of Bogota, Colombia, where through immersing myself in the culture of the community, I became fluent in the Spanish language. This influenced the Bishop of Brooklyn, who upon my ordination as a Catholic priest in 1961 assigned me to assist in the formation of a new parish in the Astoria Houses Project, which housed a large Hispanic and African-American population.

What can I say of my sexual development from adolescence into adulthood? During the 12 years of seminary life I was in the company only of other males, both my fellow students and faculty of priests. The teaching on sexuality during those years emphasized the virtues of a celibate life and the suppression of normal expressions of sexuality.

The significant part of my formal education began in elementary school. As seven siblings had preceded me in the elementary school I attended, there was immediate recognition and acceptance by the faculty, many of whom had taught all seven siblings. Whether through genetic gifts or unconscious sibling rivalry, I excelled scholastically to such a degree that I skipped a grade three times so that I was 12 when I began high school. Scholastic competitiveness marked my educational career as I went on to achieve four degrees. I hold degrees in philosophy, theology, social work and psychoanalysis. While all siblings completed high school, the only sibling who completed college was the first-born, my sister Maria. These educational accomplishments were one clear path to surpassing my siblings. However, three of my male siblings have been highly successful financially and I have been conscious of that. Clearly, choosing the path to the priesthood was not a path to become a millionaire. At one point, I even took a voluntary vow of poverty.

After attending one year of high school at Brooklyn Technical High School, a highly competitive school, I consulted the local parish priest. This resulted in my decision to apply to and being accepted into Cathedral College of the Immaculate Conception. This was a minor seminary involving a daily commute for six years. Completion of these six years led to entrance in the Seminary of the Immaculate Conception. Completion of six years in this major seminary culminated in my ordination as a Catholic priest in 1961, at age 25.

Significant maturational achievements of these 12 years of seminary life included my spiritual development as daily mass including spiritual homilies, which influenced the compassionate aspects of my personality. From a secular point of view, I received an excellent scholastic education. In the six years of education in the major seminary, a major in philosophy was followed by four years of studies in dogmatic and moral theology, canon law, as well as four years of intense scriptural studies and the history of the Catholic Church.

In addition to these classroom educational experiences, emphasis was placed on our spiritual development. While there was a focus on the teachings of Jesus on love of neighbor, the teachings of the Catholic Church on the value of a celibate life were also emphasized. Such emphasis resulted in an almost denigration of normal sexual development. The denial of sexual relations with others, especially females, meant that for those 12 years of education in the seminary, classmates and faculty were other males.

This emphasis on a celibate life as the necessity in the life of a Catholic seminarian en route to life as a Catholic priest contributed to a failure to achieve mature sexual development. This had a severe negative impact on my relationships with women, as I experienced when I began interacting with females upon my ordination to the priesthood. To state it succinctly, this lack of normal development of male sexuality contributed to serious difficulties in my relationships with women. This continued through 24 years of marriage.

Once I was ordained as a Catholic priest, I was then in the company of female parishioners and female colleagues in some of my social action activities. As individual females showed romantic interest in me and I experienced romantic interest towards some of them, this provoked within me the most serious conflict in my life. I consulted my spiritual director to assist me in my struggles. He recommended that I seek professional help from a psychoanalyst. I therefore began a personal analysis.

On the other hand, those 12 years of seminary life had many positive effects on my development. Bonding with classmates in loving friendships has resulted in some friendships which have lasted 68 years. Positive aspects of spiritual development have contributed to a diminution of selfish behavior and a concern for the well-being of others, both on a material and a spiritual level. The spiritual journey begun in the years of seminary training has continued to this day, as will be described in the remainder of this chapter.

I began my personal psychoanalysis at age 30 and I remained in personal/group psychoanalysis for 30 plus years as well as in personal/group supervision for the same period. The benefits to my personal and professional life have been many. These can be enumerated in the following categories: (1) personal life, (2) relationship with women, (3) life as a parent. In my personal life, I have discovered many facets of my unconscious. Although this process of discovery continues, principal areas of revelation include the self-abasement and self-neglect of basic human needs which I had chosen in my unconscious rather than experienced rage toward my parents. As for suppression of my normal sexual needs, I hypothesize that this was the necessary accompaniment to my unconscious choice to become a priest which would confer on me a very elevated status in the local Italian community.

My need to establish a worthy sense of self and to compete with my brothers has taken the form of seeking approbation from others in all forms of social involvement I have taken in my life. I surpassed them in my academic achievements as well as excelling in three professional careers which receive much social recognition. My professional life has been expressed in my career as a priest, college professor and psychoanalyst.

Growing up in a family of 10 children, for all its drawbacks on my emotional development, helped me to be comfortable as a classroom teacher as well as in conducting group therapy. While I began training in pastoral counseling as a cleric, once I began my personal analysis, I incorporated as a new model for my personal life the example of my analyst and I decided I would become a psychoanalyst. Accordingly, I pursued a Master's degree in Social Work and completed two certificate programs in psychoanalysis as well as completing an academic program leading to a PhD in Psychoanalysis. I have held licenses in Clinical Social Work and in Psychoanalysis in NY State. Upon completing a clinical tract in the Master's program in social work, I began my psychoanalytic training at the National Psychological Association for Psychoanalysis (NPAP), which taught a classical Freudian approach, The analysts who most inspired me were a group who were trained by Hyman Spotnitz. Members of this group decided to form their own institute, and upon completing my studies at NPAP, I entered their institute, the Center for Modern Psychoanalytic Institute (CMPS). I have taught at both these institutes. At one point in my career I recognized a need for a training institute on Long Island. Together with a group of analysts, I founded the Long Island Center for Modern Psychoanalytic Studies (LICMPS). In addition to teaching at a number of psychoanalytic institutes, I have taught in the graduate department of education at Touro College in New York, where I also founded the Graduate School of Social Work.

I have also taught in the Graduate School of Social Work at George Mason University.

A major turn in my orientation both in my personal and professional life began on a week-long retreat with John Welwood, a Buddhist psychologist. I subsequently participated in a number of retreats with Welwood. Through him, I came to know of the wisdom of Thich Nhat Hanh and I participated in many retreats with this Vietnamese Buddhist monk. This has contributed to my establishing a daily practice of mindfulness meditation. I am currently enrolled in an intensive two-year training program which will lead to certification as a teacher of mindfulness education. The leaders of this program are two psychologists, Tara Brach and Jack Kornfield, who teach the practices of mindfulness meditation and the practice of loving kindness from a Buddhist psychology perspective. I have studied with many other psychologists who incorporate Buddhist psychology into their practice. These include Jonathan Foust, Pema Chodron, Sharon Salzburg, Jonathan Goldstein, Hugh Byrne, Rev. Robert Kennedy, and Rev. Michael Holleran. My interest in incorporating the latest findings in the field inspires me today to study Buddhist psychology. I am now incorporating the benefits of a mindfulness meditation practice into my clinical work.

While my maturity as a spouse developed in my marriage I did not grow sufficiently to develop a happy, fulfilling life as a marriage partner. What I have learned from my relationships with women is that I project onto my female partner the expectation that she meet the maternal needs I failed to receive in my infancy. I seek 100% approval and ongoing approbation of my basic goodness. If this was ever questioned, rage would surge. I believe that at this point in my development, I am in better touch with these issues and I am capable of forming a mature relationship with a woman. My aim is to contribute to a woman from the gifts that have matured in me over the years as well as to receive the gifts which she offers.

My career from the earliest years of seminary training has taken the form of a spiritual journey. I understand my purpose in life is to be of service to others. Consequently, upon my ordination as a Catholic priest in 1961, I was assigned by the Bishop of Brooklyn to help found a new parish in Astoria, Queens. In addition to my liturgical roles in celebrating mass daily, listening to confessions weekly, and counseling parishioners, the major part of my priestly duties took me on a daily basis into the Astoria Houses, a low-income city housing project whose residents included a large number of African-Americans and Hispanics. So involved was I that the then manager of Astoria Houses asked me to develop a community center which over the next year took over the first level of four of the 24 buildings in the Astoria Houses. I insisted on naming the community after Saint Martin de Porres of Peru, who was both black and Hispanic. Although the city of New York would not let me affix the word Saint to a city building, they did accept his name, Martin de Porres. Today, more than 50 years later, the Martin de Porres Center is still flourishing and I understand that it has extended itself so that there are now three other Martin de Porres Centers in Brooklyn and Queens.

I will name a few of the activities I brought to the program. The New York City Board of Education brought in a Head Start program. Many local teachers volunteered to tutor students in need of help. A number of athletic teams were organized. I invited nuns from the local convent of the nursing Sisters of the Sick Poor to offer health programs. In addition to my work in this community center, my spiritual journey as a priest included a serious and involved commitment in both anti-war movements during the war in Viet Nam and civil rights demonstrations. I marched in Jackson, Mississippi, in Washington, DC, as well as in Selma, Alabama, where I was granted permission to visit Martin Luther King Jr. in prison. I expressed my admiration of him for his tireless endeavors to obtain equal rights for all people. He thanked me for my efforts to fight for the rights of the poor and disenfranchised in my community.

Thanks to the Mayor of New York City, who was John Lindsay at that time, a War Against Poverty was initiated. This program encouraged local neighborhood groups to submit proposals for funds for programs they were to initiate in their community. I was elected Chairman of Qualicap, which supervised the administration of such funds for the Long Island City and Astoria communities. Programs like these, which return taxpayers' monies to local community groups, need to be expanded and be ongoing.

At age 84 today, I now live in an independent living community in Arlington, Virginia. I continue to treat a number of patients either in person or via Skype or Facetime. I conduct on a weekly basis a seminar for fellow residents. The seminar includes discussion of a chapter each week of a book based on Buddhist teachings.

The first two books studied have been *Radical Acceptance* by Tara Brach (2003) and *No Time Like the Present* by Jack Kornfield (2017). The seminar affords participants opportunities for spiritual and emotional growth as we practice mindfulness meditation and participants relate their personal lives to the contents of the book.

As I review my life, I am grateful for the many benefits I enjoy in my life. I am most grateful to my parents who gifted me with life and nine siblings. From the love of all these extraordinary people, I feel a deep sense of belonging to a very large extended family. With the help of many spiritual teachers as well as the guidance of the many psychoanalysts I have worked with, I have overcome deficits from my early developmental years. I have enjoyed love from and bonding with my siblings. I have been blessed with the reciprocal love of my two daughters. I enjoy my relationship with my sons-in-law. Together they have gifted me with five wonderful grandchildren. In my professional life I have been gratified by what I have been able to accomplish as a priest, psychoanalyst and professor. Many patients have to this day expressed their gratitude for the benefits to their family from their treatment with me. As I continue on my spiritual journey, I live with a sense of peace and love which I share with each and every person I interact with on a daily basis.

References

Brach, T. (2003). *Radical Acceptance*. New York: Random House.
Kornfield, J. (2017). *No Time Like The Present*. London: Rider.

Chapter 10

Wilderness and psychoanalysis

A journey of aesthetics, desire, and ethics

Joseph Scalia III

> Some see Nature all Ridicule & Deformity ... & Some
> Scarce see Nature at all. But to the Eyes of the Man of
> Imagination, Nature is Imagination itself.
>
> William Blake[1]

For me, there is an inextricable link between mankind's autochthony and his transcendence. That link has (in)formed my psychoanalytic journey for decades. I take a bit of liberty with the word *autochthony*, by which I mean that aspect of us which intersects at the place of our human, savage origins and our more recognizable self of civilization. Already, as I write those words, I see how much more I mean by the term, and then how immediately problematizable too is the term *civilization*. So, I will trust the context of my usages to informally define my terms.

As a young man looking for my way in a world that promulgated vacuities as the stuff of life, I intuited a path of Thoreau's before I knew of him: "Eastward I go only by force; but Westward I go free."[2] At that time, I had a certain fierceness and fearlessness, but no reliable direction except a geographical and a Leopoldian land-ethic one: that is, I experienced an inviolability and integrity, if you will, of wild land, unable to be improved upon by man. My wife and I fled the city as mere youngsters and landed quite by choice in the wilds of Montana, finding an opening onto something beyond language and the pretenses of society's various proffered wisdoms, its pretendings that had already made me sick. Here I found the writings, and sometimes the writers themselves, of the remaining lower-48 wilderness: Edward Abbey;[3,4] Howie Wolke[5] – imprisoned for his activism in Wyoming's Wind River Mountains and Wilderness; Doug Peacock[6] – who treated his Vietnam experience by numerous encounters with Northern Rockies grizzly bears; Scott Nearing;[7] Rick Bass;[8] Barry Lopez;[9] to name a few.

Before that, there had been my protective maternal grandfather, a building contractor, Birtles Langenhennig, who died when I was 12 – at which moment I remember uttering to myself "How am I going to live now?" And there had been the chaplain at Jesuit High School in New Orleans, a renegade Jesuit priest, Joseph P. McGill, whom I later realized was a liberation theologian – which, along with related critical pedagogy and liberation psychology and the imprisonments and assassinations its progenitors suffered, would later inform me – who weathered oppressions for digressing from his Order's discourse. Those two men, respectively, were my Oedipal and my adolescent guides into a world I otherwise had too pervasively experienced as violently punitive for my efforts at subjectivity, my efforts at expressing myself outside of its crushing cultural parameters. Both were gentle and kind; and both "spoke truth to power" while protecting me from that same "power." At that same time, Richard M. Neal, who was then a renegade Marine and Purple Heart and two-time Silver Star recipient from his combat in Vietnam and would later rise to second in command of the U.S. Marine Corps – had been relegated to the outback of Jesuit High's Junior ROTC (Reserve Officers' Training Corps), supported me in my rebellion against my enrollment in JROTC (Junior Reserve Officers' Training Corps); he would later also support me in my becoming Captain of that same group's Physical Fitness Team, even though I was no longer an ROTC member. How did I become blessed enough to be looked after by such souls?

In graduate school, I came upon another gentle and kind father figure, Richard Caple, a humanistic–existential student of group functioning, with whom I did an independent study that ripped open my intellectual and philosophical mind – a mind originally born in grade school conversations with my mother – and gave me the beginnings of an experiential–intellectual position from which to navigate theretofore *negatively hallucinated* mental incarcerations.

However, it took my immersion in the wilderness lands of Montana to find and solidify, albeit only partially and thus problematic, a masculinity that stood firm and secure living outside the social order. The wilderness gave me a place to stand, a place to make a stand.

Wet behind the ears, full of physical prowess that I didn't know I was conflating with wisdom, I sometimes ran roughshod over others. Lynne, the girl who captured my heart and held it through thick and thin, has been my partner in the affairs of the heart, in the wilds of the land, and in numerous battles with societal oppression. She is the one who has known best both my gifts and my blind limitations, the one who sees my best self, and the one who suffered most my immaturities and misguidednesses. The latter is the greatest regret of my life, although today, 41 years married, no such blunder exists and she and I now soar on exalted ground together, day in and day out.

Our core wilderness experience together still emblematizes our journey, and supersedes our faux pas. We lived the first two years of our son's life in a rustic and wildlands log cabin in snowy mountain country, with no electricity or running water, cutting our own firewood, hauling water from the creek, and hunting our own meat. I practiced psychotherapy two days a week, Lynne worked with the economically disadvantaged one day a week, and we lived wild the other days, she and I and our cherished son. Mingling closely with black bears – and now and again a grizzly bear or two, bull elk, spectacular deer, and cougars – we hiked and skied and backpacked untold wilderness miles in the most arduous and often untrailed terrains, and felt serene and secure there.

It was from that placeholder, during that time, that I found my way into psychoanalysis, and ultimately into manhood, constrained by mentors there, by our devotion to our son, and by Lynne herself, who found her own way to accept nothing less of me, and thus ensured an ever more passionate embrace of each other.

I stumbled upon a supervision group, held by phone, with Missoula psychotherapists consulting Robert Langs. Sometime thereafter, I discovered the Colorado Center for Modern Psychoanalytic Studies, and found Jan Middeldorf, Faye Peterson, Robert Marshall, and Phyllis Meadow. In my personal analysis, I found the space of the Freudian Pair, and a kind of wondering/wandering beyond any judgementalism; that is, I found my way to the wellspring of the unconscious. It was largely that experience that opened my mind to my first book, *Intimate Violence: Attacks Upon Psychic Interiority*.

Toward the end of my formal psychoanalytic training, I landed in a control analysis with Christopher Bollas,[10,11] and continued weekly supervision with him for five years, later editing an anthology, my second book, *The Vitality of Objects*, following his writings. During these years, I traveled to Boulder, Boston, New York City, Philadelphia, and London. Bollas opened my mental world to an experience-near reception of Klein, Winnicott, Bion, and Lacan. He provided me with a theoretical and clinical sophistication that is simply "in my bones." I cannot imagine my psychoanalytic self without that opening! And it was he who first told me of GIFRIC, and its Lacanian analysts' extensive work with psychosis. He also became a lifelong compatriot of mine, as well as a family friend. I remember well the moment my son and I sat next to each other on a couch across from him, as the two of them talked about universities my son might best attend. I grieve the day when one of us will no longer be traveling the world at the same time as the other. He continues to this day to be one who holds my feet to the fire. Plus, he knows the beauty of harsh, wild land!

I have never been long away from the wilds of Montana, and my family and society that have stood apart somehow from the rest of the world. As my son grew into adolescence and then adulthood, he and I shared an ethics and a physicality honed not only day in and day out but also during many long jaunts into wild country. Recently, I faced a most disturbing set of events which necessitated my containing all sorts of unnameable dread. One of my most comforting and grounding moments was a conversation about that with him, now Professor Joseph Scalia IV, already at 33 a traveled man of the world. Only this visit was in the Colorado Rockies town he now calls home. As he received me and rejoined my account, his own ethics and resoundingly unpretentious fearlessness filled me with a relief and a gratitude I cannot begin to describe.

In the midst of studying, practicing, and traveling, I also met and was deeply influenced by Paul Geltner, Traci Morgan, Jeff Eaton, and Charles Turk, all colleagues and all friends.[12] I should say that these analysts derive from differing schools of thought, especially Freudian, Lacanian, Modern Psychoanalysis, object relations deriving from Winnicott and Bion though deeply influenced by Klein. I have been chillingly filled with a multitude of *savoirs* hard won by these souls.

And most recently, I have been challenged by theory and practice *after Lacan* by GIFRIC analysts Willy Apollon, Danielle Bergeron, and Lucie Cantin, traveling to their seminars in Quebec over a 12-year period. My metaphor of holding one's feet to the fire emerges again here, as they not only made Lacan and their own extrapolation of him really available to me, but put desire, ethics, and aesthetics front and center in what had been my longest-standing blind spots.

Coextensive with those Quebec trips, I made some 40 jaunts to Boston, where I earned my Doctor of Psychoanalysis (PsyaD) in Psychoanalysis, Society, and Culture, in some ways interrupting work I'd have otherwise done, but broadening my apprehension of what the world is, and its profound and fundamental contingent nature. Deconstructing the world's derailments, and its transformations or becomings, were indelibly etched in me there for whatever time remains to me on earth, as I studied with Siamak Movahedi, an Iranian-American sociologist and psychoanalyst and Chair of my Department; Stephen Soldz – who was one of the spearheads of exposing the complicity of the American Psychological Association in torture of detainees at Guantanamo; and Jorge Capetillo-Ponce, a sociologist on the forefront of systemic injustices and exploitations suffered by migrants; and the felicitously renegade Charles Lemert.

In Boston, too, I visited often with Rocky Mountain-born and - raised philosopher Geoff Pfeifer, as we worked over Althusser, Badiou, Zizek, Marx. I later found the young Montana philosopher, Joseph Anderson, also deeply moved by Badiou, Marx, and Althusser. Confluences of land, confluences of thought.

In my sojourns among Montana, Boston, and Quebec, my friend, Charles Turk, now in his ninth decade, all along buttressed – and continues to complement – the Quebecois take-no-prisoner manner with his singularly understated way of making the unthinkable simply matter-of-fact. I have faced a few demons while strolling the sublime byways with Charles in seminar sites in San Juan, Chicago, Bozeman, Quebec, and Toronto. Charles has a way of remaining unflappable in the face of what seems catastrophic, an outside-of-time way of seeing and being beyond the imaginary and symbolic orders that can otherwise seem they are about to crush one's soul. He and I have alternated presenting cases to each other now for perhaps seven or so years on a monthly basis, extending me an ongoing and grounding analytic space apart from the everyday. I can only hope that I have approximated something equally valuable for him.

My dear friend of nearly 40 years, Bill Goslin, and my former teacher, Marianne Spitzform, another friend of four decades, are also crucially there inside me. Both fellow Montanans, they have been and continue to be among those who trouble my false certainties and shoot me out of the cannon barrel of closed thought into ever broadening experience.

And it was Bill, a longtime Bitterroot Wilderness Ranger, who, more than any other, taught me the ways of the wild, of the backcountry, hunting, shooting a recurve bow, being not only safe but at home in arctic cold, how to use a chain saw ... Bill has been my friend in my most troubled times, and has been a rock – a sob of gratitude hit me as I wrote that. A daytrip almost to the summit of Montana's Granite Peak, an after-work 30-mile hike along Montana's State Line, the Bitterroot Divide, those are but two of the many backcountry excursions that he and I have made.

What is it to have a backbone? The Blackfeet Indians called the Continental Divide in Northern Montana "the backbone of the world." It is one of the places my son and I have backpacked, both with others and just the two of us. Once, 10 miles from the nearest trailhead and without any cell phone or other connection to the outside world, 100 yards from where we would make camp, fresh on the heels of reading aloud together *Beowulf*, we encountered a large, lone grizzly bear track, evoking Grendel in today's backcountry. Chilling. Sublime. Beautiful. The wild sustains a human.

I am a "recovering environmentalist," a former President of Montana Wilderness Association, fighting for the preservation of unmolested wildlands. "Keep it as it is" was the ethos of Teddy Roosevelt and Gifford Pinchot. Looking back, I see that sometimes my environmental work has been true, sometimes it has been unwittingly complicit with oppression and exploitation. There are various ways one can be unwittingly complicit with those forces. I gambled on ethics in the following.

I met and befriended some who would do away with preserved wilderness as it is designated in the 1964 Wilderness Act. They are motorized recreationists and right-wingers, so ideologically different than my left-wing self. Yet I reached out to them, Mark Hoffman and

Kerry White. They challenged me, would only meet with me if I would go with them on a dirt-bike motorcycle ride in their version of the woods, their version of how the land should be used. So I did! And I didn't even wreck the bike or otherwise hurt myself, though they took me on mountain trails that were sometimes on the edge of my ability, to say the least. We became human to each other, and remain on good terms years later. That was one of my more moving lessons in civic life. I hope that some of my love of unmolested land found its way into their bones. Still, I must simultaneously face the ongoing assaults on wildlands conservation that I know that Kerry White is actively undertaking. I must consider that it might only have been his idiom, character form as opposed to psychical or mental contents, that allowed us a mutual humanization, and that he – as a Montana State Representative – may enact practices that are hateful to the land. How do I reconcile that?

Another such time, Lynne and I met with a white supremacist whom we thought had been responsible for vandalizing the building of Northern Rockies Psychoanalytic Institute, the small training center and analytic outpost in Bozeman, Montana that I founded. Although we fell out of touch, living in different states and perhaps his group leading him away from us – maybe he was "at risk" of becoming a "recovering white supremacist" – he and Lynne and I experienced, there too, a mutual humanization. How possible is such a thing on a grand scale?

What does it take to move a group away from destructive "basic assumptions" toward Bionian "work groups" that tolerate ambiguity and uncertainties along with "the inherent trauma of being human," as Christopher Bollas once put it to me? Most of my small-group knowledge (K) of this comes from existing in O, if you will, in psychoanalytic groups with anorexics and bulimics, whose symptoms, I believe, are mute protests against and deliverance from navigations of threats of interpersonal and social hegemonies and injustices, psychic disintegration, and the insatiable longing of our beings. I have led such a group of eight women now for two years and have been moved over and over by their tenacity in collectively insisting upon eschewal of facile basic-assumption space. To have done this has occasioned many, many painful experiences of manifold sorts that have no ready resolution or relief. A recent instance of this was an hour and a half of unplanned disclosures dealing with rape, rape culture, including not only being raped but also recognizing oneself as having raped. As one member after another shared their experiences of the unspeakable, we all were drawn imperceptibly farther and farther into another world, a being drawn into something beyond our control, a world of no safety, no illusion of protection from others, of also no safety and no illusion of protection from our own selves. This was the most painful group I have ever been in. I, and everyone in it, felt "shell-shocked." My work then was to sit with this agony that outstripped spontaneous assimilability. It was to bear a helplessness to provide relief, a borne helplessness that itself, paradoxically, provided the only True movement toward relief that was possible at that time. Receptivity. Reverie. Letting go of symbolic and imaginary markers of security. And being then and there nonetheless, or rather, precisely then and there secure, secure in helplessness, and horror, and unbearable pain. That was what mattered. That is what so often is the Thing that matters!

I wrote the above paragraph before and after a pit stop in rural Wyoming en route to Colorado for Thanksgiving with our son and daughter-in-law and granddaughter. In an unappealing concrete lot, crouching down to the level of and cuddling with our two Siberian Huskies, waiting for Lynne and feeling her presence, I was transported with those beautiful and dear otherworldly wolf-dogs to a plane of being that is exultant but cannot be described.

Two years ago, in response to four suicides by hanging by belt, of two teens and two adults over a several week period in the 7500 population Livingston, Montana – where Lynne is undauntable and inspirational Principal of now both the high school and middle school – and after a Confederate flag demonstration at another time of the year, we held "town hall" meetings. A local psychologist, Rachel Jergenson, and Lynne and I facilitated these meetings. Each was initially filled with a great deal of enmity and contempt and outrage expressed and seeking targets of blame; but each was filled, too, with hope and a wish to transcend simplicity and hatred and to find collective respect. The latter won out. I later learned that Christopher Bollas's forthcoming book, *Meaning and Melancholia*, will address precisely such waters as those we navigated above, arguing that democracy is not only a political concept but also a theory of mind.

When might a group be able to give up its Kleinian paranoid–schizoid positions and its members individually and collectively tolerate the angst of independent thought?

My son comes again to my mind, both social critic and engineer that he is; and his wife, Nikki, also an engineer and a social critic. Over some years now, they have often tempered some of my impulsively interpreted *faux* left positions by filling in left-out nuanced, transformative considerations that did not fit the party line. What does it take for any of us to stand corrected by information that had theretofore existed only in darkness for us? What does it take for a psychoanalyst to speak to and be received by an other who is so deceived?

When Lynne and I first came to Montana, once, after a rift had momentarily struck us, I went out into –20°F, crystal clear skies below a Milky Way I reached out and touched, and an enormous canyon on the horizon, backlit by the universe. I lay there, knowing how easily I could freeze to death and feeling the gift of life's ephemerality.

The ability to contain powerful and disturbing emotion, to move from simplicity and easy and selfishly gratifying discharge of emotion and blame to embracing ambiguity and not-knowing, with attendant aloneness and at times the remorse and mourning of discovering one's own destructivity when it had been thought otherwise: these are some of the crucial and vital capacities of the psychoanalyst that are also necessary to a social life of a collective that can evolve and advance. To know well, to be serene even in the knowledge of one's own damaging errors and those of a society, these are part of what has grown in me in the life of the West, both its wildlands and its wild societal life.

Those first two years of our son's life, we lived tucked in to a canyon so narrow and whose walls were so high that the sun did not touch our cabin for a full month of winter. Two thousand feet up on one side, three thousand on the other. There I decided to take a midnight pee off the porch, not even though I encountered a black bear 20 feet away looking right at me, but because he was there! There too we encountered mountain lions on two occasions. I stalked to within literally arm's length of two large bull elk on our "lower" ridgetop, reached without the aid of trails.

Felling giant tamarack snags on steep hillsides, bringing in the year's firewood, running now some 85,000 miles – an embodiedness begun in latency on a sole 20-mile hike alone with my father for a Boy Scouts merit badge across the city of New Orleans and back, a father who also embodied a matter-of-fact and indomitable determination in life ... The coldest wind-chill weather I have ever encountered was three days' worth of –80°F in the Missoula Valley, where the wind was unrelenting and the air was biting to breathe. One's skin unexposed could become frostbitten in no time at all. Again, because of, not in spite of, this historic cold and blowing snow, I ran – bundled up to be sure! – 20 miles in those three days. It was as though running on the moon, or some lone planet where marginal living conditions would make life barely tenable moment to moment. Another time, in the Crazy Mountains, a friend asked when I whisked off my pack at the sudden sight of two black bears 50 yards away clashing their jaws together if I were getting out bear spray; I said, "No! My camera." Such times have always given me an aliveness that I think must be akin to D. W. Winnicott's meaning in his, "Oh God; let me be alive when I die!"

How blessed I have been to have been welcomed by persons like James Grotstein and Michael Eigen, both of whom I lunched with, in their respective hometowns, their graciously helping me form links between my wild Montana and their urban psychoanalytic worlds. I recall clearly James Grotstein driving me around in his little, restored convertible Jaguar sports car, zooming through traffic in his Los Angeles, the wild man in him emerging from his erudite self!

I look back on my adulthood and feel a mourning for so many of my actions and thoughts that robbed me, and others around me. Yet that is inextricably part of my *savoir* now. It has aided a capacity to leave always open the possibility that I am being blind and presumptuous, and to be comfortable discovering the times that I am, that is, to not efface myself then but rather to simply caress my humanity, my humility. This is crucially part of holding others' feet to the fire! Constraining one and oneself to full speech.

Plato's *forms*, Kant's *noumena*, Lacan's Real, post-Lacanians' *hors langage*, Bion's "O," Freud's *beyond the pleasure principle*. There are always "thoughts without a thinker" to be heard, if only we can listen. There is an insatiable longing in humans that most of us mis-identify and search in vain after objects to gratify it, terminal objects leading ultimately nowhere. Leaving the grip of this dead-end behind and embracing the human quest has made all the difference! It has allowed me to comfortably know and notice the moments of flight into primitive thought and its easy access to gratifications like arrogance and like contempt or dismissal of others, and to easily return to complexity and its phenomenal sequelae like ambiguity, love, humility, gratitude, and subtlety. That is, living in a space that is "outside the social order," where the greatest joy is found beyond the pleasure principle, freed from society's inculcations of what I should desire, brings me back again to the wild.

Imagine oneself suddenly living in a civilization wholly dissimilar to one's own. Imagine living on a planet nothing like what we find beautiful about our own. Where would one's center be found? To fully embrace what we cherish, while being free to imagine an entirely different cherishable life: then one's self has nothing especially to do with the things with which one identifies, nothing much to do with inculcated objects of desire or morality! Freedom to dream, and to be, in the profoundest of psychoanalytic meanings of the terms!

It's another paradox that the less I need to be knowledgeable, the more I live in Truth and the more I truly love. The less I am me, the more I am myself! The less I am identified with anything, the more I cherish the ephemeral beings and things around me. The less I need to know, the more I know. The less I must be right, the more Faith I have in Truth itself, the more settled in I am to at-one-ment, or becoming O. The less I try to be a psychoanalyst, the more I am a psychoanalyst!

Notes

1 Blake, W. (2015 [1906]). *The Letters of William Blake*. London: Forgotten Books.
2 Thoreau, Henry David (2010 [1862]). *Walking*. Cricket House Books.
3 Abbey, Edward. (1968). *Desert Solitaire*. New York: Touchstone Press.
4 Abbey, Edward. (1975). *The Monkey Wrench Gang*. New York: HarperCollins Publishers.
5 Wolke, Howie. (1991). *Wilderness on the Rocks*. A Ned Ludd Book.
6 Peacock, Doug. (1990). *The Grizzly Years: In Search of an American Wilderness*. New York: Henry Holt & Company.
7 Nearing, Scott, and Nearing, Helen. (1970). *Living the Good Life*. New York: Schocken Books, Inc.

8 Bass, Rick. (1991). *Winter: Notes from Montana.* New York: Houghton Mifflin Company.
9 Lopez, Barry. (1978). *Of Wolves and Men.* New York: Scribner.
10 Bollas, Christopher. (1989). *The Shadow of the Object: Psychoanalysis of the Unthought Known.* New York: Columbia University Press.
11 Bollas, Christopher. (forthcoming). *Meaning and Melancholia.*
12 Geltner, Turk, Eaton, and Bollas all traveled to Montana to lead seminars at the Northern Rockies Psychoanalytic Institute, pushing into the interstices of the hegemonic and oppressive mental health ideology of the day.

Chapter 11

My path to and within psychoanalysis

Frank Yeomans

The question of my route to psychoanalysis involves not only my path but also, to some degree, the way psychoanalysis has evolved over the years. My path began during my years working toward a PhD in French literature at Yale. Earlier, in college in the late 1970s, my choice of a major had been guided more by what I enjoyed studying than by practical career plans. French literature appealed to me for many reasons but mostly because, like other great bodies of literature, it was a window into the heart and mind. The French Department at my college, Harvard, while solid, was not at the avant garde of the field, but allowed me to get a good foundation in that area of study. However, it did not prepare me for something of a shock when I moved on to the more sophisticated Department of Romance Languages and Literature at Yale to find that the traditions of literary study that had led me to the field were considered outdated and irrelevant. Studying literature to understand the human experience, society, and history had been replaced by the deconstructionist movement. As I look back at this now, it is hard to imagine that major academic departments had become dominated by faculty who promulgated that the future of literary analysis was to proudly undo the meaning of texts – and yet this tradition lives on even now in some ways. Before losing the thread of this article, it is important to explain that my escape from an intellectual movement that seemed both inexplicably dense and ultimately nihilistic was to read Freud. And yet ... the origins of the deconstructionist movement – Ferdinand de Saussure's linguistic theory – still resonate in my understanding of our psyche's indirect grasp of experience: it does seem to be fundamentally true that our experience of reality is inevitably mediated by the symbols of language.

Part of my work in graduate school included my first readings of Freud: Dora, Anna O, the Essays on Infantile Sexuality, and the Interpretation of Dreams. The discovery of these texts was a turning point that, combined with a number of other events, led to my leaving the field of literature after completing my PhD and moving on to medical school to become a psychiatrist. The most personal event motivating my decision was witnessing the manic episode of a long-time friend. She had come to visit in New Haven and, over the course of a weekend, had become increasingly manic: rapid, loud speech lasting all night long. She was hospitalized. This experience drew me toward the idea of working to help those with mental illness (with, at the time, little to no awareness that psychoanalysis would not do much for a full-blown manic episode).

A second event was meeting a man who would become a life-long mentor: Stanley Leavy. Stan was a senior analyst at the Western New England Psychoanalytic Institute who was curious enough, open-minded enough, and humble enough to audit a graduate student seminar in the French department because it was the only place at Yale then to learn about Jacques Lacan. I got to know Stan, told him about my growing interest in working clinically in psychoanalysis and received his encouragement about applying to medical school. But the coast did not seem clear for a number of reasons, including my being gay, which I worried would bar me from the career of psychoanalyst. I was discussing my concern about whether I should come out to Stan with a close friend; she said "I don't think you have a choice. My boyfriend's in analysis with Dr. Leavy and has told him all about you." It was my good fortune that Stan was particularly open-minded for an analyst of his day.

A third event during my years in graduate school that had an impact on my thinking about psychoanalysis was the influence, mostly negative, of Jacques Lacan. Lacan's writings were prized by the avant garde in the French Department. I could get through "Le stade du miroir" and "le séminaire sur 'la Lettre Volée'," but much of the rest of Lacan seemed impenetrable. The sense of obscurity only increased when I attended, along with 500 others, his "seminar" in Paris when studying there from 1974 to 1975. That year was a turning point. Thoughts of changing my career from literature to psychology or psychiatry took center stage. In order to better inform the decision, I enrolled in all the courses needed to get an undergraduate degree (D.E.U.G.) in psychology at the University of Paris. In addition, I worked as a volunteer in a psychiatric hospital, helping the woman who offered patients a form of poetry therapy and psychodrama. That practical experience reinforced my questioning of the obscurity of a Lacanian approach, in contrast to the stark suffering I saw in the patients, and led me to decide to pursue psychiatry rather than psychology because of the increasing role – now unfortunately overemphasized – of medication in mental health.

Upon return to the US, it took two years to complete my PhD while simultaneously taking pre-med courses and applying to medical schools. My dissertation was a psychoanalytic reading of Flaubert's short stories, *Les Trois Contes*, which I recommend to anyone who has not read them. The first, *Un Coeur Simple*, continues to fascinate me as, among other things, it challenges the reader on whether to respect or question defense mechanisms. During those last years in graduate school, I had been awarded the Mark Kanzer Fellowship for combined work in psychoanalysis and the humanities, a fellowship that included attending the first-year curriculum of the Western New England Psychoanalytic Institute. The curriculum focused mostly on key texts of Freud and greatly enhanced my interest in his work. My presence as a non-MD in the seminars was not welcomed by all the analytic candidates at the Institute. It was an experience of the rigid boundaries of institutional psychoanalysis. I began to get used to my role as an outsider in relation to the field.

I should mention my own experience of therapy as another factor in my route to psychoanalytic work. I began as a senior in college and continued for part of my time in graduate school. The three trainee therapists who treated me over those years seemed to be a combination of Rogersian and Freudian and helped me a great deal with the "ego-dystonic homosexuality" that had brought me to therapy. However, much more important than that was the introduction to exploring my unconscious.

I went from graduate school at Yale to that university's School of Medicine. It was the ideal medical school for me because of a strong psychiatry faculty that included many analysts: Ted and Ruth Lidz, Marshall Edelson, Samuel Ritvo, Sid Blatt, Richard Isay, Richard Munich, William Sledge, Betsy Brett, Sid Phillips, and Harriet Wolf, among others. Upon finishing medical school, it was tempting to continue at Yale for my psychiatric residency, but I was drawn to New York by my partner, now husband, a psychologist I met in 1976 who had come from Argentina.

My psychiatric residency was at the Payne Whitney Clinic (PWC) of the New York Hospital–Cornell Medical Center (now the New York Presbyterian Hospital–Weill Cornell Medical College). This department of psychiatry provided the opportunity to learn from some of the best psychoanalysts in the field: Robert Michels, Arnold Cooper, Otto Kernberg, Ted Shapiro, and Dan Stern, among others. A major decision with regard to my future in analysis came in 1982 when I decided to begin analysis. Armed with recommendations from the PWC faculty and my Yale mentor Stan Leavy, I met with a number of analysts to decide on the best "fit." A dilemma arose because the analyst I thought would be the best was not a training analyst. It had been my assumption that I would enter into analytic training at some point. However, then, as now, I placed clinical priorities over institutional/organizational ones. I could not have guessed what a central role my analysis would play in my life. It has had three chapters. The first was my formal analysis – on the couch, four times a week for the first years, lasting eight years. In addition to helping resolve conflicts and inhibitions, it became a way of thinking and reflecting about experience, both my internal experience and what is happening in the world.

I have sought further therapy with the same analyst on two occasions since I terminated formal analysis in 1990. The first was around my decision to leave my academic career within the department of psychiatry, a decision described below, and on to a combination of private practice and teaching as part of the voluntary faculty. It seemed wise to explore this plan before acting on it to avoid the possibility of a self-defeating move. The second return to therapy, which continues, was linked to wanting to reflect on issues of aging and mortality. Each return to analytic work has opened up more exploration and understanding than I anticipated. Each return has also been a reminder of how much we inevitably leave unexplored as we go through our daily lives and how the mind never ceases to be a dynamic mix of wishes, fears, anxieties, and urges that need to be balanced as best we can. One particular balance seems to be between understanding defenses and respecting the need for them.

Thoughts about changes in the role of psychoanalysis in mental health and in society

By the end of psychiatry residency in 1985, my thinking had begun to evolve. It was clear that the role of psychoanalysis in psychiatry was declining but opportunities to do psychoanalytic work within psychiatry were still available. A commitment to working with the seriously ill led me to take a job on a long-term inpatient unit at the Westchester Division of New York Hospital–Cornell. While this career choice made it possible to continue to learn analytically based skills, it did not allow the time to pursue analytic training. However, my 10 years there included supervision with Otto Kernberg, Paulina Kernberg, Richard Munich, Michael Selzer, Michael Stone, Ann Appelbaum, Herb Schlesinger, and other analysts or analytic therapists. As I kept deferring full analytic training, I reassured myself that this level of supervision, combined with my personal analysis, was helping learn what I needed to know to be effective clinically.

One of the most formative experiences in my years working at the Westchester Division was two weeks spent at the "Leicester Conference" in England, the annual marathon experiential learning event sponsored by the Tavistock Institute. It is not an exaggeration to say that I have never learned as much in two weeks as I did in that exercise in learning about the functioning of groups and organizations and about one's own functioning within them.

The development of my career path has been closely linked to my work with Otto Kernberg. My first encounter with him had been as a psychiatry resident. His lecture on object relations and borderline pathology offered a conceptual structure for understanding personality disorders that continues to guide my professional thinking. My work at the Westchester Division of New York Hospital, where he was the Medical Director, allowed more regular contact with him. From the start, I became part of his study group on borderline personality disorder (BPD). That group was a turning point for me and, I believe in a small way, for the development of psychodynamic psychotherapy. In addition to Otto himself, the group included Paulina Kernberg, John Oldham, Ann Appelbaum, Michael Selzer, Lawrence Rockland, Steve Bauer, Arthur Carr, Harold Koenigsberg, and John Clarkin. Over the years, the group, which became the broader Personality Disorders

Institute in 1995, grew to include Diana Diamond, Monica Carsky, Jill Delaney, Kenneth Levy, Eric Fertuck, Barry Stern, Lina Normandin, Karin Ensink, Kay Haran, Eve Caligor, and Alan Weiner, among others.

John Clarkin's role was essential in the development of the group. He was head of psychology at Cornell. He had been trained in a CBT tradition but was intrigued with Otto's ideas and brought his talents as a research psychologist to the group. Coming from the Menninger tradition of the day, Otto Kernberg understood the need for psycho-analysts to get involved in research in a way that was rare for analysts in 1985. Even now, some analysts consider research to be antithetical to analysis and even blasphemous.

It was hard to imagine how important the decision to embark on research was. Without research to support it, psychodynamic therapy could not be taught now in graduate departments of psychology accredited by the American Psychological Association; nor could it be reimbursed in many countries whose national health services demand that covered treatments have an evidence base. The current emphasis on evidence-based treatment is controversial and I share many concerns about it (Shedler, 2015; Lazar et al., 2018). Principal among those concerns are (1) that real patients are more complex than the subjects in many randomized controlled trials (RCTs) that, in their effort to study a single disease entity, screen out patients who may be more representative of those encountered in clinical practice, and (2) that it is much more difficult to rate and study the complex processes central to a psychoanalytic understanding of the mind (e.g., the impact of the therapist's interpretations or the level of the patient's defenses) in contrast to the more concrete elements of cognitive behavioral therapy (e.g., assigning homework or counting symptomatic behavior). In spite of these reservations, I believe research has advanced our field and can do so more successfully as more sophisticated research methods are developed.

Our group's research efforts were complicated by the evolving landscape throughout the field of mental health and, in particular, at the National Institute of Mental Health (NIMH). Our study group received some funding for a pilot study but, with time, the NIMH, under Thomas Insel, turned largely away from treatment research and toward brain research; it awarded the little money it allotted in the area of treatment to CBT research. Our group began to increase its involvement in research just as the door for government-sponsored funding started to close. In a way that reminds me of what we hear of Florence in the Renaissance, our main funding for research has come from private benefactors: the BPD Research Fund and the Dworman organization.

The RCT we carried out in the early 2000s (Levy et al., 2006; Clarkin et al., 2007), put us on the map of evidence-based treatments. It was in organizing that research that we were forced to come up with a name for the psychoanalytically based treatment we had developed for borderline personality. I say "forced to come up with a name" because Otto Kernberg always considered his work an extension of the application of psychoanalytic work and not a separate form of therapy. That view remains accurate. However, the rigor of the research world requires that a treatment be manualized (described in a systematic way) and that the therapists who provide the treatment in a study can be rated for adherence to the treatment model. Such rigor requires defining the boundaries of the treatment and naming it. Based on the nature of the work, we chose to call it Transference-Focused Psychotherapy (TFP; Clarkin, Yeomans & Kernberg, 1999, 2006; Yeomans, Clarkin & Kernberg, 2015).

By the time we completed our RCT, we had begun to teach in other countries. Colleagues in Munich and Vienna carried out a second RCT (Doering et al., 2010). The publication of that study led to formal recognition of TFP as an "evidence-based treatment."

As I moved on in the field, my approach to psychoanalytic thinking became more focused on the object relations and structural model as developed by Kernberg's carrying forward the work of Fairbairn, Klein, Jacobsen, and others. While one of Kernberg's main contributions to the field of psychoanalysis was to propose a bridge between object relations theory and ego psychology (Kernberg, 1980), the object relations perspective seemed especially to resonate with working with patients with severe personality disorders. As our group's work progressed, our understanding of the therapeutic process has increasingly appreciated and emphasized the importance of combining interpretation and experiencing the affect related to the material being interpreted in here-and-now of the session (Caligor et al., 2009). This has been quite a shift from my early thinking that the therapeutic process was all about intellectual understanding – an idea that suits an academic more than it does a clinician. Traditional interpretation of genetic material, as interesting as it may be, never seemed, in my own analysis or in my practice of therapy, to effect deep change in a person's appreciation of self, others, and their place in the world. Rather than delve into the far corners of the patient's history, it seemed, and seems, more important to have the patient's internal world unfold in all its intensity in the therapeutic interaction.

As the Personality Disorder Institute's (PDI's) work developed, I found myself at the crossroads between the world of psychodynamic therapy and the world of specialists in personality disorders (PD), especially BPD. Aside from my work with the BPD study group, my "day job" at the Westchester Division was on a long-term unit for seriously ill patients. Over time the unit changed from having a mixed population of psychotic and borderline patients to having exclusively borderline patients and my role changed from assistant unit chief to unit chief. That situation offered a rare opportunity to work with some of the most difficult cases in relatively safe circumstances with an extraordinary clinical team.

Being at the crossroads of the analytic world and the "personality disorder world" created challenges and opportunities. It may have been more comfortable for me to remain exclusively in dialogue with my analytically oriented peers, but the field of personality disorders became an increasingly rich area for various schools of thought to try to understand that particular form of psychopathology and develop more effective ways to treat it. This led to a sort of battle brewing in the world of PDs. The kind of work that analysts focus on – neurotic patients – was not at the forefront of funding by research organizations or insurance payers. The world of PDs became an important area for staking the validity of one's treatment approach – a battle that seemed to be almost won by CBT-based treatment models. We were going against the tide. Speaking at conferences beyond the boundaries of the analytic world revealed the degree to which analytic approaches were considered outdated and irrelevant by many in the field of mental health. The criticism of psychoanalytic thinking has, at times, been quite extreme. The publisher of a book I co-wrote with John Clarkin and Otto Kernberg in the late 1990s responded to the manuscript praising the book but suggesting that we "take out all the psychoanalytic language"; we did not. Colleagues in departments of psychology reported that they were personally committed to continuing to write analytically oriented articles even though these articles might *count against them* in their efforts to get academic tenure. Nevertheless, years of presenting at meetings seems to have convinced an increasing number of students, and even some colleagues from alternative models of treatment, that psychoanalytic thinking should not be relegated to the history of psychiatry. It seems that, at least in the area of PDs, the different models of treatment are now engaging in a mutually respectful dialogue.

Ironically, while others in the "personality disorder world" often looked askance at me and my colleagues and thought we were hopelessly vague and imprecise compared to a CBT approach, many of our analyst colleagues dismissed our work as too methodical and even reductionistic. While never claiming to compete with psychoanalysis per se, our group does believe that we can work with our patients at a level that respects the complexity and individuality of unconscious processes. Recent developments seem to support that belief. Some of our students in the residency program at PWC and Elizabeth Auchincloss, their training director at the time, wrote an article arguing that TFP is an excellent way for residents in psychiatry to be introduced to psychoanalytic thought and work in general (Bernstein et al., 2015). More recently, in addition to our teaching at the Columbia Center for Psychoanalytic Training and Research, we have begun to teach TFP at the New York Psychoanalytic Society and Institute, often considered the most traditional of American institutes.

While I tend to be an optimist, I continue to be concerned about traditions that are being lost. The prime example of this, in my experience, is the tradition of long-term psychoanalytically based inpatient treatment. The Yale Psychiatric Institute was an example of this treatment model. The model appealed to me since my days at medical school. It provided the challenge of intensively treating the most severely ill patients from a multidisciplinary approach that included exploration of unconscious conflict and the meaning of symptoms along with attempting to achieve major changes in the patient's life. My work on such a unit at the Westchester Division brought together an exciting group of colleagues and supervisors. However, after 10 years of immersion in this work, managed care appeared. It was hard to imagine its ultimate impact. The extent of the threat to long-term inpatient treatment became clear the day a reviewer said to me: "It would really help your patient's case if you could tell me she'd made a suicide attempt in the past week." It became clear that reviewers did not have patients' interests in mind. It was chilling. I left my hospital position when staffing was cut to the point that I could not provide the kind of treatment on my unit that I believed my patients needed.

Moving on from that position, I thought of the words of one of my supervisors: "The key to mental health is the ability to adapt to the circumstances you find yourself in." My colleague Diana Diamond, a psychologist, and other refugees from the vanishing long-term inpatient work, began to try to treat the challenging patients we had got to know during our inpatient days with what we referred to as the "hospital without walls" model. This consisted of twice-weekly individual therapy, structured with whatever treatment parameters and ancillary treatments (e.g., family therapy or treatment for substance abuse) might be indicated. In general, we have had success with this model. Nonetheless, the damage done by managed care to a form of treatment that had a long and honored tradition has left me very wary of ongoing and possible future threats to the survival of analytic work. In essence, the mission I am dedicated to in my career is to help the invaluable contributions of the psychoanalytic tradition continue to be available to clinicians and, especially, to patients. I think of the help and richness this tradition has added to my life and worry that economic and other forces threaten this type of thinking and work. Beyond the economic forces, it continues to be the case that many individuals, including many in the field of mental health, seem threatened by the Freudian revolution and the idea that forces within us that are beyond our awareness have a major impact on our lives (in spite of daily evidence to support that view).

Since those dark days in the mid-1990s when managed care was introduced, the PDI's experience has been more encouraging. Requests for training multiplied. Teaching introductory workshops has led to the establishment of TFP groups in Germany, Austria, Canada, the Netherlands, Mexico, Italy, Spain, the United Kingdom, Switzerland, Poland, Hungary, Turkey, Greece, Chile, Argentina, Uruguay, Australia, Israel, Russia, and China. It was especially gratifying to hear from our Mexican colleagues, based at their National Institute of Psychiatry, that it was the first time in 50 years that there had been psychoanalytically based teaching at their institute. They told us this was possible because TFP had established an evidence base. Another special experience was in Poland where our third conference there, in 2017, was attended by 1500 people. Poland, like other countries previously under Soviet influence, could not develop a healthy psychoanalytic presence during the Soviet years. After the fall of the USSR, therapists in those countries were hungry for learning how to practice analytically but, in many cases, those people understood the wisdom of focusing on psychoanalytic psychotherapy rather than psychoanalysis. This "jumping" to focus on psychoanalytic therapy in contrast to pure psychoanalysis could be lamented, because full psychoanalysis is a precious art that should not be lost. However, a number of reasons suggest this is a positive development. One reason is that, in most countries, the demand for psychoanalysis has decreased dramatically. Another reason is the way in which psychoanalytic work is developing. At the PDI, we have studied the process of our therapy as well as the outcome. In our supervision groups, we discuss the moment-to-moment interactions in the recorded sessions we observe. We also look at the big picture of the therapy: what diagnostic understanding do we have of the patient and what treatment goals can we jointly agree upon? It seems that in the course of this process we have helped deliver an analytic approach somewhat more efficiently. The time it takes for our patients to demonstrate change seems shorter, on average, than it used to be. As I write this, I anticipate some readers will find talk of "diagnosis and treatment goals" antithetical to psychoanalysis. However, it is hard for me to understand why analysis should be different from other fields where possible advances are seen as potentially beneficial rather than regarded with suspicion. It is, of course, the risk of dogma over science.

Over time, my commitment to focusing on the application of analytic techniques to those with severe PDs, and the time that endeavor required, made me finally decide that full analytic training would not be the most effective use of my time. I made this decision with regret. Nevertheless, I have found it possible to have mutually beneficial contact with my analyst colleagues and with analytic institutes. In 2012 I was awarded honorary membership in the American Psychoanalytic Association. This outsider (a theme from my analysis, of course) was invited in. I hope that my perspective can help advance the analytic endeavor. My position is by no means unique. One of the most important resources to have developed over recent years is the Psychodynamic Psychotherapy Research Listserv on the internet. Started 10 years ago by Andrew Gerber and Mark Hilsenroth, this online community includes approximately 400 psychotherapy researchers around the world. Many are psychoanalysts; many are not. One of the challenges for psychoanalysis as it moves forward is to define its boundaries. Tolerance is essential. When I go to certain analytic meetings, I question discussions of cases that present process with no mention of diagnosis, treatment structure, or goals – but there is room for that kind of discussion. Sometimes when I present, listeners question my use of diagnosis, a treatment contract, and goals – I hope they can agree there is a place for this.

As a way of concluding, I'll go back to the beginning: my studies in French literature. For many of years, I had thought that those studies, while personally enriching, were not immediately relevant to my work as a therapist. That view has changed. After spending a great deal of time reflecting on the "mechanism of action" of therapy, it seems clear that a major part of what leads to change is helping a patient achieve a coherent personal narrative. This may be especially true of patients with severe personality disorders who, by definition, have a fragmented and non-continuous sense of self. A key part of the work is helping the patient understand the dynamic resistance to achieving a sense of coherence and unity.

On a practical level, the education in French has allowed me to teach in that language extensively in Québec, in Switzerland and, to some degree in France. It is gratifying to hear some French therapists express an appreciation for analytic work that is more dedicated to clinical change than Lacanian analysis. On the level of psychotherapy as helping the patient develop a more coherent narrative, I have been surprised by a recurrent experience at national and international conferences: I have found myself in the position of giving a lecture that follows a masterful presentation of research, data, and statistical analysis. In contrast to this "scientific rigor," my message will be one of theoretical constructs still largely in search of an evidence base and, above all, case histories that tell the story of an individual. It is always a pleasant surprise to see that that level of discourse – even in the age of the brain, the need for evidence in the narrow sense, and the pressures of managed care – continues to stimulate vibrant interest and discussion.

References

Bernstein J, Zimmerman M, Auchincloss EL. Transference-focused psychotherapy training during residency: an aide to learning psychodynamic psychotherapy. *Psychodynamic Psychiatry* 43(2): 201–222, 2015.

Caligor E, Diamond D, Yeomans FE, Kernberg OF. The interpretive process in the psychoanalytic psychotherapy of borderline personality pathology. *Journal of the American Psychoanalytic Association* 57: 271–301, 2009.

Clarkin JF, Levy KN, Lenzenweger MF, Kernberg OF. Evaluating three treatments for borderline personality disorder. *American Journal of Psychiatry* 164: 922–928, 2007.

Clarkin JF, Yeomans FE, Kernberg OF. *Psychotherapy for Borderline Personality*. John Wiley and Sons, New York, 1999.

Clarkin JF, Yeomans FE, Kernberg OF. *Psychotherapy for Borderline Personality: Focusing on Object Relations*. American Psychiatric Press, Washington, DC, 2006.

Doering S, Hoerz S, Rentrop M, et al. Transference-focused psychotherapy vs. treatment by community therapists for BPD: randomized controlled trial. *British Journal of Psychiatry* 196: 389–395, 2010.

Kernberg OF. *Internal World and External Reality*. Jason Aronson, New York, 1980.

Lazar SG, Bendat M, Gabbard GO, et al. Clinical necessity guidelines for psychotherapy, insurance medical necessity and utilization review protocols, and mental health parity. *Journal of Psychiatric Practice* 24(3): 179–193, 2018.

Levy KN, Meehan KB, Kelly, KM, et al. Change in attachment patterns and reflective function in a randomized control trial of transference-focused psychotherapy for borderline personality disorder. *Journal of Consulting and Clinical Psychology* 74(6): 1027–1040, 2006.

Shedler J. Where is the evidence for 'Evidence-based' therapy? *Journal of Psychological Therapies in Primary Care* 4: 47–59, 2015.

Yeomans FE, Clarkin JF, & Kernberg OF. *Transference-Focused Psychotherapy for Borderline Personality Disorder: A Clinical Guide*. American Psychiatric Publishing, Washington, DC, 2015.

Chapter 12

The scarecrow's search for a brain
A gay man's odyssey for validation as a psychotherapist

Harold Kooden

History of this chapter

When Arnold Rachman, one of my dearest friends since college, proposed that I contribute to his edition of this journal, I was very interested. His idea was to present a collection of the unusual paths that some psychotherapists have taken in developing their careers. He knew that I had been one of the first White, openly gay psychotherapists in New York City since the late sixties and had been continually active in the local, national and international LGBT community since then. He also knew that I had been involved in establishing a movement for a positive gay psychology. In the late sixties and early seventies, none of the traditional, postdoctoral programs had the reputation of admitting openly gay candidates since we were then seen as mentally ill. As I was out of the closet, I made the decision not to apply and be rejected. I felt that, because of the homophobia in the field, I would have to create an alternative path for my advanced learning and training. When I accepted Arnold's writing assignment, I was primarily focused on telling my story about something that happened in my past—a unique piece of history about my search for professional validation. Much to my surprise, when I seriously started thinking about this chapter, I came to the realization that this one moment in my history was actually a reflection of a lifetime pattern of decision-making and of coming to new insights that are still ongoing at age eighty-one.

Shift in perspective

In talking about history, it is important to realize that, other than specific dates, all history is really a subjective story about events in the past from the perspective of the teller of that story. Though we would like to think that history is to be viewed objectively, no one is immune from putting their slant on these events in terms of their own interpretations, experiences and definitions of reality. I am saying this since I am writing about events that happened many years ago and my perspectives have changed over time. I was not necessarily totally conscious of what I was doing nor had I a full understanding of my actions. I just seemed to keep taking the next step forward. But for so many years, when I would tell the story of my life, I would stress the deprivation and traumas in order to elicit sympathy about how much I had to overcome. Though I generally am a positive person and am seen as optimistic, in spite of all my accomplishments, I could not help myself in telling how bad things were, which was really a "poor me" narrative. Over the years as a psychotherapist and author, I have developed a theory on how our lives become like a tapestry that has a discernible pattern composed of the many threads of our life experiences that may, at first glance, seem disconnected. Many times, this pattern is not discernible until much, much later. Sometimes the pattern does become clear until we develop new interpretations or perspectives. For example, about seven years ago, I was fortunate to be a member of a group specifically dealing with LGBT aging and spirituality. Hearing others' histories, I made a life-changing decision that I would start presenting my story from a completely opposite perspective beginning with one of the most significant events in my life. Rather than seeing it as the tragedy, I now redefined it as a blessing in disguise!

Early history

When I was fourteen years old, I was arrested for being actively gay. It was a clear case of police entrapment that was continually covered up by the police and throughout all the subsequent court hearings and sentencing. Because I would not give names, the book was thrown at me. (Los Angeles was a police state for gays in the fifties. If a man was arrested for being gay, everyone in his personal phone book could be arrested on the possibility of being gay, and if an adult was found having sex with a minor, it was either life imprisonment or permanent incarceration in a mental hospital.) Though the entire experience was devastating at the time and eventually led to my almost successful suicide attempt, it also paved the way for my leaving home when I turned eighteen and I was no longer a ward of the court. Besides not having to deal with the coming out issues to my family, it also gave me a clear understanding of oppression and a subsequent identification with oppressed minorities. Living in fear was a constant in my entire life until only recently when no longer was "homosexual panic" an accepted legal defense for assault and even murder—this legality has only changed in recent years. Though I graduated high school at age sixteen, my very low self-esteem made it easy to quit my first year in college and start working. (It is important for you, the reader, to realize that for practically every gay child, there was the constant feeling that there was a basic and bad part of themselves that had to be hidden from the family—hence the adage that all gay children are orphans.) In my early teen years, my immediate family consisted of a loving older sister, a schizophrenic mother, an absent divorced father, and a Marine sergeant, homophobic older brother. When I was four, he began his intense belittlement of me as a sissy, which began the new feeling that something was inherently wrong with me; a feeling that was further compounded when I started realizing at age six my attraction to men—a secret that I instinctively knew I had to keep hidden. In addition, I did not receive support for being intelligent. In fact, when I asked questions or contradicted adults as children can do, I was called stupid. Though I enjoyed school, I remained a B+ student even though I skipped two grades. So I grew up with the feeling that I was a hardworking, not particularly good student who always had to hide who he was from everyone, especially family.

Later, as I approached my eighteenth birthday, I felt that if I stayed in California I would be "smothered." I had no other word for this feeling but that I would suffocate if I stayed. So even though I was very scared and highly anxious, I took a chance and moved to Chicago where I had the possibilities of a potential lover. As I now understand, this physical move to a different life began a pattern of my being very frightened but still taking action in order to open new doors of opportunity for me. I did not see this as a courageous act since I was too scared and upset. (It took me many years to realize that courage is taking action while still being frightened.) I had made the right choice to begin a new life in Chicago without my family and this gave me the space to create a new world for myself. This is another instance of my changing perspective on past events. Instead of focusing on this as rejection by my family, I now see the freedom that this absence-of-family gave me to begin a new life without interference. Through my lover, Joe Reed, and his friends, I was exposed to a world of culture and functioning adults, so I became like a sponge absorbing and living in this new reality. Joe was a perfect role model for me in that he was a caring, insightful, very intelligent, openly gay man who had meaningful relations with his family. Though he was thirteen years older than I, I was the sexually aggressive one who pursued him.

After arriving in Chicago, I immediately found a job and we established a life living together. (Let me digress for a moment to present a singular incident that led to my lifetime of questioning what I am supposed to believe as the only reality. While on a job as a packer in a warehouse, I became friends with a coworker, Jimmy Smith, a Black, Korean War veteran. One night we drove to his home for dinner in order to meet his wife, Barbara, a schoolteacher. I was absolutely shocked at seeing the vast extensiveness of beautifully maintained homes and apartment buildings in this all-Black neighborhood, Chicago's Southside. Heretofore, all I had ever known of Black neighborhoods was the slum buildings alongside the railroad tracks on my daily commute to my job. This was the common image portrayed in the White press and television. Seeing this shocking contradiction to what I knew, started a lifetime process of questioning the "reality" that was being presented to me as fact.) After a couple of years of working, Joe and his friends convinced me to go back to college and pursue my childhood dream of becoming a psychiatrist. As I came from a family of physicians on my mother's side (two uncles and grandfather), I was programmed early to become a physician—when I was age five, my first gift was a play "doctor's kit"!

Academic history

Much to my surprise, I discovered that I did very well in the premed program at the Chicago branch of the University of Illinois. I assumed that I got all A's simply because I was a very hard and focused worker. I commuted to the campus daily while living in the home that Joe and I had created. In my second year, I took my first psychology class, which I thoroughly enjoyed. One day, we had a substitute teacher who struck me as very approachable and understanding. I explained to her that my goal was to become a psychotherapist after finishing my psychiatric training but I felt there was too much emphasis on physiology, psychopharmacology and the physical body. I wanted a much broader background in subjects like sociology, political science and anthropology. She told me of a program at the University of Chicago called The Committee on Human Development (HD) that was an interdisciplinary committee where the student minored in the social sciences, physiology and genetics as well as took the committee's core courses. These courses encompassed the entire life cycle, in which the individual was seen as a psychological being living in a physical body that was influenced by his/her culture/society. The HD student would also be able to take the university's clinical psychology program, resulting in a doctorate in Human Development and qualify to be a psychologist. I knew that I had a good memory and would be able to finish premed and medical school, but I was frightened of the idea of having to write a master's thesis and dissertation. That took real intelligence that I did not feel that I had. Intrigued by HD, I went for an interview, was accepted and actually received a full two-year scholarship. So from a chance encounter with a substitute teacher whom I never saw again, my life changed direction and I was now on the path to becoming a psychologist.

The next major and extremely difficult step was my decision to leave the home that I had established with Joe and move to a rooming house near campus. I knew that if I treated this next phase of my education as a commuting student, I would not be free to take full advantage of all the potential directions that might open up for me, though I couldn't explain it more clearly than that. I am astonished that I could make these forward-thinking decisions all the while beset by almost overpowering anxiety and abysmally low self-confidence. I was simply terrified, but I still made this decision to move out on my own and continue working while going to school. Luckily, one emotional support for me was Joe since he and I remained friends until his premature death years later. (In fact, I am still very close to his niece, Laura, whom I met when she was four and I was eighteen.) So began my ten years in HD that became one of the seminal influences for the rest of my life.

Specifics of academic history

In order to better understand my professional path, it is essential to understand the uniqueness of this program. This was the model that Harvard used for its similar program. The psychology department at the U of C was a very traditional one with the emphasis on psychopathology, experimental psychology, psychology as a science and statistical research. It was so traditional that, though there were gays and lesbians in the program, they had to stay completely in the closet or risk being expelled. This was completely different in HD where even some of the staff were known to be gay. (Let me introject a distinction between simply not talking about being gay but not denying living with a man, as in HD. In contrast, students in the Psychology Department had to hide and "date" and present themselves as heterosexual. So though I was not out publicly, I hid nothing about my lifestyle. It was not until later in New York City that I actually came out publicly in all aspects of my life.) Now back to HD and how it stressed the relationship among all the physical, psychological and social factors affecting human development. This was the first time I started hearing about the flight or fight response, the immune system or the possible connection between cancer and psychic factors. Class, race and religion were also studied as they influenced people's behavior—the individual was always to be seen in a socio/political context. HD also had core courses that focused on each phase of the life cycle with all its concomitant influences beginning with conception through childhood through the teens into young adulthood, adulthood and then into old age. What was also significant about each of these courses with their specific readings, research and theories, was we had to learn different ways of observing and doing research: from developing observational techniques based on theories on child development; from observing students in their classwork and their interactions with friends in order to make a psychological report, and from developing a guide to interview a three-generation family in order to understand family dynamics. In each of these courses we had to present a comprehensive report based on what we had learned about our subjects and the relationship between the theories we had studied and what we had empirically observed. So we had to learn different kinds of observational skills as well as how to integrate theory with practice.

Besides taking many classes in sociology and studies of social and class structures, we also had a number of visiting professors that were eminent in their fields, such as child development, cognitive thinking styles, genetics and abnormal psychology. This type of exposure was essential in expanding our thinking so that we could look at controversies and come to our own conclusions. One such example was a course taught by the anthropologist Oscar Lewis, who was known for developing a theory about the disintegration of a culture. His primary example was of a small town in Mexico that had been studied at the same time by another prominent anthropologist, Robert Redfield, another former professor of mine. My chosen term paper was on how two people could study the same town at the same time and come up with totally opposite conclusions since Redfield's research was a presentation of a theory about how a village remains stable and perpetuates itself! This is a perfect example of HD's emphasis on teaching its students to think for themselves and learn how to deal with what seemed irreconcilable realities.

As I mentioned before, I was working and going to school. One summer, instead of my usual job as a short order cook, I was able to get a job as a research assistant on an HD research project. Unfortunately, the pay was not great, but I was learning a lot about interviewing and how research was developed. A month into the job, I received a letter telling me that I had been awarded a renewable United States Public Health Fellowship that covered full tuition and a stipend. I had absolutely no knowledge of how I got this as it just appeared "out of the blue." You can imagine my shock when I found out that a professor of mine, Bernice Neugarten, initiated all this. After reading my final assignment in her class on adulthood and aging, she wanted to find out who I was since I had been completely silent in her class. She had gone to the bursar's office to read about me and found out that I was self-supporting, so she applied for the fellowship for me. I had never spoken up in her class, as I felt so intimidated by her. She was a brilliant lecturer and is considered a founder of the field of gerontology in the United States.

Her class was one of the most stimulating and illuminating ones I had ever taken. Of extreme importance was her research that stressed how people keep developing as they age so that growing old was a constant process of growth and development—a positive take on aging.

And contrary to current mythology, people did not automatically become conservative as they aged; they only became more of what they already had been. My final project, which was over 300 pages, was an analysis of a three-generation family in which I had developed a very thorough interview guide using a variety of theories on family dynamics and individual psychology. This meant using the guide to interview the two living grandparents, two parents and their four children. Needless to say, I did my very best on this project and yet was surprised to receive an A+ grade. Typical of me, I thought that I got it because I simply worked very hard. I am going into this in detail because she became very important in my career. She was a lifelong mentor for me, and in the late nineties, when I wrote my book on aging in the middle-aged gay man, I dedicated my book to her.

Her faith in me helped me to get through some very difficult moments in my life. When I finished most of my postgraduate classwork and had to start thinking of taking the doctoral exams and doing a dissertation, I was fearful that I could not adequately do a dissertation nor pass the doctoral exams. Though I had passed the master's exams with honors, I still doubted my abilities. Talk about emotional scars! By this time, I had also taken the necessary physics and organic chemistry courses to complete premed requirements. I could easily get into the U of C medical school and then later go back for my PhD. When I explained all this to Bernice, she wisely counseled me not to drop out of HD but to finish with my PhD and then, if I still wanted the MD degree, go to medical school. She was convinced that I would not go back for the PhD once I had my MD. She was very compassionate about what I could do and assured me that I would be able to finish successfully. She was now head of HD, and her support helped me make the decision to stay and go for the PhD—a decision that I have never regretted.

Academic work and psychotherapeutic skills development

Simultaneous with the HD core courses were the clinical psychology program's requirements. One option that I chose was to do a year's practicum at the U of C Counseling Center founded by Carl Rogers. Though he had left, the center still was a bastion of client-centered psychotherapy. This practicum involved coursework as well as actual counseling experience with supervision. It was my first exposure to an academic program that focused on how to listen empathically to the client and her/his experiences. Besides giving me an intimate glimpse of one form of psychotherapy, it also led to a research assistant job studying the process and outcomes of psychotherapy. After intensive training, my job was to classify a client's recorded statements according to four categories of voice quality or modes of talking. These four were 1) highly emotional, 2) tentative and thoughtful explorations, 3) storytelling and 4) low energy. As expected, the second category was the one most indicative of successful psychotherapy. None of these categories had to do with the actual content of what was being said. The number in each of these classifications was then statistically related to already established measures of success or failure in psychotherapy. I learned how to listen carefully to the client's way of expressing her/himself without being distracted by what was being said. As you can imagine, this was a learning experience that proved to be invaluable for me throughout my career as a psychotherapist. It taught me how to listen carefully without being confused or distracted by the words or extreme expressions of emotionality. In addition, it taught me to pay attention to what was happening to the client beneath the surface of the words or overt communication.

Another requirement of the clinical program was a one-day-a-week year's externship at a psychological facility in Chicago. Most of the available externships were at traditional psychological departments in hospitals or clinics. For the first time, there was a new choice within the Municipal Court , which I chose as I felt it would give me a different kind of experience than what I was already receiving in my classes.

Unfortunately, I was the only one from my university who made this choice. The assignment was in the Psychology Unit that saw all males who were sex offenders or were deemed "psycho" by the arresting officers. The psychologist who headed the unit had only a master's degree in psychology and yet was probably one of the most perceptive diagnosticians I have ever encountered in my entire career. He had developed his own testing protocol that consisted of a photograph of a familial scene, a Rorschach-like drawing and four questions similar to ones found in the standard IQ tests. These were given during the forty-five minute interview with fifteen minutes to write up the final report on the mental status of the interviewee! It was overwhelming to watch this man do all this and come up with a comprehensive and detailed diagnostic report. By this time in my schooling, I had already taken courses in administering and analyzing the results of Rorschachs, Thematic Apperception Tests and IQ tests. We had many hours to learn about test administration and analysis of the results with intensive supervision over a period of weeks. Now here was a man who clearly understood the fundamentals of these testing techniques and had reduced them to their basics. He had honed his analytic and listening skills so that his results were reached in a matter of minutes and not hours or days. Needless to say, I was extremely impressed with his abilities and forever saw him as a role model of perceptivity and sensitivity—someone to emulate. (Though I have never forgotten this experience, I regrettably do not remember his name.) By the end of the year's assignment, I felt confident in producing a meaningful written report within the hour allotment. Clearly this was another significant lesson about developing my skills in how to interview, listen and understand the complexity of the person in front of me without having the "diagnosis" as my main focal point. I learned how to let the "diagnosis" emerge after observing, feeling and not leading with my intellect. What a golden opportunity I had been given!

Besides this testing experience, another life-changing moment happened during this externship. One afternoon, there was no one waiting to be interviewed. The director suggested that I observe one of the juvenile courts. Since I was seated to the side of the judge, I could see both the judge's and defense attorney's faces. I had a devastating experience in seeing the overtly racist behavior of both the judge and the public defender in the different ways they treated Black and White juvenile offenders. The differences in sentencing was totally outrageous. For the first time, I emotionally understood and identified the similarities between racism and homophobia. I now saw with my own eyes how both Blacks and gays, regardless of race, were treated differently and subjected to a different set of rules than those reserved for non-gay Whites. This was one of those "aha" moments that has remained with me until today, and this awareness is still one of the motivating forces in my continued activism.

Due to my interviewing skills, I was able to continue being an interviewer on a variety of research projects in HD. A study of high-level federal executives in Washington, DC, taught me how to interview older, accomplished people. Following this project, I was hired for exploratory interviewing on a proposed study of new and seasoned psychotherapists. There were four categories of interviewees: psychologists, psychiatrists, clinical social workers and self-identified psychoanalysts. The assignment was to interview psychotherapists in San Francisco to find out what kind of questions needed to be asked to understand who they were. From the results of these preliminary intensive interviews, an interview guide and questionnaire were developed that were then used for psychotherapists in practice in Chicago, Los Angeles and New York City. My later work in these four cities gave me the opportunity to observe these professionals closely since the interviews were lengthy and sometimes conducted over two days—this was an opportunity for them simply to talk about themselves.

Though the book on this research was published years later (Henry, 1971), I had already come to my own assessments about the variations in this group of professionals. Regardless of discipline, there were those who worked all the time and had little time for their families. It seemed their entire emotional life was wrapped up in their work with little energy left over for their loved ones. Some were very focused on making as much money as they could, so there seemed to be little free time for any outside interests. The ones who seemed most contented were those who put limits on the amount of time they spent in their practice so as to make sure they had physical and emotional time with their families. One group stood out as being the most emotionally constricted in their lives and they were the hardest to reach as an interviewer—these were the self-identified psychoanalysts. Again, regardless of discipline, there were those who were very impressed with their power over their patients' lives, how much control they could exert as experts in their field and their strong belief in being the true arbiters of what constitutes mental health. Another characteristic that stood out applied to the ones who had been politically active in their undergraduate days and remained committed to their beliefs in terms of financial donations and/or pro bono work. These therapists seemed to make sure their professional work was not in conflict with their political beliefs and that they had a life outside of just being a therapist. Regardless of income or discipline, this group seemed both happier in their personal and professional lives as well as seeming to have a positive attitude about their patients.

Seeing such a conglomeration of professionals from such an intimate perspective, I had the opportunity to see which kind of professional I wanted to be. It was still not clear to me exactly how all this would manifest itself, but I saw what I did not want to be. I was also very influenced by a famous research study that investigated new disciples from a variety of schools of psychotherapy (Fiedler, 1950). Research showed that these disciples were found to be much more dissimilar than similar to each other. At the same time, the same measures were given to the founders of these schools and/or other old-timers from these schools. The findings showed that the seasoned therapists were more similar to than different from each other—the complete opposite finding for the recent graduates. So for me, knowing these results combined with my own experience in the aforementioned interviewing only made me very cautious about exclusively following only one school of psychotherapy, especially psychoanalysis. It also told me that to be a successful psychotherapist, I had to develop internal skills and a way of relating to my patients/clients in a way that could only come from actual experience, and that I had to have a life outside of what I did professionally. Though I was learning about the therapists' lifestyles and different therapeutic approaches, I still had to discover what these professionals did in their therapy that made them good psychotherapists. I believed that part of this learning would come from my yearlong internship. And so another story about the uniqueness of the U of C.

Though almost all clinical internships are done before graduation, the U of C permitted it to be done postdoctorally. I had watched so many of my fellow students do their internship while trying to finish writing their dissertations. The results were that they made little progress on their dissertation and they did not devote all their energies to their internship. I decided to finish my dissertation, graduate and then treat my internship as my first year of working as a psychologist. I had chosen to apply for an internship in New York City and felt that this would give me a base from which to look for a permanent job. I chose New York City as I had visited there when I was twenty and knew that this is where I eventually wanted to live. I also had another long-range goal in mind. I wanted to work for the United Nations in helping developing countries create their mental health systems. While I felt that the United States had experience in how to set up these programs, I was convinced that what constituted the unique mental health standards of that country had to come from the country itself. The United States could not superimpose its concepts of mental health on another country—each country had its own definitions. I felt that the newly emerging field of community mental health could teach me more about this process.

Internship

I was accepted into the internship program at Albert Einstein College of Medicine's Jacobi Hospital in the Bronx. I had the option to choose how much time I could spend in community mental health in addition to the usual testing, therapy and supervision requirements. I chose 50%—the only other intern out of ten interns who made a similar choice selected 10%! We were assigned to work in a newly created community mental health center in a working-class neighborhood, and it was also expected that the required testing and supervision would be done at the center. Though we had to attend our weekly intern meetings at the hospital and other scheduled meetings as part of the internship program, the other intern and I were seen and treated as part of the working staff of the community mental health center. As I was older (thirty-one) than most interns and already had a doctorate, I was accepted as a staff member and received minimal supervision as an intern. It was a trial by fire. Whereas older, trained psychologists were now being permitted for the first time to work in the emergency room in Jacobi Hospital, I was already seeing patients immediately in the walk-in clinic at the center. Though supervision at the clinic was extremely limited, I was outspoken on one issue, which led to problems with one of my temporary supervisors, an Israeli psychoanalyst. He had been helpfully supervising me with the dynamics of a Black couple that had been having marital problems. In talking about our last session, he believed that I had been inappropriate in spontaneously asking them about their feelings concerning the assassination of Dr. Martin Luther King Jr. the night before. Though the session with the couple ended well, he believed that I had no right to bring up this topic on my own and that I was violating the therapeutic contract. On this issue, I stood my ground and presented arguments counter to his. The final outcome was that he conceded that this was a cultural difference between him and me. This discussion taught me an important lesson about cultural relevancy and the dangers of strict adherence to absolute rules in psychotherapy, regardless of context. In many ways, the contrast between my experience and that of the other interns at the hospital was almost laughable. Whereas they were lucky to see a few patients in their last months of their internships and would spend weeks going over one Rorschach with a supervisor, I had patients and supervision from the very beginning. In fact, because of a lack of time, some of my testing supervision was done in the evening at my supervisor's home in Connecticut. The internship program required that all interns observe a family therapy session at the affiliated mental hospital. Not only could we observe this very skilled therapist, we also had the chance to talk in depth with him. Needless to say, I learned much from this opportunity. Not only was he skilled in understanding and explaining the psychodynamics of family interaction, he also effectively taught us to observe nonverbal interaction, such as how to interpret how an infant was handled in this family setting!

Another advantage of working in this community mental health program was that when I started looking for a permanent job, I was able to get an advance notice of another potential community mental health program at Lincoln Hospital. This was in a very poor Hispanic and Black neighborhood that was considered one of the worst slums in the Bronx. There was already a smaller, mental health clinic at Lincoln that was run by the Albert Einstein College of Medicine. This new program would be a very expanded program with storefront clinics out in the community as well as having a training program for community residents to become mental health workers with the potential of their going to college. With all my recommendations from where I had done my internship, I applied for a job as a line-staff psychologist. That I also spoke a passable Spanish also worked in my favor, as the majority of the clientele were Puerto Ricans, many of whom spoke little English. (Another benefit of the U of C was that, as I had anticipated working in a Spanish-speaking community, I successfully petitioned to take my required doctoral language exams in Spanish rather than the usual French or German.) Though I was hired, I did not hear about the certainty of the funding until the last day of my internship. Now

I could take a real vacation before beginning my first official job as a psychologist where I would actually earn a decent salary. (It had been a standing joke at the facility where I did my internship that my intern stipend was so low that I was the only staff member actually on Medicaid, as were most of our clients.)

While at this internship, I had one of those moments of awareness that woke me up to something that I could not quite figure out but knew that I was on to something important. I and the other intern, who was also White, were invited to an evening Christmas party by our clinic's director, who was also White. When we got to his home, we discovered that his wife was a Black woman and that the party was actually an annual gathering of her sorority. Arriving at the party, we saw that we were the only Whites out of probably 300 to 400 people.. Everyone seemed to be dancing, even one man in a wheelchair moving while his partner danced around him. I had never seen such a large crowd of middle-aged people dancing with abandon and having such a good time. Looking at all the fun everyone seemed to be having, I had such an envious feeling and I remember thinking, "They know something that I don't and I want to find out what that is." It took my coming out in all aspects of my life to discover "what that is!"

First job as a psychologist

If anyone had told me that the actions I would take on this job would thrust me into the national limelight and start me on a lifetime of prominent activism, I would have been in total disbelief. I have told you of my many learning experiences and constant changes; it is important to remember that I was constantly plagued by self-doubts, insecurities and feelings that I was not intelligent—I just had a good memory and was a very hard worker. In looking back on what I have written about my Chicago life, it seems quite ridiculous that I could not recognize my accomplishments. But, as I have said before, this is now from a different perspective. So I began my new job in earnestness and quickly saw gross inequities in how people from the community were treated, whether they were patients or staff. The vast majority of my patients were Hispanics, who seemed intimidated by the White professionals and were usually given heavy medications by the Spanish psychiatrists, who were known to only work half days but dressed "properly" in suit and tie. I soon started dressing more casually as it seemed to relax my patients, but then I was called into the administrator's office about my violating the dress code for professionals! I knew I was a hard worker and said that when as much attention was paid to the quality of one's work as to the way that one dressed, then I would comply. The administrator knew I had a point since most of the Spanish psychiatrists were known to be nonworkers; the issue was never brought up again. What further upset me is that Hispanic women were invariably diagnosed as hysterical, given heavy medications and sent home or immediately hospitalized, whereas the few, young White women were diagnosed as schizophrenic and immediately assigned to have psychotherapy.

I had a very strong belief in the importance of understanding and dealing with the world that a patient lives in and understanding her/his successful coping mechanisms. My caution in not superimposing my prejudices or value system is best exemplified in the following example for which I was almost fired. At our weekly staff meeting, I presented a recent case of mine. She was a Puerto Rican woman who was a devout Catholic and spoke little English. She had been referred a second time by her non-Spanish-speaking parish priest. Many months prior, she told him that every night after she went to bed, Jesus came down in a chariot and took her up to heaven where they had very enjoyable sex and he then returned her home. The priest was alarmed and referred her to our clinic where one of the staff psychiatrists, a Spaniard, diagnosed her as psychotic and prescribed Thorazine. She dutifully started taking it, but then stopped because it made her too drowsy and left her unable to take care of her ten children and also deal with her physically and sexually abusive, alcoholic husband. Her mother suggested she stop the prescribed medication and take an herbal tea from the local bodega that would help her sleep comfortably. She did that and her life went back to her "normal." Recently, when asked, she told the priest that she had stopped the medication but was taking the tea and that Jesus still visited her every night. So he referred her back to the clinic where I was on call that morning. As the chart had very minimal notes other than a diagnosis of psychosis and the prescribed drug, I carefully listened to her story and could find no evidence that she needed to take an anti-psychotic medication. Jesus only came to her after she went to bed. Her nightly adventure was pleasant for her and helped her tolerate a difficult life situation, all the while living in slum housing and competently taking care of her children. As the person on call, I was free to make any changes that I felt necessary. I told her to continue taking the tea and if she ever wanted to talk to me again, she just had to come to the clinic and I would see her. The only other time I saw her again was when she brought a friend whom she felt would benefit from talking with me. I told this story at the staff meeting as an example of why we professionals needed to understand the world in which a client lived. Was this client dreaming or having hallucinations? In either case, it was her way of successfully navigating through her difficult life situation without endangering herself or others. The aforementioned psychiatrist, who had a reputation of being very arrogant, was outraged at what I did and immediately went to the administration with the frustrated intent of having me fired.

I have gone into detail in the above story as it reflects a constant theme that is very relevant to this chapter about the different paths that we therapists take. What I did not realize at the time of this incident was that it also reflected on my own life. I still had not found any path in psychology or psychotherapy that reflected my own gay experience from a positive perspective. At this time, in 1968, gays were still seen as mentally ill and/or criminals, so our true selves had to be hidden. Though I was not out at the time, and had not been out professionally since graduate school, the Hispanic staff accepted me as I spoke Spanish and worked hard. I was similarly accepted by the Black staff that sensed in me a kindred soul who actually tried to make a difference in my clients' lives. In retrospect, I am sure they all knew I was gay and saw that I was a competent worker who respected the people I worked with as well as my patients.

The professional as activist

All these good feelings came in good stead when a short time later, most of the staff rebelled against the pay inequities, the amazingly privileged position the White and Spanish psychiatrists held and the evident racism in patient care. This eventually led to a sixties-type rebellion where sides were drawn and led to a walkout and the beginning of the creation of an alternative, community clinic. This led to a crisis moment when the administration advised the protesters that the police were going to be brought in to make arrests. One night .

during the protests, I was called to come in the next day in order to be arrested, as I was one of the few White professionals who supported this work action. I spent a completely sleepless night pondering my future and knowing that I was putting my entire professional future at risk by this action. Though I kept saying that this was just not the right time as this was my very first job as a psychologist, I also knew that if not now, when? So I made the decision that I would be arrested and when I came in the next day, the organizers told me that they wanted me to spend my time raising bail money for the arrestees. This action thrust me into a leadership role in this work action for which all of us were suspended for six weeks though, eventually, everyone was rehired. There was now a permanent demarcation among the professional staff between those who supported and those who did not support this work action. Because of this community mental health center's prominence in the field and its having won the American Psychiatric Association's annual award for best community mental health center in the United States, city, state and federal authorities were eventually brought in for a very thorough investigation—and some of the claims of the protesters were substantiated. Having made that momentous decision to put principle before job security and future, most subsequent decisions were much easier. Making this decision enabled me to start taking chances and not be too worried about the consequences, as I always seemed to land on my feet. This protest and work action eventually put me in touch with local psychologists/activists dealing with the American Psychological Association (APA). They had formed the Psychologists for Social Action (PSA). One of the cofounders was Doris Miller, past president of the New York State Psychological Association, who became another of my mentors and a lifelong friend. (She had a long history of activism beginning when she was one of the first professionals to stand up to Joseph McCarthy.) What was also relevant for me was that she was a well-known and respected psychologist who reflected my beliefs about seeing clients in the context of their entire life situation and not simply as a diagnosis. Through her guidance, I eventually became national coordinator of the PSA. This also meant synchronizing actions with the national Medical Committee for Human Rights—all of which put me in contact with activists from other health-care disciplines. This was the activist time when many organizations were cooperatively working together. At the same time,

I was starting a radical mental health organization composed of other mental health workers that was focusing on developing new forms or perspectives on psychotherapy. Unfortunately, I was still in the closet, so much of my work was seen as my working for others' constituencies. In 1970, besides our very intense weekly discussions about radical mental health, I decided to organize a weekend conference devoted to radical mental health theory and practices—a first in this country. This invariably meant investigating new forms of therapy that stressed looking at all the power dynamics in the therapeutic relationship between therapist and client.

At the conference we discussed much of this new perspective that was coming from the developing feminist movement—it was making misogyny and power relationships part of the dialogue about therapy. As I had already seen the evident misogyny in my workplace and the homophobia of professionals, I began to see the relevance of feminism to my thinking and practice. I began to understand that if a goal of psychotherapy was to raise a client's self-esteem and help them no longer feel powerless in the world, then it was incumbent upon the therapist to look at the power dynamics in the therapeutic relationship. The therapist, as authority figure, had to look carefully at how the therapeutic relationship perpetuated the one-down feeling of the client. Though this is now seen as part of the therapeutic challenge for many therapists, in the early seventies this was a revolutionary way of thinking. This was also the beginning rumblings of questioning professional homophobia and the pathologizing of what was considered "deviant" behaviors of women, mental patients and homosexuals (Kooden, 1987).

It was also at this conference that I came out and, much to my surprise, I did not experience any loss of standing or disrespect from any of the conference attendees. Another lesson learned about being honest about myself! I was now becoming more and more comfortable presenting myself as a gay man in a non-gay situation (Kooden, 1975). But having come out also meant that my future plans of ever working at the United Nations had to be given up. Though the first secretary-general of the UN, Dag Hammarskjold, was known to be gay and living with his lover, the current UN did not allow any openly gay person on staff.

Coming out and career choices

Having come out professionally had many ramifications that are very relevant to the story of my path to becoming a qualified therapist. I have been telling you most of the historical antecedents so that you have a better understanding of my particular journey. So far in this writing, I have chosen to take a more linear, unfolding approach in order to establish the foundations for what I eventually did. From this point on, my story will be more organized in terms of specific content areas (organizational work, seminars and workshops, readings, my writings, personal therapy and the intersection of community mental health work with the Black and Hispanic working class and private practice with White, middle-class gay men). This will cover many years but will, I hope, give you the essence of what I did and will continue to do in my never-ending work in trying to be a better therapist.

Another monumental effect of having come out professionally meant that I could not go into the postdoctoral program in which I was most interested—the William Allison White Institute. At that time, openly gay men were not admitted even though one of the principal founders, Harry Stack Sullivan, was known to have been gay. Luckily, this policy has now changed. I had also ruled out going to any of the psychoana-lytic institutes for the same reason as well as my feeling that I did not like the kind of therapist that these institutes produced. I knew too many gay men who had gone to psychoanalysts with the unsuccessful intention of changing their sexual orientation. In fact, I also knew a few gay psychiatrists who had completed their psychoanalytic training while never revealing their being gay to their training analyst!

In hindsight, it is evident to me why I made these decisions. I have consistently said that I did not go for advanced training because these programs would not accept me as a gay man. I was not aware of it at the time but there was another reason why I did not pursue the more traditional path. At that time, I was not aware of any existing school of psychotherapy that incorporated my own personal experiences as a gay teen or adult in a positive way that would be a valid component of their program. The concept of diversity training and theory had not yet reached these programs.

I wish I could have been more articulate to myself about this, but I was still carrying the scars of my past. In spite of all my bravado,

I was still beset with inferiority feelings and my own internalized homophobia where I felt I was a lesser-than male—I could not call myself an adult man yet even though I was now in my mid-thirties. So as you now can surmise, my search was not only about how to become a better therapist but also how to feel as a legitimate man in a homophobic culture. I did not feel yet that I was a full citizen of the country in which I lived—I was still seen as inadequate by my profession as well as the rest of the world. I had yet to locate myself. How could I value myself when I was seen as pathological, a deviant criminal, immature and immoral by my own profession? Luckily, I sensed that one of the ways out of this dilemma was for me to build relationships with the developing gay community and non-gay allies.

My community mental health experience had begun to teach me the importance of this sense of belonging and the crucial importance of being involved in community organizations for optimum mental health, be it church, social clubs, friendship circles or neighborhood associations. I had witnessed how these networks had given people who were living in deplorable conditions an ability to survive with a positive outlook on their lives. As I have said, these people had been living in an area of the South Bronx known as Fort Apache, which was considered the worst slum in New York City. Despite the poverty conditions with constant financial, housing and discrimination problems, many of the people I knew found sustenance and support from their belonging to some or all of these groups as well as having a sense of being a member of a family and/or a culture. They knew how to find their necessary safe spaces to relieve the tensions in which they lived. This developing awareness of mine helped me see that coming out as a gay man and identifying with a community were critical for my mental health. And so began the solidification of my becoming an activist/psychologist within the gay community and using what I had learned in community mental health work. I more clearly saw that being labeled a homosexual was only a signifier of sexual activity but being gay was an active identification as a member of a community. As you will see, this importance difference was a determining factor in my lifelong dedication to community building both within and outside the profession.

During this time, the Stonewall Uprising had just happened and radical groups were burgeoning all over the country. I was still the national coordinator of the Psychologists for Social Action. Through my involvement in the radical mental health movement, I became aware of a brand new activist organization, Mental Patients Political Action Committee (MPPAC), composed of previously hospitalized mental patients who saw themselves as belonging to an oppressed minority. After an initial screening, a radical psychiatrist and I became the only two professionals allowed into the group. This was another experience in hearing about experiences "from the other side of the couch" and incarceration in mental hospitals where all power was in the hands of the mental health professionals. As a result of our very open and revealing meetings and our protests at psychiatric conventions, I became further exposed to our profession's biases toward another group of people.

Also, around this time, a group of gay Gestalt therapists and volunteers had begun to organize a walk-in service for gays and lesbians (Identity House) that provided consciousness-raising groups, short-term counseling and referrals to qualified therapists. When I got involved, I was the only PhD volunteering in this service. I also believed that it would be important to have a state-certified psychologist on board. At that time, I did not need the certification for myself as I was working in a state-certified mental health program as staff psychologist. So I studied for and passed the state exams, which now certified me as a psychologist volunteering in this community organization. Ironically, this action later proved to benefit me personally when I wanted to start a full-time private practice.

Consequences of nomenclature change on homosexuality

Simultaneously, in this time period, the American Psychiatric Association was now being confronted with its diagnostic classification of homosexuality as a mental illness. Intense pressure was being put on them that resulted in the change in nomenclature. The American Psychological Association (APA) had yet to take this step. As I was also one of the cofounders of a national organization of gay and lesbian psychologists (ALGP), I was chosen to be the first openly gay psychologist to speak at the annual APA Council of Representatives when a vote was to be taken to establish that homosexuality was not a mental illness. One of my significant allies in this action was my aforementioned mentor, Doris Miller, who had a recognized voice at APA. The vote passed successfully with a later recommendation for a task force to study the topic of gay and lesbian psychologists.

I am going into detail about this sequence of events, as it is very relevant to the theme of this chapter on alternative paths to legitimacy. So APA created a special task for this study and I was appointed as the permanent chair. Once we convened, our group decided to make this a rotating chair so that the task force was a truly participatory one for every member—a new concept in the APA but one to which they acceded. Ironically, though the APA supported the creation of this important task force, it claimed not to have the money for its funding. We had to raise the research money through our own activist organization, the aforementioned ALGP! This APA task force became a five-year research study of gay and lesbian psychologists and their histories. The final report emphasized that APA had to take a more active stance on backing its new position on homosexuality and supporting new research and theories on homosexuality (Kooden et al., 1979). Thus began the years' long process of creating a new APA division on homosexuality as a legitimate area of professional study. As I was on both the committee to create this new division and then on the board of the new division, I came into intimate and prolonged contact with many other lesbian and gay psychologists and came to know about their experiences as professionals within the gay community. Especially important to me was my learning how other gays dealt with their internalized homophobia. The more I learned about their experiences and how they diminished their own negative feelings about themselves, the more it helped me feel better about myself. Of course, in retrospect I now understand better what all this meant to me. I thought I was just taking the most logical, next steps in my activism but actually I was trying to create a world for others that was not there for me when I could have used it. I was helping create a positive path for younger, openly gay professionals in relevant research, teaching and practice as valid members of the profession.

In the seventies and following the Stonewall Uprising, another movement was happening in the academic community. The Gay Academic Union was formed, which brought together gay professionals from many academic disciplines. I joined immediately and participated in many of its events. One day, as I was leaving one of its all-day conferences, I had another impactful moment of recognition where I realized that for the entire day I had felt as a whole person. Heretofore, at any professional meeting, I had always felt as an outsider or "not one of them" or less than. At this one special moment in time, I realized that I had been participating as a member of workshops and a professional leader of other workshops as well as socializing with friends. At no time during the day had I felt as an outsider but just as one of them. I had no sense of any contradictions in any part of my life. I have never forgotten the feeling of that blissful moment of recognition when I felt entirely as a whole, worthy person with my being a professional, a member of a community of peers and as a gay man. It had taken me almost forty years to have that experience. I vowed at that instant that I would do all that I could so that my gay brothers and sisters could have these moments earlier in their lives and not have to wait as long as I had.

Now, I would reframe that moment in time as my becoming totally conscious of the many failures of psychological theories and practices in developing a positive framework for the gay experience. As I have said before, I now see that so much of my focus has been to expand the parameters of psychological and psychotherapeutic thinking so that gays and lesbians (and now transgendered persons) are positively seen as part of the human experience. As you will see when I discuss the many groups, workshops and seminars that I participated in, I was always trying to expand my knowledge and experience AND find a place within which I could be comfortable and feel legitimate.

Augmentation of training and knowledge

During the ten years that I worked in community mental health programs, I was adequately supervised in a very traditional way that focused on the client's psychopathology; I felt there was so much more to learn. For years, I was in consciousness-raising groups that were based on feminist theory. This meant looking at how power dynamics were manifested in all relationships, especially psychotherapeutic ones. I would say this feminist perspective was one of the most influential ones affecting how I understood the therapist-client relationship. Since my university training had sensitized me to the relationship between the physical body and the psyche, I continued to take many courses and workshops in bodywork, yoga and meditation through-out my working career. Yoga, in fact, is still a part of my weekly gym routine that also includes aerobics. Holistic health was also another interest of mine, so I pursued that as well. I had already been exposed to alternative modalities through intensive workshops on healing mas-sage and biofeedback. Much of this I incorporated into my own life as part of my own health regime in dealing with my being HIV positive since 1987.

But long before this, I took a variety of programs that introduced me to other psychotherapeutic modalities in Gestalt therapy, trans-actional analysis and neurolinguistic programming. Many of these ranged from repeated intensive weekends to months-long supervised training to yearly programs. I found a year's course in psychodrama extremely useful, as there was both exposure to the technique and intensive supervision of our practice. I discovered that I did have a pro-pensity to work in a Gestalt modality since it gave me another work-ing model on the use of empathy in a new way. During one intensive group session, the leader was directing one of the participants to have a verbal dialogue with her father in which she said all that had been unsaid with him. She tried many times but always unsuccessfully to have a cathartic experience. We all knew that she was a hearing person but used American Sign Language (ASL) at home. I suggested that she have her conversation with her father in ASL even though all of us would not understand what she was saying. As expected, she had the intended experience and it was a significant breakthrough for her. It was not necessary for any of us to know what was going on—it was her experience that was the focus, which the group leader fully supported. For me, this was another example of the therapist's need to really listen to the client's world even if it meant not fully comprehending it.

Though I saw the value of all these courses and seminars, I still did not find any one approach that made me feel that I wanted to be a disciple of "that school." My goal was to incorporate into my practice what I had learned so that I could offer more treatment options to my clients. This learning also enabled me to make referrals to therapists in other modalities who could better serve what my client needed. Much of this learning and experience working in the gay community was very relevant to the workshops or programs that I gave every year at the annual APA conventions. And for many years, I was involved in a variety of men's groups composed of gay and non-gay men; a special one was one in which I was the only gay man among the other male psychologists. These weekly, yearlong groups were usually peer led and functioned as group therapy for all of us.

Developments in the client-therapist relationship and private practice

When I gave Arnold the first draft of this chapter, he was extremely complimentary about what I had written and, as a good editor, he said that there was a significant piece missing. He wanted me to write about how my work in community mental health working with primarily non-gay, Black and Hispanic working-class and poor people influenced my later work with primarily White, middle-class gay men. I knew he had put his finger on what I needed to say about how I had developed my own style of being a therapist and how these two seemingly disparate work situations had similarities—the common denominator was me as a thinking, gay man who had started making connections between people's experiences.

My last job was as director of a day hospital in a community clinic. The director of the entire mental health program had worked with me at Lincoln Hospital, and after he left, he tried to get me to work for him. After a number of years, I finally did agree and had my interview as an openly gay psychologist with his staff hiring committee. I was a staff psychologist for a couple of years before being made direc-tor of the day hospital. During this time, another incident happened that will also help explain something about the way I functioned as director and worked with my clients. In order to make a potential client and family members comfortable, I always had a community mental health worker in the interview with me—the usual practice in the past was that the director would be the only staff member in the interview. After one of these intake interviews, the worker, Mamie Pearson, said she had a question for me. She, a Black woman, had been a hotel housekeeper for over thirty years before coming to work in our program. She was also a deaconess of her church and, though I know she liked me and approved of my work, she was outspoken about her disapproval of homosexuality. After this interview, she said she was puzzled by the fact that she had never had seen a White man with so much understanding of Black clients and their lives. I told her that I was not trying to be Black but simply used my experience as a gay man to better understand their experiences. I could see the light bulbs go off in her eyes and from that moment on, our relationship was immeasurably changed for the better. As I have said before, calling upon my experience as a gay man gave me great insight as to "the other side of the couch." I thoroughly enjoyed working in this program as a clinician, but there were administrative problems for which I was not adequately trained. Though there never was a problem about my clinical decisions, I did make an administrative error for which I was appropriately fired.

Of course, I was devastated since I was now forty-one and very doubtful about my future career. Except for unemployment insurance, I had no income, so I started to develop a small private practice while I was planning to go back to college for a master's in public health. I put out the word to all my contacts that I was opening a practice. Since I was well known in the community as an activist, I received so many referrals that within a couple of months, I had a full-time practice! I soon realized I enjoyed this lifestyle and, to be consistent with my political beliefs, I operated on a sliding scale for payment—no one was rejected for financial reasons. Because most of my referral sources were White gay physicians and other activists, my clientele was predominantly White gay men who were either working or middle class. What surprised me, at that time in 1977, was that over half of my clients were men who had been in psychotherapy and/or psychoanalysis to "cure them" of their homosexuality. It was critical to them that they were now seeing an openly gay therapist.

This meant that much of my initial work was reparative therapy in helping them recover or develop a positive sense of self. It was already clear to me how society's negative valuation could impact one's self-esteem and how essential it was to find a safe place to be one's self and to have a positive role model (Kooden, 1994). This sense of safety in the world was mandatory. From working with an oppressed population in either the South Bronx or Manhattan, I knew that my work was to aid their recognition and development of their internal strengths to help them survive and thrive, a concept that was central to my later book on aging (Kooden, 2000). And it was also essential for them recognize the oppressive conditions around them that fostered their low self-esteem and the sense that something was inherently wrong with themselves—a common reaction that I saw wherever I worked.

Another focus that I inherited from my community mental health work was the psychological importance of community building. Given the lack of support from established churches, family and society, it was clear that we gays had to build our own community beyond the bars and bathhouses. We had to come up with our own social clubs, agencies and meeting spaces. Here is where my activism and profession intersected. I knew that helping my clients find their sources of community was essential to their growth as unique individuals. As "orphans" bereft of family support, these men needed to create their own chosen families and a sense of belonging somewhere. My having worked with people who existed on the fringes of society and were considered outliers or non-English speaking immigrants, I could see the negative effect of feeling themselves as damaged or lesser-than persons.

Another benefit of working in Spanish was that I could not use clichés and intellectual wordplay. I had to be simple, direct and to the point. My vocabulary was limited, so I could not use coded language or psychological jargon or "psychobabble." By and large, I was not working with a psychologically sophisticated population, so I had to learn how to speak so that I could be understood in very simple terms. This eventually gave me the ability to be equally direct in English as well. Another very important carryover lesson was my making sure that we had the same definitions of common words. I no longer was assured that we both had the same definitions of common words such as anxiety, depression, impotence, anger, fear and so on. Carefully making sure that we were using words in the same way proved to be an invaluable therapeutic tool since I no longer made an assumption we were talking about the same thing.

Another carryover experience was my going on home visits. When I worked in the South Bronx, I would walk the neighborhood to get a sense of where and how people lived. By invitation, I would also go to Santeria ceremonies at night, which were very crowded, and I was usually the only White person there. I found it essential to see people in their homes in order to get a sense of their living conditions. Sometimes the total contrast between the disrepair and neglect of the building and the clean condition of the apartment told me much about the client. Also, meeting the other family members in their home setting gave me additional information that was sometimes very relevant to my work with that client. I could easily understand some clients' need to leave the home for therapy or hospitalizations either through episodic explosions or psychotic behaviors. Their homes were overrun with other people and children barging in and/or simultaneous television(s) and radio(s) always on. It was easy to see the total lack of private space. Since I made home visits, clients would refer me to clients who would only see me in their homes. Sometimes this was for psychological reasons and sometimes it was because they would not leave their apartments empty for a moment for a genuine fear of burglaries in their absence (this was not a fantasy!).

I continued this practice into my private practice. Though there were time limitations, I did try to do this with as many clients as possible. I found this very rewarding as I discovered information about them that was useful in our therapy—information such as the luxury apartment with a highly designed interior by my client who presented himself as an extremely negative and impoverished man. This discrepancy gave me a clinically effective way to alter my work with him. Another was seeing the cut flowers (a weekly constant) in the home of a man who presented himself as a totally left-brained intellectual who seemed bereft of emotions. Simply seeing this floral display was a critical indicator of what I had been missing in our office visits where he presented himself as living in a totally gray world with no sense of color. Each of these were points to be expanded upon and opened new areas of inquiry and movement in our therapy.

My comfort in seeing clients out of the official setting was also put to the test since the gay community was small so that clients and therapists would sometimes be in the same social situations. More often than not, this was not disruptive to the therapeutic process since we would talk about our reactions to seeing each other outside the office. Sometimes this could lead to my making therapeutic-relevant observations. For example, my seeing my client joyously dancing in a disco was very revealing since he always presented himself in the office as a very depressed and almost suicidal person. My confronting him on this discrepancy was a significant turning point in our therapeutic work. In addition, clients seeing me in these social settings, while initially uncomfortable for some clients, only reinforced the fact that I was part of their community and not some distant authority figure. While I still remained an authority figure to my clients, my learning to be comfortable in being with clients outside the office setting was definitely something I began learning in my community mental health work.

My clients seeing me outside the office also reinforced for me the therapeutic value of having a therapist who was open about being gay. This aspect of self-disclosure was still a hotly contested point, which I had to defend publicly since there still were many gay therapists who were in the closet to their clients. Their defense was the dictum concerning "not interfering" with the transference process in the psychotherapeutic setting, whereas I stressed the beneficial use of clinical disclosure. I eventually wrote papers about this position that clarified this judicious use of disclosure. I showed how it benefited the client by enhancing the therapeutic relationship and made transference issues much more obvious (Kooden, 1991). In actually knowing facts about me and being able to see the contradictions between these facts and their own transference, clients were more able to understand their transference issues. This writing explicated how a clinically based disclosure of the therapist also helps minimize the inherent power dynamics within the therapeutic relationship. In addition, I wrote on the importance of positive role modeling for a gay man's mental health in which I elaborated on the relationship between the therapist's self-disclosure and the availability of positive role modeling (Kooden, 1994).

In all my work with clients, I relied on another essential process of judiciously looking at my own associations and feelings to better understand what was happening with my clients. I was first exposed to this concept through my academic studies (Whitaker and Malone, 1953). At that time, I did not have enough experience to know how to separate my feelings and associations from my thoughts in clinical work. Once I started working with clients who were of such different backgrounds and ethnicity from me as well sometimes speaking Spanish, I found myself floundering as to what was happening. When I began to reflect back to my clients the central themes of what I was experiencing, I discovered the accuracy of what I was saying. I was not interpreting back to them what I was thinking but sharing with them from emotional space. In time, I learned the accuracy of this form of reflection that was beyond language and intellectual thoughts. So many times, it was the only way I could "put my finger" on what was happening. This was an invaluable lesson for me, so I could feel secure when I was working in my private practice with clients where we spoke the same language but I still found myself not sensing what was happening.

Expanding model of psychotherapy and AIDS

Over time, it became more and more evident to me that the field of psychotherapy had yet to catch up to the actual experiences of gay men and women. This discrepancy between theory and practice only gave me more motivation to continue my educational work in our community with organizing national and international conferences in gay mental health issues through an organization, The National Gay and Lesbian Health Foundation, of which I was one of the six cofounders (Kooden et al., 1984). These conferences, and many more like them, were happening within all disciplines throughout this country so that a body of research and academic studies was being developed. We were not yet mainstream, but paths were being created in academic and professional circles so that younger gay and lesbian students could study gay and lesbian issues on their path to becoming professionals.

As I have said previously, my work in community mental health had greatly sensitized me to focus on the incredible strengths that my clients showed while living in deplorable conditions. I saw that focusing on helping them take charge of their lives was absolutely necessary in order for change to take place—taking charge became of primary importance in what I felt I could teach them. The private practice model of "talking about their inner feelings" was second-ary to making concrete changes. As I would say to other profession-als, if I could give them decent housing, education, employment and childcare first, then maybe psychotherapy would be useful. I learned very dramatically about what priorities to start with. First, we had to do what was necessary to minimize a client's anxiety and tired-ness about keeping the rats off her children's beds and having enough food to feed her children. Talking about it simply was not enough. The dictum of the psychotherapist "not giving advice but only listen-ing" was one I had a hard time with in these situations. I gradually learned when it was appropriate or not appropriate to give advice. And much to my surprise, I discovered that what the client listened to and resonated to was some knowledge that was already inside them. I only connected with what they instinctively knew but hadn't acknowledged to themselves.

I found this principle of "taking charge" was easy to transfer to my private practice clients, though the problems were very different as well as the life circumstances. I had already become very aware of the mind/body connection and the relationship between mental and physical health. This approach became very useful when I was confronted with a new, fatal disease emerging in our community, the Gay Related Immune Disorder (GRID). The medical profession couldn't identify the cause, nor was there any standard medication that could be prescribed—a diagnosis was considered a death sentence. I began to notice a definite pattern emerging in my clients and friends once they were diagnosed. Though they all became depressed, I was seeing a difference between those who died soon after and those who continued living. Those who died seemed to have no hopeful sense of a future and totally turned all decision-making over to their physician. The ones who continued living had a hopeful sense of a future and took their health care into their own hands in terms of decision-making—their physician was only one of the consultants they listened to. I wrote about these differences in our local gay publication as I felt that this represented another aspect of gay men's resilience and how taking charge was a game changer (Kooden, 1983).

Taking charge of one's health care was a new concept for many. A perfect example of this were two clients who both were diagnosed as having GRID and were told by their physician that they probably had only a year or two to live. They were referred to me about the same time to deal with their "depression." Both were ordained Presbyterian ministers in their early forties. I told both the same thing: let us focus on how to live their lives using all the strengths that they had already shown. Both were surprised by my position but reacted very differently. One said that he was more scared of becoming an old gay man than he was of dying—he continued to use cocaine and he took every medication his physician gave him without question. He died within the year. The other man admitted he was very challenged by what I said and he began to look at how he had been living his life, which meant making some significant changes in his medications, food habits and work. He began to have a sense of a future rather than the death sentence he received from his physician. He eventually moved to Colorado and was still alive in 2010.

Taking charge also had a very personal meaning to me. Having found out that I was HIV positive in 1987 and that this was an immune disorder, I made the decision to do all that I could to strengthen my immune system. I rejected taking AZT, the only medication that physicians were desperately giving since they did not have anything else to offer. AZT was a cancer medication that had been taken off the market because of its toxicity. Since its negative effects were bone marrow and liver damage, I felt the permanent damage to my immune system was not worth the risk, though it was said that it would extend my life by a year. I chose nontraditional methods of supporting my immune system. In 1993, I had to make a decision when I was hospitalized for pneumonia, which was not HIV related. Because of two misdiagnoses by an incompetent hospital physician (whom I later fired), I was put on medications that almost killed me. Heads of other departments actually came to apologize for his mistakes! I made the decision to stop the medications since I concluded they were inappropriate for me. This decision saved my life, and I have been in good health since recovering from the onslaught of these potentially lethal medications! As you can see, taking charge of one's life is not a meaningless statement for me.

In the early eighties, the world outside our community was unaware of the devastation that was occurring, though much creative mobilization was taking place. (Remember that at that time even our president refused to talk about AIDS.) An incredible number of lesbians became involved in providing health care to sick gay men while public services were not being mobilized. Much of this happened based on the health and mental health care network that we had been developing in the seventies. AIDS also brought many closeted, middle-class gay men into our AIDS fight and propelled our issues into the public sphere because of their connections and professional standing. Coming out was becoming more common, though sometimes involuntarily. We were being listened to in a new way that meant much of what we had been saying was now being taken very seriously. From my perspective, as an activist who had been on the front lines for many years, I could say that we were slowly being given credence and acceptance at a heretofore new level. We were being recognized for who we were and not because we were just trying to act like them.

One of these shifts began with the NYC AIDS Network, of which I was one of three cofounders. Our initial mission was successful in having all the AIDS organizations in New York City meet together for the first time. The next step was for us to meet with the *New York Times* so that AIDS would be written about. Concomitant with this was successfully meeting with the New York City mayor. As a result, all relevant city agencies became involved in our meetings, including the Department of Mental Health. Over the ensuing years, it also became evident that the Department of Mental Health needed to have within its permanent structure a committee specifically focused on gay and lesbian issues. With the support of the department's commissioner, this committee was created, with my being appointed as the first chair. This meant that gays and lesbians were no longer invisible to the largest agency in New York City specifically focused on mental health issues—this committee still exists today in 2018. From my many years of activism, I could now witness the speed with which we went from being outside agitators to becoming a legitimate part of the establishment. Inherent in this process is that our voices were being heard. Professionally speaking, this meant our research and theorizing was becoming relevant and accepted. More paths were being solidified in academic and professional circles. Concomitant with this was the continued development of gay and lesbian community mental health centers and clinics throughout the United States. Seeing this happening gave me another insight about how my dreams had come true.

You may recall when I earlier said that my undergraduate goal was to work at the UN in assisting developing countries in the creation of their mental health system. I was very clear that the United States could provide the technical knowhow for this structure but it had to be based on each country's own concepts of mental health. I now suddenly realized that I had achieved that goal, but that it was no longer about developing countries but about the gay and lesbian community and our unique theories about what constituted mental health and life experience for gays and lesbians! Yes, my dream had come true but in a form I could have never imagined years ago. And I had been an integral part of this process. So by helping others, I was clearly helping myself feel better about me and realize my dreams.

Activism and writing

It was becoming more and more clear to me that my activism was about community building as well as broadening the many paths leading to our own self-acceptance. I also saw that this kind of work had worldwide implications beyond the borders of this country. In 1985, I became interested in working with the International Lesbian and Gay Association (ILGA), an association then of about a hundred LGBT organizations around the world. Given my interest in the UN and the fact that I lived in New York City, I then initiated the successful process for ILGA's finally becoming an UN Non-Governmental Organization (NGO) in 1993. Equally important to my continued activism was my involvement in Services and Advocacy for GLBT Elders (SAGE). Aging issues had become very important to me in both the personal and professional spheres. As I was entering my sixties, I knew that aging, especially in the gay male community, was a critical issue. Since we lived in a youth-oriented and homophobic society, I knew intimately how aging was seen and experienced negatively by so many within our community. This awareness dictated my commitment to SAGE that has continued to the present time. Whether it was in conference planning or workshop organizing or strategic planning, my work within SAGE has been to advance an agenda for more appreciation of our own uniqueness and worthwhileness. As an elder, I could easily understand our negated standing in our society as well as how much we had to offer.

My recognition of the negative effects of internalized ageism in gay men and their struggle with aging successfully led me to also start writing about this subject in the nineties. Based on my professional experience, my own personal experiences and my university training, I created a model of developmental stages in aging for gay men (Kooden, 1997). After being published in a professional journal, it also became the foundation for my book, *Golden Men: The Power of Gay Midlife*, which was published by Avon Press (Kooden, 2000).

I purposely wrote it as a book that both therapists and non-therapists could use on how to positively age well and thrive. Much detail was given on how internalized ageism works to make aging well a very difficult task for gay men. Since gay men already had to deal with coming out, they have had the experience of making a life-changing decision about being honest to themselves and the world. This is a moral decision about honesty being of primary importance in their life in which I also show that this action can be later used to facilitate their aging well. Of interest is that internalized ageism in gay men is now a concept that has been shown to be a valid research topic (Wight, 2015). I also introduced a number of new concepts that would help gay men better understand the complexities and discrepancies in their development that can result in the many contradictory feelings they may have as adults. One singular aspect of my book is that I only used the words "gay" and "non-gay" to describe people. I wanted gay men to read a professional book in which, for the first time for many, they were the normal center of the book and the outliers were the non-gays. There was no need to translate to another frame of reference as was most typically done in most professional books. Given my history of publications on ageism, I was asked to write the section on ageism in an encyclopedia on LGBT issues (Kooden, 2009).

As you can see from my going into detail about my activism and writings, there has been a constancy in my developing a body of theory and empirical evidence for a positive approach in discussing LGBT matters that could be incorporated into all schools of psychological theorizing, especially around positive aging. I had learned early in my academic experience to see the flaws in much of psychological research. Knowing how "scientific research" on homosexuality was typically based on clients in psychotherapy or mental hospitals or prisons and usually reflected the researcher's biases, I had good reason to be suspect of other absolutes as well. I also knew that the only unbiased research on homosexuality that proved no differences between gay and non-gay men who were not in therapy was carefully suppressed until the seventies (Hooker, 1957). So I knew the dangers of developing a psychological theory based on a client population of one or on one subset of a group and extrapolating to an entire population or, even worse, basing a theory on prejudices about people from a different class or ethnicity of the researcher.

From my initial work in community mental health clinics where there was no transfer of money, I found that many "therapeutic rules" simply did not apply. Having to pay money in order to benefit from therapy did not hold since there was the usual bell curve of clients who made progress and those who didn't. I was also indoctrinated in the rule that there should never be physical contact between therapist and client. A turning point for me was working with client who lived in a rat-infested and partially burned-out building but was not eligible for city housing because, according to housing rules, she would have needed a three bedroom apartment for her and her children. She was desperate to move and felt totally overwhelmed by the city ruling that kept her where she was since the waiting list for this kind of apartment was many years long. She was intelligent and understood the outrageousness of the situation; she knew that her limited income made a more decent rental impossible and her children did not mind sharing bedrooms. At that moment, I felt she needed a supportive hug more than any words I could offer. My instincts were to stand up and give her a hug, which I did and, at the same time, I actually fantasized the ethics committee of the APA barging through the door and condemning me for my action! This did not mean that I hugged everyone. Touching, like almost everything I do in therapy, is the judicious result of a clinical decision rather than imposing a rule on myself or my client.

In like fashion, I discovered in my private practice that many rules were for the therapist's benefit. When I gave clients the option of coming in during the day at a lesser fee since the evening hours were at a premium, it was amazing how many were able to shift their work schedule around to come in during the day. Clients were flexible about each week since most could not guarantee the same time every week, nor did they feel they needed to have the same time each week. Since I knew the degree of flexibility of my clients, I could call them if I needed to shift their time. Practically all were amenable to this since they could be the one needing a shift the following week. I also found that having to pay for consultations inhibited people from seeing more than one therapist in order to find the appropriate one. If someone asked what I charged for a consultation, I said there was no charge as both of us had to find out if we could work together. If they decided to work with me, then the consultation would constitute the first, paid-for session. But there was no fee if she/he decided to go elsewhere. Yes, over the years there were a few who shopped around, but they were the bare minimum. And lastly, I found another "absolute" about clients in therapy that did not hold up. After my hospitalization in 1993, I went on disability and worked from my home. I had a reduced schedule and only saw clients that I felt comfortable seeing in my home. I did not adhere to a "fifty minute hour" but let the session go on as long as I felt work was being accomplished. There was a clear ebb and flow to the sessions with significant material coming out and, yes, it was after about forty-five minutes or so for some. What I realized was that clients did not necessarily wait to the end of a session before revealing significant information or feelings—it was just a natural process that took that long. The "fifty minute" was an arbitrary time that interfered with this natural flow. After seeing that most clients reached their peak between seventy to eighty minutes, I adjusted my schedule accordingly. It has always been interesting to see how many rules in therapy are for the therapists' comfort level, ease in scheduling and/or finances.

As you have probably realized, the community mental health experience continually reinforced my looking for those positive elements in a client's life that heretofore had been masked. This became very evident to me when, in the late eighties, I got a reputation as the "Mineshaft" therapist. The Mineshaft was a gay space known for uninhibited sexual activity and considered extremely seedy. Some of the habitués came to me because of their obsessiveness in going there every night and it began to interfere with their functioning elsewhere. I was very direct with them in stating that I would not work to eliminate a "negative" behavior until we discovered what "positives" they were getting from that very same behavior. It turned out that it was only at the Mineshaft that they could feel totally relaxed and be themselves with another man—nowhere else was this possible. So I suggested that we focus not on eliminating the Mineshaft from their life, since they were going there for a positive reason, but work toward their being that relaxed and uninhibited in their own bedroom. They were intrigued. As they found themselves not needing to go there every night and enjoying themselves in their own bedrooms, they talked with other men who seemed to have the same compulsion and also wanted to stop. Hence, my reputation as the "Mineshaft" therapist who was not judgmental about their behavior but helped them to understand the positive motives for a behavior that they initially condemned. (As you will see, this was something that I had initially learned from my own psychotherapy.)

This reframing process also led me to actions that were initially met with resistance from some clients when I suggested that they terminate therapy before they felt they were finished. A number of gay men entered therapy because of their inability to establish a long-term relationship since they were inexperienced with intimacy and open communication. With a few men, I saw that their relationship with me had become paramount in their lives and was preventing any other meaningful relationship. I suggested they take a six-month, vacation break from therapy and simply live their lives. Though some were not pleased with the idea, I was adamant. As might be expected, most found that once they opened up that space in their lives, they were eventually successful in establishing long-term relationships, having learned how to communicate and be open in a relationship. For some men, therapy was the first time they had ever had the experience of being listened to and feeling understood. Having worked with clients of different ethnicities, classes and races and even languages, I had to learn very fast how to accurately listen to my clients. This meant suspending the initial impulse, as I was taught, to make a diagnosis as soon as possible. I learned to put the need for a diagnosis "on the back burner" and just let a diagnosis emerge from what I was hearing. This meant not pathologizing the person in front of me but trying to understand who they were and, if possible, recognizing the metaphors they used in their lives. I found that, over time, I might not remember certain facts of their lives but the metaphors remained and became a significant communication between us. This reminds me of a statement made to me by a psychologist whom I had supervised. Since I knew he had been supervised by a brilliant colleague of mine in another psychological setting, I asked him about the differences between us in how he had been supervised.

He chuckled and said that he had learned from the other psychologist about how to think about his clients to make a diagnosis and, from me, he had learned how to love his clients.

Personal psychotherapy

Personal therapy is a requirement for most training programs—a maxim that I fully support. I actually began my own therapy when I sought out psychoanalysis when I was still at the university. It was not a good choice for me as he was a non-gay, traditional psychoanalyst with a couch and a chair behind. As I was in my twenties and very much in constant stress, I actually needed a more direct approach rather than the countless hours spent free-associating with no direction or interpretation. This was a very frustrating experience for a number of years, but I felt my lack of progress, whatever that meant, was entirely my fault. At the university, I was doing the practicum at the Counseling Center in which I had practice sessions with a non-gay female therapist. I revealed to her a behavior of mine that I condemned and put as a failing on my part. She, in a very open and nonjudgmental way, expressed a totally different perspective that put my actions in a very different light. The comfort and her positive and direct responses to me freed me in a way that I had never felt with my psychoanalyst. It was very evident to me that this was what I needed and I then successfully petitioned to have her as a therapist. I immediately started therapy with her and made progress. I continued with her until she moved from Chicago. This was another invaluable lesson about going toward what I felt worked best for me. I stopped blaming myself or my psychoanalyst for the lack of movement but realized that what worked for me in therapy was feeling better about myself and, with direction, seriously looking at what I was doing that perpetuated my feelings of inferiority and prevented me from feeling good about myself.

Even before starting psychotherapy, I had had a personal experience in my teens that revealed to me how a positive authority figure's insight could dramatically change one's life. After my arrest and involvement with the courts, I was assigned to an overtly homophobic probation officer. He was eventually replaced by Mr. Serota, the head of the department, who had become interested in my case. He became a lifeline for me as he saw what was going on in my family and the ramifications of my sentencing by the courts. He interceded at a critical point and he became the only one I could count on. A year into my case, and when I was back in my high school and living with my mother (who had previously disappeared twice during this period), he commented to me that he had never seen an ambulatory schizophrenic as disturbed as my mother outside a mental hospital. With that one statement, I physically felt an incredible weight leave my shoulders and from that time forward, my anger and outbursts against my mother simply stopped. Someone else in the world had confirmed for me what I had felt about my mother but was denied by everyone else. Her "etherealness and illogical behavior" was excused as a kind of ditziness to be expected from a very beautiful woman. Once my feelings were confirmed, I immediately started treating her differently by taking care of her. Though it was painful, I no longer had expectations about her as a nurturing or reasonable mother. Mr. Serota's one statement taught me how a valued person's observations can have a life-changing import of feeling understood—a lesson that I used throughout my life, especially as a psychotherapist. Sometimes, it takes only one other person to relieve that feeling of being completely alone in the world. I knew from this early experience how feeling understood can begin a self-healing process when what is being said resonates with something inside though not yet articulated. In retrospect, I can easily understand why I so clearly was drawn to the forms of psychotherapy that focused on empathy and understanding the world of the person in front of me.

Having the kind of mother that I had obviously influenced my desire to be a therapist who communicated clearly and directly. My desire to have direct communication with her was thwarted with her never being quite present—she always seem to be talking from some other place. This was clearly evident after she had surgery for brain cancer, which was equivalent to a prefrontal lobotomy. After a subsequent phone conversation with her, I commented to my partner that I felt I had actually had my first adult conversation with her. Unfortunately, it was the only time as the cancer returned and she died shortly afterward in 1965. This was another lesson about the different levels of communication and instilled in me a lifelong desire for clarity in my communication and looking at what I was doing that thwarted that intent. As you will see, this is possibly another reason why I was drawn to the kind of supervision that focused on what I needed to learn about myself.

Once I came to New York City, I discovered that many of the consciousness-raising groups that I was involved in were a different form of group therapy without a specified leader. Of course, there were the newly emerging encounter groups that I participated in for a number of years. I also found that the supervision groups connected to the community clinics for which I was volunteering also functioned as therapy groups for me. Or at least, I used them that way. Throughout my work as staff psychologist, I received the more traditional kind of supervision that focused on the client and his/her problems. Once I was in private practice, I sought out peer supervision groups that focused on the therapist as the source of the particular problem that was occurring in the session. This was in direct contradiction to the former kind of supervision that focused on the psychopathology of the client rather than what was negatively stimulated in the therapist and needed to be looked at. Though I had intermittently worked with two other therapists, I eventually had the luxury of working with a very well-known, gay Gestalt therapist, Frank Donnelly. I felt totally relaxed with him as a personal friend, and at a very important transition time in my life, I sought him out as my therapist. Besides his perceptiveness and acute abilities as a therapist, he had developed a model that made the sessions extremely impactful. He videotaped the session. I would get there an hour early and watch what had happened the week before so that when I went in to see him, I was primed from what had just happened on the tape and began the therapy session at that high level of awareness and focus. I must say that in all my years of different therapists and forms of therapy, this was one of the most effective modalities for producing insight and change.

Personal life

In case you think that my entire life has been spent only in activism and professional work, I want to assure you that I have been fortunate to have a very full life with a close circle of friends, lovers and both chosen and blood family. What is important to me is that my friendships are all inclusive: Black and White, gay and non-gay, women and men, older and younger, professional and non-professional, blood family members but, unfortunately, none of different political persuasions! And yes, over the years I have been reconciled with my family and am now a much-loved and respected elder. In my thirties and early forties, I had a series of younger boyfriends with whom I played out the role of the older man who would rescue someone who needed help.

Though it took time and much emotional effort, I eventually outgrew this dynamic and was able to establish a more peer relationship. I met my lover, Jim Black, who unfortunately died ten years later due to complications from AIDS, as did my three closest friends by 1994. Jim and I were already dealing with his father's cancer diagnosis when we received Jim's diagnosis of AIDS and mine of being HIV positive. This led me to start volunteering with his father's hospice program and eventually with Jim's hospice program as well since I had learned much from the combination of being Jim's primary caregiver and my own professional and personal experience dealing with AIDS.

As fortune would have it, I met my husband, John Hunter, in 2001— we were actually introduced by non-gay friends who thought we might be interested in each other. At that time, I was 65 and he was 59. For the first time, I was intimately involved with a Black gay man. He was then an associate dean at the university where he had been chair of the art department and an art historian specializing in Italian Renaissance art. Though the topic of racism has been central to my activism, this relationship necessitated that I explore in depth all aspects of my own racist feelings and the benefits of my White privilege. These discussions parallel some of the same discussions that you have been reading about in this chapter. It is also reflected in the conflict between assimilationist and liberationist thinking in the gay community since Stonewall. Can we only be accepted if we act like them, or can we strive to be seen and accepted for our uniqueness? As you the reader must have surmised long before this, my path has been as the liberationist. I have had to forge my own path mixed with my own desires to be accepted on my terms. It is not that I have rejected all the standards set by my profession, most especially the one for the therapist's own therapy. This dictum of "know yourself" has been absolutely essential for my own development and is central to the theme about which you are reading. In addition to psychotherapy, there are additional modalities to further our knowledge of ourselves.

Relationship between travels and psychotherapy

In further discussing my personal life, I feel it is important to mention one feature that has greatly influenced my perspectives—my travels. As you might have gathered, I am not a "sit on the beach and chill out" kind of person. From my first trip outside the United States in 1969, while sitting in an outdoor café in Venice, I realized that I wanted my travels to expose me to new ways of seeing or acting that I could incorporate into my life back home. Travels were not simply vacations to relax in new settings—they were a way to "broaden my horizons." I know it is a cliché but it is a meaningful one for me. So before John and I began our yearly, month-long trips, I had already spent time in Mexico, Guatemala, Italy, Ireland, France, Portugal, Greece,

Germany, England, Saint Vincent, South Africa, Morocco, Peru, Ecuador, Bolivia, Spain, Argentina, Brazil, many Caribbean Islands, Yugoslavia, Cuba and Turkey, some of which I did by myself. These trips always seem to have a very personal meaning for me beyond the simple accumulation of beautiful memories. They enabled me to see beyond cultural differences without judgment and accept that there are very different realities by which people live successfully and happily.

This reminds me of another personal anecdote. Years ago, a friend once asked me if I got bored listening to people telling me about all their problems. My immediate response was "no"; it was like reading a new book when each is different and memorable. (In fact, I also said that the only time I get bored is when my clients are not working or connected to what they are saying. When I start planning the dinner menu, I know that I am bored!) So travels have the same impact on me of the discovery of other realities, especially since I have gotten older. Since John and I love exploring cultures, our travels have led to my eventually writing personal travel narratives about each trip, which are greatly enhanced with his photos. Together, we have gone to Mexico, China, Bali, the Philippines, Japan (with my sister, Dianna), Greece, Jordan, Turkey, Brazil, Egypt, Morocco, Ecuador, Peru, India, Argentina and Iran. Our trip to Iran was a very unique one in that the decision to go there prompted much soul-searching before and during, as homosexual acts there are punishable by death. The resulting travel narrative took all this internal dialogue into account as well as the joy of meeting a new people and seeing a country of which I knew so little. Hopefully, these narratives about my external and internal travels will enrich our next travel destination of West Africa. We both are very interested in how he, as a Black man, will feel in a totally Black culture and I, as a White man, will feel in the same circumstances.

These extensive travels are, for me, part of that continual learning process of how to be comfortable in the world and continuously have new experiences. It helps me see the world through their eyes, a gift for better understanding. An additional benefit to all my travels is my learning how to feel comfortable and have a strong sense of myself without the usual supports of my home environment. Seeing the variety of ways other people live also reinforces my belief that there are many other standards of what constitutes mental health. We in the United States or similar countries are not the official arbiters of what constitutes mental health. So much of this depends on the culture and what standards our profession is attempting to reinforce. There is a reason that some refer to mental health professionals as "soft policemen." An often cited example of this use of a profession to maintain social order was the 1880s medical designation of "drapetomania, an inborn tendency of slaves to run away from their owners." This was one of the examples used to help declassify homosexuality as a mental disorder. Or what about the psychologists who had "scientific evidence" of the intellectual inferiority of Blacks? Though we can now easily laugh at these examples of prejudice being disguised as scientific evidence, it is always essential for us mental health professionals to question any broad judgments we make about any group of people. And my many travels have only reinforced this strong belief of mine.

Importance of reading

In telling you of my history, I nearly forgot to mention the extensive reading that I have continually done. It has been so much a part of my life that it is like the fish that does not recognize it is swimming in water. Since my late teens, there has never been a time when I have not been reading in order to expand my thinking and become aware of new fields of inquiry. I had an explosive experience when I first read *On Liberty* by John Stuart Mill in an undergraduate English class, I was completely bowled over. I had never read a book that kept opening my eyes and gave me so much to think about in each page and almost every paragraph. The "light bulbs" were continually going off with excitement at the sheer volume of new concepts, ideas and formulations. So many new perspectives were presented that touched on incipient ideas I may have felt but could not articulate. It was a watershed experience, as this became the model as to how I approached reading for the rest of my life but especially when I entered HD.

Luckily, this program at the university pushed the envelope on new dimensions on the mind-body connection that has now become a strong interest of mine. But then, the medical establishment ridiculed the idea of an immune system since no "organ" could be pointed to as the seat of that system. Thankfully, we now actually have a recognizable field of psychoneuroimmunology. Though we studied the many different personality theories, it was only at the counseling center that the actual practice of therapy was studied. Once I came to New York City, I never stopped exploring professional books and journals that dealt with individual, group and family psychotherapy. I was intrigued by alternative modalities of therapy, though my practice remained mostly of a verbal, talking kind. I have always had eclectic interests, so humanism and holistic health continued to be primary interests. Since this was the time of the "New Age" in thinking, there so was much to explore. Luckily, I was exposed to the newly emerging, scientifically valid research on healing touch and focused meditation for physical healing. This awareness of the relationship between one's active participation in the healing process has become a guiding principle in both my personal and professional life. I was able to expand my psychodynamic therapeutic approach by teaching relaxation techniques that incorporate deep breathing and meditation.

Eventually I became interested in reading about the intersection between spirituality and health. Because of this interest, I eventually convened the first meetings in New York City for gay men on the relationship between spirituality and mental health. In my thinking about the coming out process and the decision to make honesty a primary value in one's life, I saw that this was a moral/spiritual decision about one's life. Coming out as a gay man is a declaration of what is important in one's life—that the quality of one's life is paramount. Over the years, I have witnessed the fact that, once having made this life decision as to what constitutes a good life, subsequent decisions are made easier. Coming out as a gay man means identification with a community, whereas a statement of being a homosexual is only self-referential. Though both are positive moves toward better mental health, the involvement in community has been shown to be an important ingredient of lifelong good mental health.

Unfortunately, in the early seventies, there was a paucity of professional literature with a positive stance on homosexuality. A few years later, a local bookstore had an entire display window filled with the emerging field of professional books, journals and literature that dealt with homosexuality. I felt so good because I recognized everything; I had read all of the books and magazines and knew practically every author and researcher. Within a few years, that would have been impossible, as the field had so greatly expanded. Not only does our own APA division have its own journal but also one can find research on homosexuality in a diversity of professional journals.

Since I am talking about over fifty years of reading, I can only give a very broad overview of what I have read, but I am sure you can surmise what kinds of reading I have done and incorporated into my practice and personal life. I still am not convinced that any one program could satisfy all my interests and beliefs. From a recent experience at a prominent training institute, I was a witness to recognize professional programs that do incorporate a positive gay psychology but do not deal with the power relationships characteristic of the client/therapist relationship. As I learned years ago, good therapists learn more from their total experience than from any one school. Each psychotherapeutic program has something to offer—psychoanalytic, Gestalt, hypnosis, biofeedback, client-centered, self-psychology and so on. In this sense, there is always something more to learn, to be the best psychotherapist we can be. It may be our next and most difficult client who teaches us what we needed to learn!

Conclusion

At this point, you might wonder when did I start believing and feeling that I was gifted. It was at the end of a process whereby I made another dramatic shift in my life. In my early forties, I finally became aware that the extremely difficult and painful lover relationship that I was in, was an echo of the relationship I had with my mother. What I had thought was sanity and a feeling of being at home was really insanity given the home life I had experienced. This realization was part of that dramatic process of finally "leaving home" and letting go of much of the damage inflicted there. In a subsequent conversation with a highly intelligent new friend, I had another revelation after I had minimized my intelligence. I had justified my not being intelligent since I could point to two people in HD whom I thought smarter than I was. In this moment, I saw the absolute ridiculousness of my thinking. HD was one of the hardest departments in the social sciences at the U of C and yet, I put myself at the bottom because I was not at the absolute top—there was no middle ground. This was a moment of clarity accompanied by our laughter at the reality that the only stupidity present was about the way I was thinking.

All this talk of supervision, readings, therapy and transformative insights brings me back to the "why" of this chapter. About four years ago, Arnold Rachman suggested that we talk regularly each week as a form of a co-created analytic experience. Some call this mutual analysis. He was then living in Florida with his wife; I had been best man at their wedding. I was honored, touched and scared about this invitation. The vestiges of my insecurities came up. Arnold was a training analyst with all the necessary credentials and a published author of many articles and books. He was internationally known and highly respected. Though we had been friends for over fifty years, we had never talked about therapy and professional issues, though I had read much of what he had written. I knew what I could gain from this new aspect of our relationship but sincerely doubted if I could be of help to him. I explained all this to him and we plunged in with our weekly, hour-long phone sessions. Within a few years, he and his wife moved back to New York City, and we began weekly, two-hour sessions in person. It is obvious that we both have benefited from these sessions, and I have seen, or should I say experienced, what he has gained from my participation. Whatever final doubts I may have had about my training or qualifications have clearly receded. He has already talked about our writing about our experiences in this mutual process, which only reinforces my feeling that he sees me as a colleague. This peership is further highlighted in his asking me to write this chapter as an example of a qualified psychotherapist who has taken an unusual path. As the scarecrow in the Wizard of Oz needed some external indicator of his having a brain, I, too, had been looking for that signifier. In serious contemplation about this chapter and seeing all that I have accomplished, I am amazed and pleased. In reviewing my life at this age, I can now say that I have achieved my goals and have a good sense of self-validation. So, Arnold, thank you for your loving support in this process of validation.

References

Publications

Fiedler, F.E. (1950) A Comparison of Therapeutic Relationships in Psychoanalysis, Non-Directive and Adlerian Therapy. *Journal of Consulting Psychology*, 14:6, pp. 436–445.

Henry, W. E., J. H. Sims, and S. L. Spray (1971). *The Fifth Profession: Becoming a Psychotherapist*. San Francisco: Jossey-Bass.

Hooker, E. (1957). The Adjustment of the Male Overt Homosexual. *Journal of Projective Techniques*, 21, pp. 18–31.

Kooden, H. (1975). On Transiting. In H. Kooden (Editor), *Gay Psychology: Coming Out. Social Action: Newsletter for Psychologists for Social Action*. VII, Letter 1.

Kooden, H. et al. (1979). Removing the Stigma. *Final Report of the Board Social and Ethical Responsibility: Task Force on the Status of Lesbian and Gay Male Psychologists*. Washington, DC: American Psychological Association.

Kooden, H. (1983). AIDS and Stress: An Unexamined Link. New York City: New York Native, Vol. 66.

Kooden, H. et al. (1984). *Gay and Lesbian Mental Health 15 Years after Stonewall: Sourcebook on Lesbian and Gay Health Care*. National Gay Health Education Foundation, First International Lesbian & Gay Health Conference, June, pp. 101–104.

Kooden, H. (1991). Self-Disclosure: The Gay Male Therapist as Agent of Social Change. In C. Silverstein (Ed.), *Gays, Lesbians and Their Therapists*. New York: W.W. Norton, pp. 141–154.

Kooden, H.(1994). The Gay Male Therapist as an Agent of Socialization. *Journal of Gay & Lesbian Psychotherapy*, 2 (2), pp. 39–64.

Kooden, H. (1997). Successful Aging in the Middle-Aged Gay Man: A Contribution to Developmental Theory. *Journal of Gay & Lesbian Social Services*, 8 (31), pp. 21–43.

Kooden, H. (2000). *Golden Men: The Power of Gay Midlife*. With C. Flowers. New York, Avon Books.

Kooden, H. (2009). Ageism. In J. Hawley (Ed.) *LGBTQ America Today, An Encyclopedia*, Westport, CT: Greenwood Press, pp. 24–27.

Whitaker, C. A., and T. Malone (1953). *Therapeutic Roots of Psychotherapy*. New York: Blakiston.

Wight, R. G. et al. (2015). Internalized Gay Ageism, Mattering, and Depressive Symptoms among Midlife and Older Gay-Identified Men, *Social Science & Medicine*, 147, pp. 200–208.

Educational Videos

Kooden, H. (1987). Narrator. Diagnosis Today. "Women and Mental Health", Politics of Diagnosis", and "Revising DSM-III". Intelligence in Media.

Kooden, H. (1987). Narrator and Discussant. Homosexuality. "What Science Understands" and "Before Counseling Gays and Lesbians". Intelligence in Media.

Conclusion

Melvin Bornstein

To write about the poignant chapters in this book, I will begin with what it is like to feel alive and a whole human being. I discovered after being a psychoanalyst for almost 60 years that the core of psychoanalysis is being human, loving life, and being creative.

I also knew that to be able to understand what the authors were expressing I needed to look within and seek similar experiences that I could use. Each author's story is written about a whole human being within a flowing narrative. This is not how psychoanalysis is usually described and taught, yet being human strongly influences the way psychoanalysis is actually understood and practiced. Being human is the lens that I will use in discussing the papers in this book. Being human is subjective and holistic. Humans are continually moving within time. Humans are motivated to bring together the complexity of the present, past, real and not real into a coherent whole, which is used to reach out to communicate to others with intense discharge of emotional tension. Humans can also discharge tension in states of disarray through behavior or directing the tension into the body. Because emotional discharge in states of disarray is aberrant it generates pain and frustration.

Much of psychoanalytic attention has been devoted to the parts of being human with a heavy objective perspective. We learn about symptoms, dynamics, relationships, a Self, intersubjectivity, understanding and insight, but the humanness is frequently given little if any attention.

Turning to my humanness which will be my lens for this discussion: I fell in love with psychoanalysis in my first year of medical school (falling in love is all about one's inner life). It was when I listened to John

Dorsey who then was the Chair of the Department of Psychiatry at Wayne State University Medical School. He lectured weekly to our class for two years. He was a psychoanalyst. He had been sent to Vienna on a sabbatical to be analyzed by Freud. In his lectures he spoke about one and only one theme—we are whole; we are the source of everything we know and experience. In other words, everything that we experience starts within ourselves including internal and external reality.

Sometimes we put outside of ourselves things that are painful that we do not like. We say this is not us. We are being hateful to ourselves and others which is the cause of mental illness. "We are our own everything," Dorsey would say. If we embrace the meaning of this phrase that he repeated frequently we would live caringly and lovingly.

Truthfully, I didn't know what this man was talking about, but I knew he was right. This was 70 years ago. I will explain why I knew John Dorsey was right and how his ideas has changed my life. They helped me create my lens to see my inner and outer worlds and enable me to help others change their lives. I was a 22-year-old medical student who was learning how to become an adult and physician while experiencing an incessant inner force to create coherence out of an array of feelings, thoughts and fantasies which included repetitive patterns.

Along with my growth I married and developed intrusive repetitive thoughts that my new wife was going to develop a terminal illness and die. Within a short time, this was organized into an irresistible desire to have a doctor reassure me that she was OK. I understood that I was being overwhelmed by a peculiar state that seemed nonsensical. I was looking for reassurance. No matter how reasonable physicians were, it did not last. I realized I had to keep much of this to myself. I was concerned this was going to seriously interfere in my sense of well-being and capacity to be productive, creative and, most of all, interfere with loving my wife.

It was because of this that I sought analysis, which has continued to this day, initially in the form of two formal analysis and a daily period of self-analysis including my daily experiences and my experiences conducting supervision and analysis.

This is what I have achieved in my ongoing analysis. I learned that packed into my phobic, inhibiting, low self-esteem symptoms was my narrative about my mother who was engaged with me enough as an infant, but when I was six years old she began losing interest in me, along with life itself, because of early traumas and upheavals in her life. She found embracing life and making joy and creativity out of her traumas and upheaval was too difficult and not working.

She withdrew and immersed herself in her fantasies, masochism, and biological proclivities while I became phobic toward her. This was 65 years ago. Her treatment and care were primitive, which I am sure made her worse. She was institutionalized and had a lobotomy. My father did what he could. He remained committed to her; encouraged me to remain in contact with her. Although he had his limitations, he became a model for me of honesty, courage, and love.

In the unpacking of my symptoms I discovered the fundamental nature of repetition which enabled me to feel it was possible to stop time, rewrite history in the form of my transferences and fantasies. By repeating traumas, I was protecting myself against feeling like myself, fully alive in the present with my narrative, including my pain and suffering and, most importantly, in touch with many of my feelings. My powerful desire to develop and live life well demanded work and courage.

So, today, I can be in touch with the traumas of early neglect and the upheaval of my mother's psychosis, unconscious communication of her terror, defensiveness of my repetition against feeling alive. Also, I can be in touch with my longing for my father to be more adequate in helping me deal with my early trauma. All this was packed into my symptoms that I still feel, but with an ability of including all that makes up my early trauma into who I am. With this capacity to reach my inner life I can unconsciously and consciously reach for greater emotional understanding of my patients and allow them to feel intimate with me.

It took me a long time because to go beyond the dynamics of my trauma which could be understood with objective formulations, I had to survive, develop a love of life and an exuberance in being creative which could only be understood with subjective formulations. I had to focus on a subjective platform of what it is like to be moving through time in a state of mind of being whole and alive as a person and agency living in the present moment and motivated to organize and understand the pressing parts of my inner life.

In other words, feeling alive and whole was different than working with an objective perspective. It was being a witness and agency to myself. It is the irony of being a human, being in the context of an incessant movement of time with feelings that cannot be directly controlled. I had to discover this part of the analytic process myself. All the theories I found and studied did not help much because the place where analytic insights arise is in the moment to moment experience of the analytic process. It is based on feeling alive and whole, growing while being in a state of weakness, inundated by a variety of feelings demanding discharge. Feeling alive is like being a person who is trying to organize a multitude of experiences to be used in showing what one understands about who he or she is. Everything is in a state of movement and degrees of transformation.

Also feeling whole and alive includes having to deal with humiliation and shame because of exposure. It has to do with finding a place for my trauma with the desire to embrace my life with energy and joy. There is a momentous transformation from objectivity to subjectivity, being an agency with the responsibility of what one does or not do and how this corresponds to right or wrong, truth or falsity, loving or degrading. It is this platform that is demanded in the analytic process.

To get to this platform by following theory is limited because it only can be found by following oneself. This is where looking inward with free associations is enabling to follow the complexity of the activities of the mind. Only by looking inward with the use of metaphors, simile, intuitions and hunches can one grasp the working of the interior of the mind within a fleeting moment.

In addition, there is the presence of the repetition of the past because when the past was the present it was overwhelming. In the repetition there is a feeling that the present cannot be dealt with because of one's past limitations that feel like the present.

I learned that to feel alive from moment to moment, I had to direct my attention to the present moment, organize the experiences of inner and outer, and communicate them to myself in my inner world and to others in my outer world. That act leads to experiences of wholeness and being alive with an exuberance of joy and love. I found that doing this brought what had been dissociated and repressed into ownership which then became part of my "infrastructure that contributes to my identity." In other words, "to who I am," which is my legacy.

Only by being immersed in an analytic process in my teaching and life in general could I develop a greater understanding and ability to move into this open mental state. It helps me write this section of the book.

So, let's turn to the papers as I responded to them using my lens. All the authors wrote with courage and love. They were exposing their lifelong commitment to organize and expose themselves with their traumas, failures, disappointments, humiliations, vulnerabilities and successes. Packed in their writings were demonstrations of how in the present moment as they wrote, they had been able to use their talents and creativity to give the reader a view of their wholeness and humanity in becoming analysts. They were showing us how they gained strength to take ownership of parts of themselves that they had not been able to reach and tame. In other words, bringing these renegade parts into their tent and make them part of who they are.

Arnold Rachman writes how he discovered the value of Ferenczi's writings as he was overcoming the deficiency of empathy in how he was taught about being a psychoanalyst. This resonated with his relationship with his father dying, a mother depressed and leaving home to begin work, but a grandmother who took care of him with enormous empathy which contributed to his inner tools that helped guide him through difficulty times. The capacity to use those tools made up his growth and whatever in his matrix that made this all happen, that included an overpowering force to live well with courage.

Harold Kooden describes a lifetime struggle to free himself from the social and internal obstacles that prevented him from feeling whole and using his power to gain fulfillment in his life which rested on his coming out. In his early life he could not do this because of family and social prohibitions which interfered with his desire to love life and live well. Instead he turned much of his experiences against himself. Psychoanalytic training was not available to him. As a young man, homosexuality was viewed as pathology in Psychology and in Psychoanalysis. The work of development continued. He became active in local and national and international LGBT organizations. We see his internal work and courage as he transformed self-criticism and inhibition into creativity and his love of life. In other words, to transform his superego into an inner strength of living.

Joseph Scalia describes his commitment to the wild land that brought him to confront his vulnerability, unpredictability, and weakness. This led him to develop an ability to tolerate the experience of the authenticity of his life by being able to be open, close, and loving. This movement is similar to the results of resolving the transference resistances leaving the patient capable of being close and authentic to the analyst not as a transference but as a whole person. In other words, to overcome the infantile terror of being alone and unprotected.

Dan Gilholey describes profound events of his early life. His father returned from World War II with a head injury, depressed and suicidal, which eventually resulted in his actual suicide. Gilholey entered early adulthood, left home and established himself as a recognized artist. He then went into training as a psychologist and psychoanalyst.

He reveals to the reader how dissociation has been part of his creative experience in his art and therapy. Using his lens formed from his trauma, he could see that dissociation was a valuable defense against making his trauma part of his joy of life. This helped him use derivatives of his life with his trauma as part of art and therapeutic creativity.

Frank Yeoman takes the reader on a journey of defining his narrative in being whole and human. He begins with his study of French Literature, which is all about being human. Then he discovers Lacan and his ideas about language. Because of Yeoman's humanness that includes his ability to create language and develop an agency, he is able work within his inner life and know the unknowable. He describes learning about the complexity of what he knows and what he doesn't know. Freud would call this enormous energy to grow and love the life instinct. Yeoman turns to Psychiatry with its opportunities to understand and treat human suffering. He is forced to deal with the social, medical, and economic demands of his work and incorporates them, adding to the complexity and demands of being human.

Clara Mucci describes that she fell in love with language as a young child. When she first read Shakespeare her vision of the complexity of life came alive. She became a language scholar which led into analysis and analytic training combined with being part of two Italian cultures as basic parts of her experience congealed.

It was in writing and her analysis that enabled her to develop the emotional ability to delve deep within her mind to grasp the mental states that contribute to being human. Writing has many characteristics of an analytic process. The gathering of inner experiences connecting them to words, creating a narrative and implementing this complex process led by her agency to communicate to another in the present moment and enabling her to be in touch with another even if the other is an anonymous reader.

With this beginning she shares her development with teachers and mentors which has enriched her understanding of the complexity of reaching toward being whole.

Simone Marshall writes her autobiography on her development as a psychoanalyst. She grew up in post-World War II Paris influenced by her father's suffering from depression as a result of manning a cannon for four years. Her story is one of becoming whole, bringing together her early life with the challenges of settling in the United States where she received her graduate education. Her story is that of finding herself and using the dissociated and repressed part of herself, the complexity of her feminine identity, her enormous inner power to develop and to live well with her inexorable creativity.

Henry Kellerman writes about his childhood with his parents and Bubba and some adults who reached out to him. He understood something about their troubles. They had fixed ideas that no amount of logic could change. They clung to these ideas because they were protective. With deep conviction and courage, he grew to understand the complexity and irony of human experience. These ideas were protective, but also damaging to these troubled adults. They contained powerful desire to live and reveal directly and honestly but also to hide as acts of cowardice.

His understanding of inner life was not only based on living with ideas, but experiences in the Yiddish theater. He became immersed in improving his mastery of Yiddish and developed an understanding of the personalities of people in transition from one culture to another.

Alan Entin describes the enormous power secrets have in shaping development within family relationships. In the presence of a secret, one feels ignored without help in dealing with the deep emotions that are generated by the secret.

Entin discovered powerful hidden messages in pictures of his family that could help him become whole. By using the pictures to do internal work of reducing the effect of dissociation and repression he got in touch with his narrative which released enormous creative energy expressed in his family therapy, photography and writing.

Fergal Brady takes us on an odyssey towards an understanding of himself and the world that surrounds him. He describes how the development of the use of words contributed to the recognition of powerful affects of pain and awe with a love of life by melding this diversity into new words and concepts that can be communicated to himself and others. The free associations in his psychoanalysis enabled him to develop a deeper appreciation of the continual diversity and transience of life. The use of poetry, music and classic literature have been wonderful tools to enhance consolidation of his inner life.

As a boy Robert Marshall was awed by jazz. He became a jazz pianist. To him jazz is all about improvisations. The musician begins with a musical idea and creates a musical dialogue with the other musicians. They creatively go back and forth elaborating on the idea which becomes a living entity enriched and a source of fulfillment and pleasure. He described the similarity with the therapeutic process which is also part of a living, growing and creative process for patient and analyst very much like playing jazz. To understand the present moment in an analysis we must reach a depth of experience described best by "heart and soul," theory is limited, loving life is more descriptive, to keep the process authentic and alive. Surprise, deep affects and intimacy are integral to both jazz and analysis.

Benito Perri had a seminarian education with secular and spiritual components which promoted his intellectual and spiritual growth. During his years in seminary life he embraced celibacy which made it impossible to integrated the celibacy with his intellectual and spiritual growth. He began analysis witch eventual led to entering psychoanalytic training becoming a psychoanalyst and devoting himself to the spirituality within psychoanalysis and the improvement of society.

The authors of each chapter are writing about themselves as whole human beings who are exposing themselves, their "hearts and souls," by describing the special routes they have taken to become psychoanalysts or psychotherapists. The lens that I have used enabled me to see that they looked within themselves to create their narratives which required considerable work and courage. They had to deal with exposure, pain, trauma, humiliation, a variety of affects and a recognition of their vulnerability, all of this had to be brought together with continual growth and creative capacities.

Most importantly, they had to deal with pain and trauma which was easier to live with in the form of a repetition. In a repetition growth is ignored with a withdrawal from reality. Numbness replaces feeling alive. With a repetition time stops and one feels that it is possible to alter past traumas and pain. One can avoid transforming experiences that once were the present, but now are the past which one has to live and grow with to be included into the whole of the author.

All of this requires work which leads to a delineation of one's identity with all the relevant painful affects that at one time was current and now must be used to contribute one's experience of life. To me this growing and transforming process has abstractly been described in Ego Psychology. I mean the neutralization and sublimation of drive energy that results in growth of the ego. I found this abstraction addresses the process of creativity, transformation and discharge of tension.

But the abstractions of ego psychology are insufficient. It does not address the reaching out and withdrawal inward because of pain and humiliation in the psychoanalytic relationship. Fairbairn had developed Object Relation Theory that is based on the wholeness of the analyst and patient reaching out to each other and withdrawing into fantasy because of pain and humiliation.

Ferenczi added to the wholeness of patient and analyst interacting with each other in his classic paper, The Confusion of Tongues (1949), in an analytic relationship there are two human brings communicating with each other. Not simply patients with their repetitive frozen experiences, but the analysts whose experience with patients are influenced by their dissociation or repression which interfere with their conducting the analysis. Also, this complimentary response to the analyst becomes a means to look within and understand the patients' experience.

Melanie Klein described projective Identification, which includes special fantasies with narcissistic characteristics. They are sadomasochistic states with primitive aggression. Because of their narcissistic features they are used to defend against experiences of unmanageable instability seen in trauma. These states are where one goes when reality is too difficult. It includes numbing oneself to reality and withdrawing into fantasy. Many of the writers described their creativity as efforts to reach out of their sadomasochistic withdrawn states which required enormous energy and courage. My entire life has been engaged in transforming withdrawn states with superego introjects into engaged creativity.

Finally, patient and analyst react in a deep subjective experience to one another which is intersubjective. Free association is the most important gift that Freud gave us. It enabled us to focus on intersubjectivity.

Everything that I have described involved whole people who are working at becoming more whole. Whole people have a Self that includes an agency. The Self is imbued with healthy narcissism. We are continually aware of receiving sufficient or insufficient narcissistic gratification for whatever we do including the external and internal work we do.

Patients who ignore us, demean us or recognize and appreciate us generate different levels of self-esteem. As an agency the emotional work that I have done regulates my self-esteem. I grew up feeling deeply damaged with intense rage and hunger. This was repressed and dissociated, but returned in the form of symptoms. My analysis, especially my self-analysis, with emphasis on the use of language, relatedness and communication in the here and now, enabled me to become whole with my traumas and pain.

The final step in analytic work and the most difficult is bringing together and taking ownership of everything that has been the result of dissociation and repression. Then doing the work, to feel open and authentic with one's analyst, to be able to own and love all that contributes to one's self as I was taught years ago by John Dorsey that has made such a profound impression on me, has enabled me to transform my pain and suffering into who I am today. This is the lens that I have used to write this final chapter.

Reference

Ferenczi, S. (1949). Confusion of Tongue Between Adult and Child. *Internat. J. Psychoanal.*, 30:225–230.

Index

9/11 30–31

Abbey, Edward 187
Abraham, Karl 2
acting 147
Active Psychotherapy 10–11
academic history, psychology 215–219
activism 221, 226, 228–230, 234, 239,
    245–250, 253, 254
addiction 44
Adler, Alfred 1
adolescence *see* childhood and
    adolescence
affect regulation theory 171, 175
aging 213, 218, 219, 238, 246, 247
Aichorn, August 3
AIDS Network 242–245
altered consciousness 83–86, 97, 98; *see
    also* dreams/dreaming; hallucinations
alternate session 21
Althusser, Louis 191
American Group Psychotherapy
    Association (AGPA) 146–147
American Psychological Association
    (APA): Entin 60, 73, 74; Guantanamo
    detainees 191; Kooden 230, 234, 238,
    242–3, 246, 247; Lincoln Hospital,
    New York 225; psychodynamic psy-
    chotherapy 204; Rachman 9; Yeomans
    209–210
anal phase 43
Anderson, Joseph 191

anhedonia 35
Anna Freud Center 174
anthropology: Marshall, Robert J. 117;
    Marshall, Simone V. 132; Mucci 153,
    158
antidepressants 35
Apollon, Willy 191
Appelbaum, Ann 203
archeology 5
army 134–135, 137–139
art: Entin 72–76; Erikson 3; Gilhooley
    81–85, 92, 98, 248; Kellerman
    106–107; Marshall, Simone V. 144
Association of Lesbian and Gay
    Psychotherapists (ALGP) 233, 234
attachment theory 171
Auchincloss, Elizabeth 207

Badiou, Alain 191
Balint, Enid 50
Balint, Michael 45, 50
banking 36, 47
Bass, Rick 188
Bateman, Antony 174
Bauer, Steve 203
Beck, Samuel 8
Bellevue Hospital 132–133
Beres, David 118
Bergeron, Danielle 191
Bhabha, Homi 166
Bion, Wilfred 190, 193, 196
birth trauma 1

Blake, William 187
Blatt, Sid 201
Blixen, Karen 167; "The blank page" 160; *Out of Africa* 165
Bloss, Peter 3
Blum, Harold 11
Bodenstab, Johanna 173
Bollas, Christopher 190, 193, 194
Bonomi, Carlo 48, 53
Boomtown Rats 33, 34, 54
borderline personality disorder (BPD): Mucci 172, 174, 175; Transference-Focused Psychotherapy 171; Yeomans 203–205, 206
Bornstein, Melvin 243–252
Boston Graduate School of Psychoanalysis 83
Bowen, Murray 58–61, 68, 75
Brach, Tara 183, 185
Brady, Fergal 30–54, 249–250
breakdown 31, 32, 33, 35–36, 42
Brett, Betsy 201
Breuer, Josef 81, 87–92, 97
Bridgman, P. W. 122
British Psychoanalytic Association 157
Budapest School 45, 46, 50, 53; *see also* Ferenczi, Sándor
Buddhist psychology 184, 185
Byrne, Hugh 183

Caligor, Eve 204
Cameron, John 39, 47
Cantin, Lucie 191
Capetillo-Ponce, Jorge 191
Caple, Richard 188
Carr, Arthur 203
Carsky, Monica 204
Cartwright, Rosalind 9
Caruth, Cathy 165
Casey, Domhnall 37, 38, 41, 51
Castoriadis, Cornelius 165
Center for Modern Psychoanalytic Studies (CMPS), New York 83, 183

Charcot, Jean-Martin 85–86, 92, 93, 94, 96
childhood and adolescence: Bornstein 244–245; Brady 31–33, 43, 53, 54; Entin 56–58, 66; Gilhooley 81–82, 248; Kellerman 103–108, 111, 112, 113, 249; Marshall, Robert J. 115–116; Mucci 150–154, 156; Perri 178–180; Rachman 5–7; Scalia 188
child psychiatry 58
child psychoanalysis 2
child sexual abuse 44–46, 48, 53
Chodorow, Nancy 161
Chodron, Pema 183
Christian Science 2
City College, New York (CCNY) 117–118
Clarkin, John 203, 204, 206–207
Client-Centered Psychotherapy *see* Person-Centered Psychotherapy
client- therapist relationship and private practice 237–242
clinical psychology: Entin 58; Kellerman 114; Kooden 216–219; Marshall, Robert J. 118; Marshall, Simone V. 131; Rachman 7, 8, 9, 10
cognitive behavioural therapy (CBT) 204, 205, 206, 207
college: Bornstein 243–244; Brady 36–37, 38, 39, 40–41, 45, 50–51; Entin 58, 59–60; Gilhooley 82, 83; Kooden 214, 215, 224–226; Marshall, Robert J. 116–119, 122–123, 133, 135; Marshall, Simone V. 131–133, 134, 135, 139; Mucci 154–160, 162–167, 169–172; Perri 181; Rachman 7–11, 13–22, 25, 26; Yeomans 199–202
Colorado Center for Modern Psychoanalytic Studies 189
Coltrane, John 125
Columbia Center for Psychoanalytic Training and Research 207
Columbia Teachers College 118, 131–133, 134, 139

community mental health 224, 225, 229, 231, 232, 235, 237, 239, 241, 242, 245, 247, 249
Confusion of Tongues paradigm: Ferenczi 13, 14, 45, 174, 251; Rachman 13–15, 16, 17, 20, 22, 26; Severn 2
Cooper, Arnold 202
Correale, Antonello 172
Coué, Emile 2
counselling 36, 38, 39, 47
countertransference: Brady 47; Freud 122; Marshall, Robert J. 122, 148; Marshall, Simone V. 132, 146, 148; Rachman 20, 21
creativity: Entin 73–74, 75; Gilhooley 83, 93, 97, 98; see also art; photographs/ photography; writing
Culler, Jonathan 161

Dartmouth School of Theory and Criticism 166
David, Henry 138
de Beauvoir, Simone 143
deconstructionism 199
de Kooning, Willem 83
Delaney, Jill 204
delusions 107–110
democratic philosophy 9
depression: as absence of imagination 97; Brady 35–36, 43, 44; Marshall, Simone V. 131, 249
de Saussure, Ferdinand 199
Deutsch, Helene 3
Dewey, John 9
Diamond, Diana 204, 208
domestic violence 153
Dorsey, John 244, 252
Doyle, Arthur Conan, and Sherlock Holmes 32, 38, 44, 50, 54
dreams/dreaming 81, 83, 84, 92–93, 98
Dublin Business School (DBS) 36–37, 38, 39, 40, 45
Dulit, Everett 121
Dunlop, Joey 34–35, 54

Eakins, Thomas 83
Eaton, Jeff 190
Eddy, Mary Baker 2
Edelson, Marshall 201
education see college; school; training
ego psychology 205, 251
Eigen, Michael 196
Einstein, Albert 123
electroconvulsive therapy (ECT) 35–36
Ellenberger, Henri 91
Elliott, Mitch 37–38, 39, 40, 41–43, 46–47, 51, 52, 53
Emory Institute of Psychoanalysis, Atlanta 164
encounter and marathon movement 10
English, Woody 140
Ensink, Karin 204
Entin, Alan D. 56–76, 249
Erikson, Erik H. 1, 2–3, 58, 60
experimental psychology 114

Fairbairn, Ronald 205, 251
family: Bornstein 244–245; Brady 32–33, 34, 35, 43, 44, 47; Entin 56–57, 59, 62–66, 74–75; Gilhooley 81–82, 84, 93–94, 248; Kellerman 103–106, 107–110; Kooden 214, 215, 217, 219, 225, 247; Marshall, Robert J. 115, 116, 118, 119, 121, 133–149; Marshall, Simone V. 118, 119, 131, 133–149, 249; Mucci 150–154, 161–162, 165, 166, 167; Perri 178–180, 181, 182, 184, 185; Rachman 5–7, 16, 247; Scalia 187, 188, 189, 190, 192, 193, 194, 195, 196; Yeomans 202
family psychiatry 58–59
family psychology 57, 59, 66, 76
family systems theory 59–62, 68–69, 75
family therapy 66–72, 225, 249
Farber, Marvin 8
Federn, Paul 3
Feldman, Betty 7, 15–16, 18, 19, 25
Feldman, Marvin 118
Felman, Shoshana 161, 165–166

feminism: Kooden 230; Marshall,
Simone V. 143–144; Mucci 160, 161
Ferenczi, Sándor: and Brady 45–46,
48–49, 50; Confusion of Tongues
paradigm 13, 14, 45, 174, 251; and
Klein 2; and Lorand 23–24; and
Mucci 167, 168, 171, 172, 174–175;
and Rachman 10–13, 14, 16, 22,
23–24, 25, 26, 247; and Severn 2, 13
Ferenczi Association 175
Fertuck, Eric 204
Fidler, Jay 117, 122
Figlio, Karl 41
Flaubert, Gustave, *Les Trois Contes* 201
Fonagy, Peter 174
food 151
forgiveness 174
Fort Dix Mental Hygiene/Hospital 137,
138
Foust, Jonathan 183
Fowler, Sandra 74
Franklin, Ben 87
Freud, Anna 1–2, 3, 23
Freud, Sigmund: birth of psychoanalysis
85, 86, 91, 92; and Bornstein 244; and
Brady 37, 40, 41, 43, 44, 46–47, 52, 54;
comparison with Sherlock Holmes 32;
countertransference 122; family pho-
tographs 71–72; and Ferenczi 12–13,
22; free association 252; and Freud,
Anna 1–2; and Kardiner 123; Library
of Congress 11; and Lorand 23; and
Marshall, Robert J. 148; miracles 97;
Mourning and Melancholia 41; and
Mucci 154, 155, 156, 160, 168, 169,
172, 174; music 123; and Pappenheim
(Anna O.) 91, 92; and Perri 183;
"The Question of Lay Analysis"
1; and Scalia 189, 190, 196; "The
Unconscious" 40, 43; Wednesday
Psychological Society 38; wishes 110;
and Yeomans 199, 200, 201, 208, 248
Friedan, Betty 143
Fromm, Erika 8, 9–10, 141

Gay Academic Union 234
Geltner, Paul 190
Gendlin, Eugene 9
George Mason University 183
Gerber, Andrew 210
Gestalt therapy 233, 236, 253, 258
GIFRIC 190, 191
Gilhooley, Dan 81–99, 248
Gillespie, Dizzy 116, 125
Goldstein, Jonathan 183
Goldstein, Kurt 118
Goodman, Benny 116, 126
Goslin, Bill 192
grandmother as therapeutic role model
5–7, 16
Grease (film) 33
Green, Andre, *The Dead Mother
Syndrome and Blank Mourning* 41
Grosskurth, Phyllis 25
Grotstein, James 196
Group Analytic Practice 39, 40
group therapy: Kooden 233, 237;
Marshall, Robert J. 118, 126–128;
Marshall, Simone V. 141, 143,
146–147; Perri 182; Rachman 19–21;
Scalia 193–194
Gruen, Walter 8
Guerney, Harold 122

hallucinations 88–92, 97
Hammarskjold, Dag 230
Hampshire, Alice 17–18, 19, 25
Hanaghan, Jonathan (Jonty) 39
Haran, Kay 204
Harris, Adrienne 24
Hartman, Heinz 3
Harvard University 199, 217
Havinghurst, Robert 8
Heaney, Seamus, *Beowulf* translation
51–52
Henry, William E. 8, 58
Herskovitz, Aron 8
Hilsenroth, Mark 210
history 5, 22, 24, 85–92; Hobson, Allan 98

Hoffman, Mark 192–193
holistic health 236, 257
Holleran, Michael 183
Holmes, Sherlock 32, 38, 44, 50, 54
Holocaust 168, 173
homosexuality: Kooden 214, 230,
    233–235, 237, 238, 247; Yeomans
    200, 201
hospital without walls model 208
human development: Entin 58;
    Erikson 3; Kooden 216, 217;
    Rachman 8
humanism 257
humanness 243–52
humor 125–126
Humphrey, T. 73
Hunter College, New York 82, 140
Husserl, Edmund 8
hypnosis 10, 85, 86, 89, 94
hypothesising 38

internship 224–226
ill health: Brady 31, 32, 33, 35–36, 42;
    Marshall, Simone V. 131, 149
imagination: birth of psychoanalysis 86,
    87, 89, 90, 92; Gilhooley 81, 85, 92,
    93, 97–99; Mucci 152, 155
impossible 86, 92, 93, 96, 97
improvisation 115, 116, 117, 118, 120,
    121, 122, 123, 124, 127, 128, 250
induced feelings 123–124, 146
Insel, Thomas 204
Institute of Liberal Arts (ILA), Atlanta
    155, 157, 158–160, 162–165
Institute of Personality Disorders
    169–171
Intensive Group Experience 10
International Lesbian and Gay
    Association (ILGA) 246
Irish Psycho-Analytical Association 37,
    39, 47, 51, 52, 53; Reading Group 41,
    46, 51; Saturday Night Group 38–39,
    40, 47, 51
Isay, Richard 201

Jacobi Hospital, New York 224
Jacobsen, Edith 205
James, William 9
Jergenson, Rachel 194
Jewish Board of Guardians 132
Johnson, Barbara 161
Jones, Ernest 2, 12, 22
Jung, Carl 1, 160

Kahn, David 98
Kant, Immanuel 196
Kardiner, Abram 122–123
Kellerman, Henry 21, 102–114, 249
Kennedy, Robert 183
Kernberg, Otto: and Mucci 166,
    169–171, 174, 175; and Yeomans 202,
    203, 204, 205, 206–207
Kernberg, Paulina 170, 203
Kerr, Mike 69
Killingmo, Bjorn 41
King, Martin Luther, Jr. 185, 224
Klein, Melanie 1, 2; 'Our Adult World
    and its Roots in Infancy' 43; projective
    identification 251; and Scalia 190, 195;
    and Yeomans 205
Klineberg, Otto 132
Knoepfmacher, Lia 123
Koenigsberg, Harold 203
Kohut, Heinz 11
Kooden, Harold 212–259
Kornfield, Jack 184, 185
Kovacs, Arthur 73
Kris, Ernst 124
Kristeva, Julia 155, 161

Lacan, Jacques: and Mucci 156, 160,
    165, 166, 167, 168; and Scalia 190,
    191, 196; and Yeomans 200–201,
    210, 248
Langs, Robert 189
language: Kellerman 103, 109, 112,
    249; Marshall, Simone V. 132; Mucci
    150–152, 154–155, 157, 158, 162, 163,
    248; Yeomans 210, 248

Laub, Dori 172–173, 175
Lavoisier, Antoine-Laurent 87
Leavy, Stanley 200, 202
legal system 214
Lemert, Charles 191
Lester, Olive 7–8
Letterman Army Hospital, San
    Francisco 135, 137
Levin, Hyman 118
Levy, Kenneth 204
Lewis, Oscar 218
liberal philosophy 9
libraries: Brady 31–32, 34, 45, 54;
    Mucci 159
Library of Congress 11
Lichtenberg, Joseph 24–26
Lidz, Ruth 201
Lidz, Ted 201
Lifton, Robert Jay 168
Lincoln Hospital, New York 225, 237
Lindsay, John 185
Liotti, Giovanni 173
literature: Mucci 151, 154–156, 158,
    159, 160, 163, 165, 167–168; Yeomans
    199–200, 210, 248
Long Island Center for Modern
    Psychoanalytic Studies (LICMPS) 183
Lopez, Barry 188
Lorand, Sándor 23–24
Lyotard, Jean-François 165

managed care 207–208, 211
Marathon Group Therapy 10
marital therapy 141
Marshall, Robert J. 21, 115–128, 131,
    133–135, 136, 137–149, 189, 250
Marshall, Simone V. 116, 118, 119,
    131–149, 249
Martin de Porres Centers 184
Marx, Karl 191
Maslow, A. 124
Masson, Jeffrey M. 22, 23
Mattick, Paul 11
McCarthyism 7, 135, 136

McCoy, James A. 162–164
McGill, Joseph P. 188
McLeod, D. 73
Mead, Herbert 9
Meadow, Phyllis 189
media 73
Medical Committee for Human Rights
    229
meditation: Kooden 236, 257; Perri
    183, 185
memory: Brady 45–46, 47; Mucci 168,
    169, 174
Menaker, Esther 22–23
Menniger, Karl 22
mentors: Kooden 219; Marshall, Simone
    V. 132; Rachman 24–26; Scalia 189;
    Yeomans 200, 202
Mesmer, Franz 81, 86–87, 88, 91, 92, 94
Meszaros, Arnold 53
Meszaros, Judit 53
Michels, Robert 202
Middeldorf, Jan 189
military service 137–139
Miller, Alice, *The Drama of Being a
    Child* 41
mindfulness 183, 185
Mintz, Elizabeth 10
miracles 85–86, 93, 95, 97, 98
mirroring 44
Mitchell, Juliet 166
Montagu, Ashley 117
Montague, John 52
Montessori Method 3
Morgan, Traci 190
motorbikes 34–35
Movahedi, Siamak 191
Mucci, Clara 150–175, 248–249
Munich, Richard 201, 203
Munroe, Ruth 118
music: Brady 33–34, 35, 48–49, 51, 54, 250;
    Marshall, Robert J. 115–117, 118–119,
    120–121, 124, 125–128, 147, 250
music therapy 127–128
mythology: Brady 52–53, 54; Mucci 165

National Academy of Design 83
National Gay and Lesbian Health
   Foundation 242
National Institute of Mental Health
   (NIMH) 204–205
National Institute of Psychiatry, Mexico
   209
National Psychological Association for
   Psychoanalysis (NPAP) 183
Neal, Richard M. 188
Nearing, Scott 188
Neugarten, Bernice 218
neurolinguistic programming 236
New Lisbon Institution for Retarded
   Males 138
New York Hospital–Cornell Medical
   Center 202, 203, 206, 207–208
New York Psychoanalytic Society and
   Institute 140, 207
Normandin, Lina 204
Northern Rockies Psychoanalytic
   Institute 193

object relations theory 2, 45, 205, 251
Oldham, John 203
oral phase 44

Papp, Peggy 66
Pappenheim, Bertha (Anna O.) 81,
   87–92, 97, 98
Pappenheim, Harriet 21–22
Parker, Charlie 116, 126
pathology 102–103, 106, 107
Paul, Robert 164
Peacock, Doug 188
Perri, Benito 178–186, 250
personal life 253–254
personality disorders: Mucci 169, 171,
   172, 174, 175; Yeomans 203–205,
   206–207, 208, 209, 210
Personality Disorders Institute (PDI)
   166, 203–205, 206, 207, 208, 209
Person-Centered Psychotherapy 9, 10,
   11, 16, 25, 26

personal psychotherapy 250–253
Pescara University 154–156
Peterson, Faye 189
Pfeifer, Geoff 191
phenomenology 8, 9, 10
Phillips, Sid 201
philosophy: Perri 180, 181; Rachman 9;
   Rank 1; Scalia 191
photographs/photography 56–57, 60, 62,
   63, 65–75, 249
phototherapy 69–72; early history
   213–215; physical abuse 179
Pinchot, Gifford 192
Pine, F. 122
Plato 52, 196
poetry 51–52, 250
politics 32
Pollock, Jackson 82
Polytechnic of Central London 156
Postgraduate Center for Mental Health
   122–123, 140, 145
Postgraduate Psychoanalytic Institute
   10, 13–22, 25, 26
Pragmatism 9
projective identification 251
psychiatry: Entin 58; Kooden 215;
   Marshall, Simone V. 132, 136;
   Yeomans 200–201, 202, 203, 207, 248
Psychoanalytic Inquiry 25
Psychoanalytic Inquiry Book Series
   25
psychodrama 236
psychodynamics: Ferenczi 13; Rachman
   10; Yeomans 203, 204, 206, 210
psychohistory 22, 24
Psychologists for Social Action
   229, 233
psychology: Entin 58, 73, 75–76;
   Kellerman 107, 110, 114; Kooden 212,
   215–220, 223–226, 229, 247; Marshall,
   Robert J. 117–118, 121, 122; Marshall,
   Simone V. 131, 135, 138, 139, 140;
   Mucci 167, 168, 169, 172; Rachman
   7–8, 9, 16, 17; Yeomans 200–201

psychotherapeutic skills development 219–224
Puysegur, Marquis of 91

Qualicap 185
Quarterman, Dale 66

Rachman, Arnold Wm. 5–26, 48, 212, 237, 247
racism 221, 254
radical mental health 230
Rank, Otto 1
rapport 94–95, 97
reading 256–258
Redfield, Robert 218
Reik, Theodore 1
Reinhardt, Ad 82
Reiss, Ted 16
religion see spirituality and religion
research: Brady 45, 47; Entin 58, 60, 62–66; Kooden 217, 218, 220–221; Marshall, Robert J. 118, 119; Mucci 157, 168, 173–174; psychodynamic psychotherapy 210; Rachman 11, 22, 26; Yeomans 204–205, 206
Richet, Charles 94
Ritvo, Samuel 201
Roazen, Paul 22, 23
Rockland, Lawrence 203
Rogers, Carl 9, 219
role models: Kooden 215, 221; Rachman 5–7, 10, 22–23, 26
Roosevelt, Theodore 192
Rutgers University 116–117

SAGE 246
St Patrick's hospital, Dublin 30–31, 35–36
Salzburg, Sharon 183
Sanders, Joseph 156
Scalia, Joseph, III 187–197, 247–248
Schillinger, Mort 121
Schlesinger, Herb 203
Scholes, Robert 166

school: Entin 57–58; Kellerman 105–106; Kooden 214; Marshall, Robert J. 116; Marshall, Simone V. 143; Mucci 151, 154; Perri 180–181; Scalia 188
Schore, Allan 174–175
Schwartz, Maurice 113
Sciacchitano, Antonello 166–167
Searles, Harold 94
Segal, Hannah 156
Selzer, Michael 203
Services and Advocacy for GLBT Elders (SAGE) 246
Severn, Elizabeth 2, 13, 25, 48
sexual abuse 194; children 44–46, 48, 53
sexuality: Kooden 233–235, 247; Perri 180, 181, 250; Yeomans 200, 201
Shakespeare, William 151, 154–156, 158, 159, 165, 167–168, 169, 173, 248
Shapiro, Ted 202
Silverman, Kaja 161
Simone, Simone 147
Slavson, Sam 132, 134, 137, 139, 140, 147
Sledge, William 201
Smith, Tony 82
social work 36–37, 180, 182–183
Società Italiana Psicoterapia Psicoanalitica 171
Society of Rings 1
sociology 216
Soldz, Stephen 191
Sorbonne 131, 141
spirituality and religion: Brady 32; Gilhooley 85; Kooden 257; miracles 85; Perri 180–186, 250; Scalia 188
Spitz, Rene 118
Spitzform, Marianne 192
Spivak, Gayatry 166
Spotnitz, Hyman 94, 123, 140, 183
Stallybrass, Peter 161
Steinem, Gloria 143
Steiner, Riccardo 156

Steinert, Joseph 118, 122
Stengers, Isabelle 87
Stern, Barry 204
Stone, Michael 203
Stonewall Uprising 232–234
suicide/suicidality: Gilhooley 81, 82,
    93–94, 248; Kooden 213–214;
    Marshall, Robert J. 127, 128
Sullivan, Harry Stack 148, 231
supervision: Bornstein 244; Brady 39;
    Kernberg 170, 171; Kooden 220, 221,
    224, 225, 236, 252; Marshall, Robert
    J. 122, 123, 125, 127, 148; Marshall,
    Simone V. 148; Mucci 172; Rachman
    10, 17–18, 25; Scalia 189, 190;
    Yeomans 203, 208, 209
Swales, Peter 11

Tavistock Institute 203
Teachers College, Columbia University
    118, 131–133, 134, 139
teaching: Bornstein 246; Freud, Anna
    1; Kooden 232; Marshall, Simone V.
    137–138, 139; Mucci 156, 157, 166,
    167, 172, 175; Perri 182, 183; Yeomans
    202, 207, 208
theater 112–114, 249
Thematic Apperception Test 10
theology 180, 181
Thich Nhat Hanh 183
Thompson, Clara 148
Thoreau, Henry David 187
Touro College, New York 183
training: Brady 38, 39–41, 46, 47,
    50–51; Entin 58; Gilhooley 83, 248;
    Kellerman 106, 108, 114; Kooden
    212, 216, 220, 224, 225, 235–237, 247;
    Marshall, Robert J. 145; Marshall,
    Simone V. 131, 141; Mucci 158,
    166, 171, 248; Perri 182–183, 250;
    Rachman 5, 7–10, 13, 16–20, 22,
    25–26; Scalia 189–190; Yeomans 202,
    203, 208
transactional analysis 236

transference 248; Bornstein 245;
    Kooden 241; Marshall, Robert J. 148;
    Marshall, Simone V. 132, 146, 148
Transference-Focused Psychotherapy
    (TFP): Mucci 171, 174; Yeomans 205,
    207, 208–209
trauma: Bornstein 245, 246; Gilhooley
    248; Mucci 168, 171, 172, 174–175
Trauma Analysis 2, 13
travel: Kooden 254–256; Marshall,
    Simone V. and Robert J. 141, 145;
    Scalia 190, 191
Turk, Charles 190, 191–192
Turner, V. 151

United Nations 223–224
university see college; specific universities
University of Buffalo (UB): Marshall,
    Robert J. 118–119, 133, 135; Marshall,
    Simone V. 135; Rachman 7–8, 25
University of Chicago: Entin 58;
    Kooden 216; Rachman 8–10, 11, 14,
    16, 17, 25
University of Chieti-Pescara 167
University of Illinois at Chicago 215
University of Sheffield 40–41, 45, 51
University of Wisconsin in Madison 58

Vecchi, J. 63
Vienna Psychoanalytic Institute 2, 3
Vienna Psychoanalytic Society 1, 2
Virginia Commonwealth University
    (VCU) 59–60
volunteering: Entin 66, 75; Kooden 233;
    Yeomans 201, 202

Wad River 31, 32, 42, 53–54
War Against Poverty 185
Wayne State University 244
Weiner, Alan 204
Welwood, John 183
Western New England Psychoanalytic
    Institute 200, 201
Whitaker, Carl 58

White, Allon 161
White, Kerry 193
Whitehead, Tim 67
wilderness 187–197, 248
William Alanson White Institute:
  Kooden 231; Marshall, Robert J. and
  Simone V. 118, 133, 140, 141, 145,
  146, 147, 148; Rachman 18
Wilson, Charles 128
Wilson, Teddy 116
Winnicott, Donald 190, 196
Wolf, Alexander 19–21, 25–26
Wolf, Harriet 201
Wolf, Katherine 118
Wolke, Howie 187
Wonder, Stevie 124

Woolf, Virginia 161
writing: Gilhooley 93–97, 98–99;
  Kooden 220–221, 226, 246–250;
  Marshall, Robert J. 118, 119–120,
  121, 123, 124, 125–126, 128, 147–148;
  Mucci 151, 157, 158, 160–162, 166,
  167–169, 173–174, 175, 248–249;
  Scalia 189, 190; Yeomans 206–207

Yale University 199, 201–202, 207
Yeomans, Frank 171, 199–211, 248
Yiddish theater 112–14, 249

Zetzel, Elizabeth 122
Zimring, Fred 9
Zizek, Slavoj 191